Find Your Career With Springer Publishing Company

101+ Careers in Public Health, Second Edition
Beth Seltzer

101 Careers in Counseling
Shannon Hodges

101+ Careers in Gerontology, Second Edition
C. Joanne Grabinski

101 Careers in Social Work, Second Edition
Jessica A. Ritter and Halaevalu F. Ofahengaue Vakalahi

101 Careers in Psychology
Tracey E. Ryan

101 Careers in Education
John S. Carlson and Richard L. Carlson

101 Careers in Healthcare Management
Leonard H. Friedman and Anthony R. Kovner

Careers in Health Information Technology
Brian T. Malec

201 Careers in Nursing
Joyce J. Fitzpatrick and Emerson E. Ea

To learn more and order, visit www.springerpub.com

101 Careers in Education

John S. Carlson, PhD, NCSP, is a professor, doctoral program director, and director of clinical training of the School Psychology Program within the College of Education at Michigan State University (MSU). He is a licensed psychologist (Michigan) and holds a BS degree in child psychology from the University of Minnesota and MA and PhD degrees in school psychology from the University of Wisconsin–Madison. He completed his predoctoral internship in the Department of Psychiatry, Primary Children's Medical Center, Salt Lake City, Utah. In addition to his faculty work at MSU, Dr. Carlson provides mental health consultation to children, families, and schools within his private practice, Child and Adolescent Psychological Services, PLC, in East Lansing, Michigan. Dr. Carlson recently finished his term as associate editor of *Journal of School Psychology,* a leading peer-reviewed journal within the field of educational psychology. Dr. Carlson has authored or coauthored over 50 articles within peer-reviewed journals and chapters within books. He recently coauthored a book titled *Counseling Students in Levels 2 and 3: A PBIS/RTI Guide.* During his tenure at MSU, he has been instrumental in proposing, securing, directing, and codirecting training and research grant projects now totaling over $4 million. Dr. Carlson's numerous positions in education over the past 25 years have clearly identified a strong need for educators and professionals who are well trained and competent to address mental health issues in school settings.

Richard L. Carlson, MA, is currently an educational consultant. During the past 13 years, he and his prior firm supported over 75 districts and cooperative service educational agencies (CSEAs) across the state of Wisconsin, helping to recruit educational leaders (e.g., school superintendents) who met the identified profile requirements of the respective entities. He holds a BS degree in business administration, a BS in secondary education from the University of Wisconsin–Eau Claire, and an MA in counseling (with certification in educational administration) from the University of Wisconsin–Oshkosh. Mr. Carlson has worked within the field of education in a variety of positions, including his working up the career ladder within schools as a high school social studies teacher, assistant high school principal, high school principal, assistant superintendent, and superintendent of the Neenah Joint School District in Neenah, Wisconsin. Following his retirement from Neenah, he served as interim superintendent within four other districts in Wisconsin and brings a wealth of knowledge to this book with respect to the diversity of careers that exist within the field of education. Mr. Carlson authored several articles, participated on numerous panels, served on many community boards, and provided leadership across the state of Wisconsin. He has served as divisional leader for the United Way and was elected as a rotary centennial district governor. In 1984 he was selected for the Principal of the Year Award by the Department of Public Instruction, and in 1988 he received the Outstanding Alumnus Award from the University of Wisconsin–Eau Claire. Mr. Carlson's positions in education over the last 50 years have clearly identified a substantial need for future leaders and administrators who have the talents, patience, and data-based decision making to bring effective solutions to tough problems facing schools.

101 Careers in Education

JOHN S. CARLSON, PhD, NCSP

RICHARD L. CARLSON, MA

SPRINGER PUBLISHING COMPANY
NEW YORK

Springer Publishing Company, LLC
11 West 42nd Street
New York, NY 10036
www.springerpub.com

Acquisitions Editor: Nancy S. Hale
Composition: S4Carlisle Publishing Services

ISBN: 978-0-8261-9984-3
e-book ISBN: 978-0-8261-9985-0

15 16 17 18 19 / 5 4 3 2 1

The author and the publisher of this Work have made every effort to use sources believed to be reliable to provide information that is accurate and compatible with the standards generally accepted at the time of publication. The author and publisher shall not be liable for any special, consequential, or exemplary damages resulting, in whole or in part, from the readers' use of, or reliance on, the information contained in this book. The publisher has no responsibility for the persistence or accuracy of URLs for external or third-party Internet websites referred to in this publication and does not guarantee that any content on such websites is, or will remain, accurate or appropriate.

Library of Congress Cataloging-in-Publication Data

Carlson, John S.
  101 careers in education / authors, John S. Carlson, PhD, NCSP, Richard L. Carlson, MA.
    pages cm
  Includes index.
  ISBN 978-0-8261-9984-3—ISBN 978-0-8261-9985-0 (e-book) 1. Education—Vocational guidance.
2. Teaching—Vocational guidance. I. Carlson, Richard L. II. Title. III. Title: One hundred one careers in education.
  LB1775.2.C38 2015
  371.10023—dc23
                                                                                    2015017182

Special discounts on bulk quantities of our books are available to corporations, professional associations, pharmaceutical companies, health care organizations, and other qualifying groups. If you are interested in a custom book, including chapters from more than one of our titles, we can provide that service as well.

For details, please contact:
Special Sales Department, Springer Publishing Company, LLC
11 West 42nd Street, 15th Floor, New York, NY 10036-8002
Phone: 877-687-7476 or 212-431-4370; Fax: 212-941-7842
E-mail: sales@springerpub.com

Printed in the United States of America by Gasch Printing.

We learn most about ourselves and others through our close personal and professional relationships. Our families and friends have taught us much and continue to teach us new things about ourselves and the world we live in. This book is dedicated to (a) our extended family members in Connecticut, Michigan, Minnesota, Texas, South Carolina, and Wisconsin and (b) especially all of the Carlsons, Johnsons, Manns, and Brabecks who established such a firm foundation for our development to become educators and to serve others.

■ CONTENTS

■ PREFACE

We are delighted that you are interested in a career in education. Educating others and helping others learn directly or indirectly are reflective of a strong commitment to others' growth and development. Based on our combined 75 years as educators, nothing is more rewarding than serving others and supporting one's personal development. We are pleased to have the opportunity to author this book and share the diverse career of education with you.

Careers in education are most typically associated with schools and school districts. In this book we devote a considerable amount of attention to careers in these typical educational settings. It is important for readers to recognize the public nature of those positions, as they are funded by local, state, and federal tax dollars. Much scrutiny is now placed on financial resources in traditional school settings and ultimately on individuals holding careers in education. Following the Great Recession (2007–2009), society is especially critical of how public monies are being used, and the returns of these tax dollars/investments are currently under the microscope in most communities. As a result, it is important for us to also focus this book on a number of alternative careers in education that occur within the private sector. The growth of educational technology and an increasing need for educators who are well trained with computers, apps, and related programs are especially evident. Using technology to impart and enhance learning is everywhere, and the potential for refinement and improvement of these methods appears unlimited within both the public and private sectors of our country.

Vision and forward thinking are essential within the field of education. In particular, leadership is a substantial growth area in education due to the pending retirements of a large segment of the baby boomer generation. The need to identify and harness the wisdom of a diverse group of individuals who are focused on bringing greater accountability to learning and education is currently paramount. Opportunities for individuals who are cognitively, socially, and emotionally intelligent exist in great numbers within the field of education. Considerable attention is paid in our book to careers of leadership, including management, innovation, and accountability, both in and out of traditional school settings. The need for an influx of our nation's best and brightest high school students into careers in education is now more important than ever.

We wrote this book to disseminate information about a diverse array of career opportunities in education. If you are interested in imparting knowledge or improving how individuals gain knowledge and learn, we are confident that you will find a career or multiple careers within this book that align well with your talents and passions. As you embark on reading or reviewing this book, it is important for you to recognize that there are four major contemporary challenges facing education within our country that contributed to our interest in working with Springer Publishing Company to create this book, including:

1. *The dearth of teacher position openings within certain parts of the country.* During the past decade or so, it has not been uncommon for hundreds of applicants to apply for one teaching position. There is a significant supply and demand issue within some communities that is forcing some with degrees in education and/or those with geographic restriction of their employment to reconsider their postdegree goals away from traditional classroom teaching positions to nontraditional educational settings (e.g., corporate trainer, religious educator, technology specialist) or alternative careers that require refinement and further development of existing skills (e.g., school counselor, school administrator, school psychologist).

2. *The high rate of turnover and challenges facing education regarding retention of entry-level teachers.* It has been estimated that 15% to 25% of entry-level teachers leave the teaching profession after less than 3 years. Rates are highest in low-income school districts, where the need for stability is greatest. Although classroom-level teaching might not best address the passion and interests of entry-level teachers, there are a variety of other education-related occupations for which their commitment to service and learners of all ages may be realized. Specialization or refinement of skill sets through graduate education such as master's or doctoral work is one alternative for these individuals that

may ultimately help them to retain the initial interests that led to seeking a degree in education. Now more than ever, individuals who are bright, who are interpersonally talented, and who bring an advanced skill set to the educational process are needed for major leadership roles both in and out of schools.

3. *There is great demand for highly qualified science, technology, engineering, and math (STEM) teachers.* Now more than ever, there is a push for students in our country to compete more effectively with students across the world. Doing so requires that students leave our K–12 educational system with more advanced skills and competencies in areas such as math, science, and technology. The U.S. Department of Education, in coordination with a number of public, private, and government agencies, has recently begun to raise awareness about the demand for high-quality teachers within our nation's schools. Microsoft Corporation's leadership in promoting www.teach.org, through advertising on social media and through traditional media including television, demonstrates the push in the past couple of years to try to inspire and invigorate highly talented individuals to enter careers in education.

4. *Accountability/budget issues.* The Great Recession (2007–2009) within the United States has created a level of scrutiny, backlash, and fervor toward public services and public education not recently seen within this country. State government budget reductions pertaining to education and resulting school district budget cuts have dramatically affected employment and job prospects in education. In parallel with less funding for public education has been a significant societal push for greater efficiency and the need for effective learning and education (i.e., outcomes and accountability). The use of technology to address prior inefficiencies within the educational process appears promising. Furthermore, the emergence and greater reliance on technology in education have resulted in significant challenges and opportunities for growth and refinement within the education profession.

We hope that these challenges, issues, and emerging needs energize you and align with your calling into a career in education. We note that despite these recent challenging financial times there are many careers in education that are truly recession proof and currently in great demand within many communities across the country (e.g., school principals, school psychologists, education technology specialists, STEM teachers).

Every career, field, and discipline goes through its ups and downs. The education field has been targeted for growth in the coming decades given the impending retirement of a large section of the current teaching workforce and the need to more effectively compete globally. Now is a great time to enter, reenter, or remain within a career in education. Helping our current and future educators meet the needs of the 21st century is clearly getting more important with every passing day. All the best to you as you carry forward your career aspirations and work toward reaching your professional goals.

■ ACKNOWLEDGMENTS

We wish to acknowledge all of those educators who have guided our work over the years. Knowledge and learning come as a result of active involvement with others. Relationships are essential for one's growth and development. Mentorship and advisement are essential to success in any career. For those relationships with past teachers, staff, parents, students, colleagues, and friends, we are grateful. A special thank you goes out to our editor at Springer Publishing Company, Nancy S. Hale. Her commitment to this project and her unwavering support of our work on this book despite a number of personal setbacks and challenges are truly appreciated. Thank you also to all of those educators who were gracious enough to share their wisdom and experiences related to our Career-in-Education Profile sections via their interview contributions to this book.

John Bell, PhD (Educational Design Studio Director)
Regina Carey, MEd (Educational Consultant/Professional Coach)
Chad Carlson, MA (Historian)
Derek J. Carlson, MEd (High School Art Teacher)
Michelle Carlson, MPA (Paraprofessional—Autism Spectrum Disorder)
Shelly Carlson, BS (Human Resource Manager)
Cindy Clement, MA (Elementary School Library Media Assistant)
Erin DiPerna, MS (Second-Grade Teacher)
Diane Doersch, MEd (Chief Technology and Information Officer)
Marianne Forman, MA (Advanced Placement English Literature Teacher)
Kerry Frawley, MSW (Early Childhood Classroom Consultant)
Julie Fricke, MLIS (University Librarian)
Kathy Jurichko, MA (Camp Director)
Marta Kermiet, LMSW (Mental Health Coordinator)

My Lien, PhD (Adjunct Professor)
Don Maslinski, MS (University Athletic Director)
Sheila Nash, MA (Special Education Teacher—Emotional
     Impairment)
Erin Seif, PhD (Teaching Assistant, College of Education)
Mary Lou Turnbull, BA (English as a Second Language Teacher)
Mike Van Antwerp, MA (Coach)
Karen Wallace, MA (Middle School Foreign Language Teacher)

We especially wish to send a special thank you to our extended family of fellow educators who contributed five of our featured interviews in *101 Careers in Education*.

I ■ INTRODUCTION TO A CAREER IN EDUCATION

1 ■ WHAT IS A CAREER IN EDUCATION?

Education is defined as the process of receiving or giving information. This information typically is given through systematic instruction or directions. Most commonly it is linked to the roles and responsibilities of a teacher. The receivers of this information are often referred to as students or learners. Advising, mentoring, coaching, guiding, and enlightening are also educational processes. Thus, in simple terms, a career in education is an occupation in which one serves as an educator or provides information to another.

A career in education can take many forms. Teachers, coaches, counselors, and consultants are specific examples. Now more than ever a career in education encompasses a number of job titles across a multitude of settings, including schools, businesses, churches, and government agencies. *101 Careers in Education* is designed to (a) give you information about an array of specific careers in the field of education, (b) allow you to see the vast diversity of careers that are available with the hope of allowing you to take away an appreciation for the breadth and depth of the field of education, and (c) set you out on a path toward learning more about the careers in education that might be of particular interest to you.

OVERVIEW

Education is everywhere, especially given the interplay between knowledge and technology that exists within today's society. Most important, careers in education are culturally dependent and tend to vary geographically. Although this book primarily addresses educational careers available in the United States, it covers educational careers that are universal and consistent with a global perspective on learning and knowledge advancement.

A career in education can be direct (e.g., teaching), indirect (e.g., supporting systems where teaching happens or where learning occurs), or a combination of both (e.g., working with learners and supporting others who work with learners). Some educators may rarely interact with learners, such as administrators, directors, or curriculum developers.

Other educators interact frequently with learners, such as physical education teachers, elementary school art teachers, and religious educators. Educators can work across the developmental spectrum with individuals ranging from very young children (e.g., preschool teacher) to older adults (e.g., adult educator). Ultimately, meeting the diverse needs of learners, wherever they may be seeking or acquiring information (i.e., classroom, school, home, community), is an integral part of a career in education.

Providing others with the knowledge, values, skills, and traditions of a discipline is an incredible service to society. Education plays a key role in making the world a better place and ultimately can be an equalizer for creating opportunities for those who can and do access it. Knowledge is power and allows one to develop the skills and abilities necessary to actively contribute to society. Careers in education are as diverse as the knowledge that exists within our world. From historians to book publishers to elementary school library assistants to middle school foreign language teachers to college presidents, all impart information to others.

A career in education is unique compared to many other fields given the significant role of public funding in financing these positions. Society has placed a priority on education through the use of public tax dollars. Federal, state, and local governments all play a major role in funding many of the jobs described in this book. The fact that many of the careers in education are financed by our neighbors, communities, and fellow citizens reflects a high level of trust in individuals who carry out the education of our nation's children. Such a role should not be taken lightly and must be recognized as a service to the country as a whole.

THE PATH TO A CAREER IN EDUCATION

It is clear that careers in education vary considerably, but it is equally important to recognize that paths to a career in education also can differ. Multiple paths ultimately can lead individuals to the same career. Some careers in school settings do not require an undergraduate or advanced graduate degree and instead may require postsecondary education to complete a certificate, specialized training, and/or an associate's degree. For example, a certificate in infant mental health might help an individual to pursue a career as a home visitor and/or a parent educator. Advanced training in early childhood mental health along with an associate's degree might allow for employment as an early childhood classroom consultant. A final example pertains to becoming a preschool or Head Start teacher, where an associate's degree in child development or early childhood education might suffice.

One of the most commonly recognized paths to a career in education is attending college/university settings to study the field of education. An undergraduate degree in education is pursued frequently in university settings across the United States and typically appears in the annual "Top 10 College Majors" report from Princeton Review, a leading provider of test preparation materials. The reason for this popularity is that a college-level degree (i.e., bachelor's or associate's degree) is the minimum education necessary for the majority of careers in education.

Typically, education degrees at the undergraduate level are linked to major fields of study such as early childhood education, elementary education, secondary education, and/or special education. Minor areas of study that are associated with undergraduate majors are also commonly undertaken, such as coursework related to a specific type of disability (e.g., autism spectrum disorder, emotional impairment, learning disabilities) or a specific content area (e.g., music, biology, calculus). A combination of major and minor fields of study allows individuals to broaden their skill sets and also helps to differentiate one's training from that of others earning degrees in education.

Undergraduate/graduate degrees are typically aligned with careers within the schools or other educational settings. They not only involve a specified curriculum and coursework but also require experience within that context and/or with the populations being targeted. Certificates from state departments of education provide accountability and recognition that this knowledge, training, and background are in place prior to allowing the individual to work within the school setting. Continuing education and professional development are often a necessary requirement to maintain certification, highlighting the importance of educators' commitment to being lifelong learners. Those who seek careers in education outside of the traditional school setting often don't need to meet the intensive requirements associated with state certification standards.

Individuals who work in traditional educational careers in school settings often complete graduate coursework and/or complete master's degrees. This additional training typically accompanies and supports their roles and responsibilities. One example of the ease of access to this advanced training is the proliferation of the use of educational technology to enhance professional development. Such continuing professional education can both increase salary and help maintain state certification credentials.

Many careers that focus on the education of school-age populations (e.g., chief technology and information officer) or the education of students with disabilities (e.g., school social worker) require an advanced degree. Specific examples include master's or doctoral degrees in educational administration and leadership, speech and language pathology, social work, and school psychology. Typically, doctoral degrees are necessary to work in the majority of higher education (i.e., postsecondary) positions found at colleges and universities.

ALTERNATIVE PATHS TO A CAREER IN EDUCATION

For those individuals who did not primarily focus on the field of education or the schooling process as a part of their undergraduate degree, perceptions are that it is difficult to enter into an educational career. Those perceptions are mostly accurate. Yet, it is also important to recognize that many undergraduate degrees do allow individuals the chance to eventually work within school-based positions after additional training. For example, psychology majors make up a substantial proportion of undergraduate degrees. Individuals who major in psychology or child psychology often have received little training in education and may have rarely taken a course within a college of education. Despite this lack of training, psychology majors can easily put themselves on a path to work in schools by earning an advanced degree in such disciplines as school psychology, school social work, or school counseling. Three additional recommendations for those from nontraditional paths who may be looking to enter into a career in education include the following:

1. Careers in education are not limited to the school setting. It is important to recognize that many industry and governmental entities need educators as a part of their organizations. For example, human resource managers help to educate a company's workforce on issues of health care, retirement, and other benefits associated with a position in the company.
2. Schools are turning to the business world for innovation and reform. Numerous careers in traditional school settings in some communities across the country no longer require a degree or advanced degree in education. For example, limited supply and increased demand of strong school district leaders who can bring a high level of accountability to education have resulted in a push to bring those with degrees in business, such as chief executive officers and chief financial officers, into positions of leadership in schools.

3. Bring your passions to the field of education. It is never too late for retraining, especially when individuals are dissatisfied or unfulfilled in the work that they are currently doing. Many indirect routes into working within schools without traditional education, background, or training are now a reality. This is especially true within low-income communities where the need for services is dire, where resources may be limited, or where persistent school achievement gaps have led to a need for significant change, innovation, and/or reform. One example is Teach for America. In this program, college graduates and professionals commit to teach in public schools for 2 years, oftentimes without appropriate state-level certification. Waivers and emergency certificates are more common than ever given pushes for school reform and issues of supply and demand of educators. A second example is private psychological consulting businesses that contract with school districts to address their special education diagnostic needs via licensed psychologists or limited licensed psychologists who often have very little or no training or background in school psychology.

CAREERS IN EDUCATION: IN DEMAND

We gave considerable thought to selecting careers to feature in *101 Careers in Education* that are currently in significant demand across the country or those that demonstrate the need for an influx of workers in the near future given the "graying" (i.e., pending retirement of a large section of the workforce) of the profession. In addition, we selected careers that have been highlighted in the media as bringing great job satisfaction to those who hold these positions. For example, we cover the following 10 careers that were recently named by *U.S. News & World Report* (2012) as one of the "50 Best Careers" in the United States:

Math teachers	Science teachers
Bilingual educators	Foreign language teachers
Corporate trainers	Day-care center operators
Educational administrators	Special education teachers
School psychologists	Speech and language pathologists

CAREERS IN EDUCATION: PERSONAL CHARACTERISTICS LINKED TO SUCCESS

Identifying careers in education that are in demand is an important step in occupational decision making. Yet, we believe it is most important to find a career that links well to your personality, interests, and passions.

This is an essential issue to consider given the challenges of retention that are currently prevalent in the education field.

Holding a career that sustains one's interest for a lifetime is rare. However, those of us in education must find individuals who want to make a life out of a career in education. The reason to address this need is simple. Those who learn to understand and thrive in an educational system are needed in leadership positions. Thus, the profession has a duty to help find individuals who will not only survive in an educational career but who will ultimately thrive within such a career.

Interest inventories are a career tool that can help individuals match their interests and talents to a career. Specifically, the idea behind these self-assessment tools is that people within the same occupation tend to have similar likes and interests. According to career/interest inventories, we know that those who pursue a college degree in education tend to be service-oriented individuals and wish to give back to others. An initial interest in becoming an educator often derives from an interest in and commitment to helping people grow and develop to their true potential; such individuals find joy in this process. Patience, creativity, dedication, enthusiasm, compassion, and strong interpersonal skills are additional personal characteristics found in those who pursue careers in service. It is interesting to note that this profile is also common for those who choose careers in health care. Those within the hospital- or community-based professions might find themselves examining employment options across settings given their interest in providing service or teaching others. The skills and interests of these individuals often transfer well to careers in school districts, educational settings, and nontraditional settings in which serving, educating, or preparing learners of all ages might take place.

Inherent in serving others through a career in education is a set of qualities that positions one to engage effectively in the teaching–learning relationship. Educators-in-training must appreciate the need for, develop skill in, and succeed in accumulating a diverse array of interpersonal skills. Examples of the skills that have been linked to high-quality teachers include the following:

- Speaking and writing effectively
- Recognizing the important contributions of all learners
- Possessing time-management and organization skills
- Understanding the importance of schooling on children's development

- Recognizing the importance of high-quality student–teacher relationships
- Being passionate about the content/knowledge you are sharing
- Thinking critically while being open to multiple perspectives
- Working collaboratively with others as a part of a team
- Finding enjoyment in working with children or individuals of all ages
- Being excited by the give and take present in the learning process
- Being flexible and adaptable to new situations
- Dealing with adversity and persevering when challenges arise
- Solving problems using data
- Being willing to actively engage in self-assessment and professional development
- Being committed to excellence and continuous improvement
- Focusing on the glass as being "half full"; being optimistic about possibilities

SUMMARY AND NEXT STEPS

So you have now been introduced to what a career in education is and the many paths that one can take to become an educator. You have also had the chance to learn some of the characteristics and qualities associated with individuals who thrive and survive within the field of education. A more thorough discussion of these important interpersonal factors is presented in Chapter 2, Linking Talents and Passions to Careers in Education. We hope you will find that chapter of interest to you and useful to your career search.

In conclusion, let us do three final things as a part of this opening chapter. These will help ready you for an efficient use of the material we present in the book. First, we provide you with an overview of the organizational structure of each of the career reviews selected for inclusion in *101 Careers in Education*. Second, we provide you with the framework of the interviews that we have conducted with individuals in what we term Career-in-Education Profiles, and we encourage you to consider using the interview questions we developed for your own interviews. Finally, we highlight key features of the book that we think help to distinguish it from others pertaining to exploring careers in education. Thank you for your interest in our book, and we wish you all the best in your exploration of and/or search for a career in education.

Organizational Structure of Each Career Review

▓ Basic Description
▓ Core Competencies and Skills Needed
▓ Educational Requirements
▓ Experience Necessary
▓ Certification, Licensure, and Continuing Education Requirements
▓ Salary/Compensation
▓ Employment Outlook
▓ Further Information for Exploration

Featured Careers: Interviews

The first step toward any career in education is to research and uncover the path (e.g., education, training, certification) necessary to successfully enter that career. Unique to our book is the inclusion of interviews with individuals who have held or currently hold the positions we review. A total of 23 interviews with individuals from a diverse array of careers in education are featured. Our interviewees provided responses to a series of questions that we think can be helpful to individuals contemplating future study or employment within these careers. A template of these interview questions is provided on the following page, as we were not able to feature as many careers as there are available. We encourage you to make a copy of that page and consider using it to interview an individual who holds a career in education that you think you might like to explore in more detail.

Summary of Key Features of *101 Careers in Education*

▓ Provides necessary skills, training, certification/licensure, compensation, and employment outlook for each career
▓ Includes career options for new teachers, those changing careers within education, and those seeking education as a second career
▓ Includes many career options outside of traditional school settings
▓ Presents interviews with individuals representing a diverse array of careers in education
▓ Provides self-assessment checklists and questions to help pinpoint a set of careers that link to one's skills, competencies, and interests

CAREER INTERVIEW TEMPLATE

Thank you in advance for your responses to the following questions. I am very interested in pursuing a career path like yours. Your thoughts are greatly appreciated.

Career in education (title):

Describe your educational background.

Describe your prior experiences and the path you took to get to this career.

Describe the work that you do.

What is a typical day like for you in this career?

What is the most challenging part of your career?

What is the most rewarding part of your career?

What advice do you have for someone in high school or currently at the undergraduate level who might be interested in this career?

What advice do you have for someone currently in a different career/ field who might be interested in your career?

If you decided to advance your career, what steps would you take and what career(s) might you seek out?

2 ■ LINKING TALENTS AND PASSIONS TO CAREERS IN EDUCATION

Attrition in the field of education is especially costly. Estimates from a study conducted by the National Commission on Teaching and America's Future (2007) found that as much as $7 billion a year is spent to replace individuals leaving the profession. Some of these costs are associated with those who are retiring. Yet, most causes of attrition are due to a poor fit between those who enter the field of education and the roles/responsibilities expected of them.

For example, many who leave a career in education decide it is not a good fit for them soon after assuming their first job. Sometimes educators lack the professional support/mentorship to succeed when first entering a career in education, but other times they realize the profession is not what they expected. Their "ideal" vision of the career does not match the reality. In other cases of attrition, educators may experience "professional burnout" after a number of years within the field—their inability to sustain their passions and interests results in fatigue and a lack of motivation to continue within the position. Finally, there is a small group of educators who are ineffective in educating others and are asked to leave or are not retained.

Your interest in this book is an exceptional example of how you are taking steps to ensure your success over time within a career that you think you might love. Exploring the diverse array of the 101 careers we feature within the field of education and working to pinpoint those specific careers that may best fit you is a great way to ensure occupational longevity. Preventing attrition is a much more effective approach compared with intervening after career match issues have already emerged.

This chapter bridges the gap between defining the field of education and the paths taken to enter the profession (Chapter 1) and a detailed description of the 101 careers selected for inclusion (Chapters 3–11). We hope you find that this chapter can further help you to (a) confirm that the field of education is a good fit for your interests and motivations and (b) link your specific talents and passions to a subset of our featured 101 careers in education.

Entering into a career that fits well with your temperament is essential to ensuring career satisfaction and longevity. As you embark on a career in education, remember to be up front with who you are, where your interests lie, and how well those interests fit with the qualities necessary for occupational success as an educator. Look for ways to ensure a strong match between a career in education and your skills, competencies, and personality.

In Chapter 1, we established that those who pursue a career as an educator tend to be service-oriented individuals who wish to give back to others, and that an initial interest in becoming an educator often derives from an interest in and commitment to helping people grow and develop to their true potential. To further examine a fit between a career in education and your interests, motivations, and passions, we present five questions that we would like you to answer honestly. Think about how you would answer these today, but also think about how you might answer these at the point when you finish your preparations to enter the field of education, as your responses certainly can change as competencies and skills change. Also consider asking your friends, family, or mentors about whether they perceive you to have these personality and temperamental characteristics. Keep in mind that we are asking about your response to these questions on a typical day—certainly there are times in our lives when it is difficult to provide an affirmative response to one or more of these questions.

SELF-ASSESSMENT QUESTIONS

	YES	NO
1. Are you an optimistic person?	_____	_____
2. Are you patient?	_____	_____
3. Are you outgoing?	_____	_____
4. Are you able to handle frustration well?	_____	_____
5. Are you results oriented?	_____	_____

We anticipate that you can wholeheartedly reply "YES" to each of these five questions given that you have read to this point, but if you can't, we encourage you to further consider why you can't and to be sure to give that reason or reasons close consideration as you review the career descriptions and career interviews that interest you within Chapters 3 to 11. In addition, if you can't answer positively to each of these questions now, think about the experiences or training that might afford you the chance to change your response from "NO" to "YES" in the future.

Next, we provide additional information about why we think your responses to these five questions are so important as you think deeply about embarking on a career in education.

1. *Are you an optimistic person?*
    Do you see the glass as half full? To be a high-quality educator, you must be a positive, optimistic person. Pessimism can be toxic within the field of education. When a pessimistic outlook on life is combined with perceived public dissatisfaction about the teaching profession, the intense pressure to demonstrate accountability for instructional practices, and a general feeling of a lack of respect from others pertaining to those working in education, numerous problems and dysfunction are sure to follow. Embracing the privilege of serving others through a career in education requires an optimistic and positive outlook on life, human development, and the power of knowledge/learning.

2. *Are you patient?*
    Can you adapt appropriately when things don't go your way? Working with others can require the patience of a saint. The moods, motivations, and personalities of learners can wreak havoc on the instructional process. Patience is a virtue when educating others. The ability to adapt to the learning context and the community of learners is essential to be successful. Expecting others to adapt "exclusively" to your methods or style of teaching is inconsistent with what is known about the importance of the teacher–student relationship in the learning process.

3. *Are you outgoing?*
    Can you be enthusiastic about your work? Teaching others requires content knowledge and understanding of the discipline. Being a high-quality teacher requires the ability to share that knowledge with others in an engaging and enthusiastic manner. Although there are some careers in education that embrace the internal workings of an introverted personality, many careers in education require a personality that is infectious and influential on others. Highly developed oral and written communication skills are typical in those who become educators. If those skills are not yet where you want them to be, that is fine. Most important is your willingness to work on them and ready them for the demands expected within the career you pursue.

4. *Are you able to handle frustration well?*
Can you remain calm when faced with adversity? The learning process can be frustrating for both the teacher and the learner. Being able to handle these challenges in a calm and cool manner is critical to working within the field of education. If you are a person whose emotions often get in the way of your ability to problem solve or think critically, this career may be especially frustrating. Reacting in an angry or irritable manner can cause learners to focus on your emotions as opposed to your content. Being distracted by an instructor's emotional state can serve as a substantial barrier to the learning process.

5. *Are you results oriented?*
Can you change your ways if your goals are not met? If you are the type of person who can embrace the importance of needing to show results for your actions, that characteristic will fit perfectly well with this profession. Being focused on an end point, altering your means to reach that end point if your prior means are determined to be ineffective, and showing others that you have reached that end point are especially important for those in education. Given that members of the public have a right to know that their tax dollars are being used effectively, being a data- and outcomes-driven individual is necessary within this profession.

Now that you have further assured yourself that your temperament and personality are aligned well or will be aligned well to the characteristics of those who find success in education-related careers, you are ready to further explore our 101 featured careers in education. To help you to efficiently approach those careers that may best fit with your interests and motivations, please consider the following six questions. These questions are designed to help you identify your preferences for educating others. Your response to each will link those passions to the corresponding chapters presented in our book.

1. Are you interested in full-time or part-time work?
a. Part-time work:
See Chapter 8.
b. Full-time work:
See Chapters 1 to 7 and 9 to 11.
2. What age groups are you primarily interested in working with?
a. Preschool:

See Chapter 3.
  b. K to 12:
  See Chapter 4.
  c. Adults:
  See Chapter 5.
  d. Any age group:
  See Chapters 3 to 11.
3. Do you prefer to work directly with learners?
  a. Yes, I like to work directly with individual learners.
  See Chapters 3 to 5 and 10.
  b. No, I prefer to work with others who directly interact with learners.
  See Chapters 9 and 11.
  c. I prefer to work both directly with learners and with others who directly interact with learners.
  See Chapters 6 to 8.
4. What types of ideas do you typically like to consider?
  a. Big ideas linked to systems change:
  See Chapter 9.
  b. Ideas linked to individuals:
  See Chapters 3 to 8 and 10 to 11.
5. With which kinds of learners are you interested in working?
  a. All children, those who are typically developing and will benefit from traditional effective instructional approaches:
  See Chapters 3 to 5.
  b. Children at risk, those who need some additional supports to be successful in school:
  See Chapter 6.
  c. Tier 3 individuals—children with disabilities and those identified as in need of substantial supports:
  See Chapter 7.
6. In which setting are you most interested in working?
  a. School/educational:
  See Chapters 3 to 5.
  b. University:
  See Chapter 5.
  c. Industry:
  See Chapter 10.
  d. Government:
  See Chapter 10.

The initial chapters (Chapters 3–7) of the book are organized via a framework that is consistent with today's focus in schools on meeting the needs of all learners. This contemporary approach to schooling is referred to as a response-to-intervention (RTI) model of education, and it brings a high level of accountability to the learning of all students.

RTI is a multitier approach to supporting students, especially those with learning and behavior needs. This framework of educational services takes much of its structure and organization from the field of public health. This public health perspective views prevention and intervention efforts along a continuum of need, or, specifically, within three distinct tiers/populations.

The first tier of services is set up to meet the educational needs of *all* individuals within a school setting (e.g., high-quality instruction, effective curriculum) or society (primary prevention). The second tier (secondary prevention) is designed to meet the additional needs of some learners who fail to respond successfully to the services provided to all in Tier 1. This group is often thought of as an at-risk group or a group that can benefit from additional services that target specific areas of need. Such services are usually provided to small groups of students. The third tier (tertiary prevention) is specifically targeted at individuals who fail to respond to the educational services provided at Tier 1 or Tier 2. This is a very small subset of the population and includes those with disabilities. Interventions at this third tier typically are intensive, require considerable resources, and are often provided on an individual basis. Special education within schools is specifically aimed at providing appropriate and effective services to this subset of the population.

We hope that we have made our 101 careers more accessible based on your responses to the questions we present in this chapter. Following the exploration of careers in Chapters 3 to 11, we conclude our book with ideas for the job-search process and discussion of the importance of professional development. Welcome to the field of education, and best wishes with your career search.

REFERENCE

National Commission on Teaching and America's Future. (2007). *The high cost of teacher turnover* (Policy Brief). Retrieved from http://www.nctaf.org/wp-content/uploads/2012/01/NCTAF-Cost-of-Teacher-Turnover-2007-policy-brief.pdf

II ■ CAREERS IN SCHOOLS: SERVING ALL STUDENTS

3 ■ CAREERS WORKING IN EARLY CHILDHOOD EDUCATION

1. PRESCHOOL TEACHER

BASIC DESCRIPTION

Preschool teachers provide education to children ages 0 to 6, in the years prior to enrollment in kindergarten. Teachers in this career work in preschools, day-care centers, or other child-development facilities. Preschool teachers provide children with education primarily pertaining to social, physical, emotional, and cognitive development. In recent years, preschool teachers have become more focused on the development of students' academic-readiness skills. This education is typically provided through structured and unstructured learning activities that encourage children to explore, investigate, and interact with their environment. Specific focus within the preschool setting is given to the development of social skills, self-regulation, communication, early literacy, and other preacademic skills. Some states now require that 4-year-old children enroll in preschool programs funded by state/federal money and run through local school districts. Most preschool teachers in those public classrooms are required to have completed additional degree/training/certification requirements.

CORE COMPETENCIES AND SKILLS NEEDED

Preschool teachers need to have an appreciation of individual differences, a tendency toward guidance and support of children's development, and a propensity for using age-appropriate language that helps children interact appropriately with their environment. Extreme patience, given the developmental nature of the population being served, and the ability to read children's cues and meet their needs are especially beneficial characteristics for those who seek out a career as a preschool teacher. Linking goals and objectives for children's growth and development to appropriate instructional methods is an important skill for preschool teachers to demonstrate. Managing the behavior of individual children and groups of children is essential.

EDUCATIONAL REQUIREMENTS

Requirements vary by state and the setting of employment (private vs. public preschool).

Typically, a high school diploma along with an associate's degree is the minimum requirement. In some cases, having a bachelor's degree can provide numerous opportunities for both entry into and advancement within the field of early childhood education. This is especially true of preschools offered within public school districts.

EXPERIENCE NECESSARY

Coursework pertaining to child development, early childhood education, and early childhood special education are common. Prior experience working in a preschool or day-care setting as an assistant or aide may be expected. Stay-at-home parents may choose to work in public or private preschools as a means to support their income while dually providing an environment of care for their child(ren) either in the preschool setting in which they are teaching or within the building in which they work.

CERTIFICATION, LICENSURE, AND CONTINUING EDUCATION REQUIREMENTS

Many states require preschool and other child-care settings to be licensed. This typically requires that preschool teachers pass background checks, have appropriate immunizations, and possess the necessary certifications (e.g., child development associate) or meet the minimal training requirements (e.g., child-care professional) expected within their state of employment. Professional development through continuing education is often a requirement of those employed in preschool programs.

SALARY/COMPENSATION

Compensation for preschool teachers is typically on the low end of careers in education. Full-time pay varies between $20,000 and $30,000 depending on years of experience and the location of the preschool setting. For example, private or religious preschool programs in urban or rural settings would typically pay considerably less than preschools in suburban settings. Salaries may be on a regular teacher pay scale (e.g., $35,000 plus) for those holding a bachelor's degree and who are teaching preschool within a school district. Median yearly pay according to the Bureau of Labor Statistics (2014) is $27,130.

EMPLOYMENT OUTLOOK

The future of positions for preschool teachers is stronger than that for most careers, both in and out of the field of education, given the increased focus and importance that society has placed on early childhood education. Low pay, high rates of staff turnover, and the challenges associated with teaching young children also result in considerable demand for high-quality preschool teachers.

FURTHER INFORMATION FOR EXPLORATION

Numerous early childhood professional organizations exist to support both early childhood education and the professionals who hold careers in the field. Zero to Three: National Center for Infants, Toddlers, and Families (www.zerotothree.org) is an example of a national organization dedicated to promoting the importance of the healthy development and well-being of young children and their families. The National Association for the Education of Young Children (NAEYC; www.naeyc .org) is an example of a professional association and an entity that provides accreditation for early childhood programs. NAEYC is focused on high-quality educational and developmental services for children from birth through age 8.

2. HEAD START TEACHER

BASIC DESCRIPTION

Head Start (for 3- to 5-year-olds) or Early Head Start (0- to 3-year-olds) teachers work within federally funded Head Start programs. These preschools are designed to meet the comprehensive needs of young children from families that are living in poverty. Head Start provides 90% of its enrollment spots based on family income level. Head Start preschool programs provide a range of services (e.g., education, health, social services) to meet the needs of children who come from financially impoverished environments. Low income has been linked to higher rates of developmental (e.g., social, emotional, behavioral, cognitive) challenges, and services provided within Head Start are perceived to be an effective form of early intervention/prevention for young children who are at risk. School readiness and child development are major foci of Head Start, and the following 11 early learning domains currently drive classroom practices: English language development (applies to dual-language learners), physical development and health, social and emotional development, creative arts expression, approaches to learning, language development, literacy knowledge and skills, logic and reasoning, mathematics knowledge and skills, science knowledge and skills, and social studies knowledge and skills. Teachers who work within the Head Start setting, as with most of those who work in preschools, provide structured and unstructured learning activities that encourage children to explore, investigate, and interact with their preschool environment. Head Start teachers work as a part of a team of providers that supports and promotes the development of the whole child. This team typically includes a teacher assistant, a paraprofessional/lunch staff, a family advocate, an early childhood classroom consultant, and other interdisciplinary staff who provide comprehensive service delivery to children and their families.

CORE COMPETENCIES AND SKILLS NEEDED

Head Start teachers not only need competencies and skills similar to those of other early childhood care providers (e.g., early childhood education, child development), but they also can benefit from having a strong belief in social justice and a desire to make a difference in the lives of young children who are at risk for later developmental challenges. Skills in managing the behavior of individual children and groups of children are essential.

EDUCATIONAL REQUIREMENTS

Requirements for education, training, and credentials are set at the national level. At least half of all center-based Head Start teachers (lead or assistant teachers) must have an associate, baccalaureate, or advanced degree in early childhood education or a degree in a related field. A greater emphasis is currently being placed on hiring Head Start teachers who have the minimum qualification of holding a bachelor's degree in early childhood education or a related field of study.

EXPERIENCE NECESSARY

Coursework pertaining to child development, early childhood education, cultural competence, and early childhood special education is expected. Experience teaching at the preschool level is also required.

CERTIFICATION, LICENSURE, AND CONTINUING EDUCATION REQUIREMENTS

The Infant/Toddler (Early Head Start) or Preschool (Head Start) Child Development Associate (CDA) credential is the minimum requirement for those working in Head Start programs, and recent policy changes now require this credential from teacher assistants as well. Professional development through continuing education is often a requirement of those employed in preschool programs. All Head Start programs are required to provide training and education to their staff.

SALARY/COMPENSATION

Compensation is typically on the low end of careers in education. Full-time pay varies between $18,000 and $30,000 depending on years of experience, the degree/credential held, and the location of the Head Start setting. Median yearly pay according to data summarized in 2011 by the National Head Start Association is $22,300 for a Child Development Associate, $26,000 for those with an associate's degree, and just under $30,000 for those with a baccalaureate degree.

EMPLOYMENT OUTLOOK

The future of positions for Head Start teachers is stronger than that of most careers, both in and out of the field of education, given the increased focus and importance placed on early childhood education. One example is the recent increase in federal and state funding for Early Head Start programs and other educational programs for young children. However, decreased federal funding, including budget cuts, has affected and will continue to potentially impact the Head Start workforce. Low pay, high teacher turnover, and job burnout are common issues within Head Start furthering the demand for high-quality Head Start and Early Head Start teachers.

FURTHER INFORMATION FOR EXPLORATION

Numerous early childhood professional organizations exist to support Head Start teachers and other teachers working with early childhood populations. The National Head Start Association (www.nhsa.org) is one specific professional organization aimed at supporting Head Start teachers and, more specifically, early childhood development and the education of children growing up under vulnerable conditions. The organization also publishes a peer-reviewed journal called the *NHSA Dialog: The Research-to-Practice Journal for the Early Childhood Field* that is available to read free of charge at journals.uncc.edu/dialog.

3. EARLY CHILDHOOD CLASSROOM CONSULTANT

BASIC DESCRIPTION

An early childhood classroom consultant, also known as early childhood mental health consultant or classroom consultant, is focused on children's social and emotional development. Early childhood mental health consultation is aimed at improving the capacity of early education teachers, families, programs, and systems to prevent, assess, intervene, and diminish the impact of mental health problems in young children ages 0 to 8 years. Classroom or mental health consultation typically takes two forms. The first is programmatic consultation, which is focused on impacting quality of care and supporting systems and services. It is provided at the system or classroom level. The second is individual teacher and parent consultation aimed at the early intervention of identified risk for a particular child. A pyramid approach to services helps to structure and guide a consultant's purpose, which is to ensure (a) an effective workforce to meet the needs of young children; (b) nurturing and responsive relationships with staff, parents, and children; (c) high-quality, supportive environments that meet the individual needs of a diverse group of young children; (d) early intervention and prevention services that are targeted at social and emotional supports for young children who have been identified as being at risk; and (e) intensive interventions for young children who display developmental delays, deficits, or behaviors that impair their functioning. Frequent classroom observations and home visits are necessary to carry out the work of an early childhood classroom consultant. Modeling, role playing, practicing, and coaching other adults are common techniques used within this career.

CORE COMPETENCIES AND SKILLS NEEDED

Early childhood classroom consultants are specialists in early childhood mental health and classroom-based supports for promoting healthy social–emotional learning in young children. Data-based decision-making skills are an essential quality of those within this career. Consultants have training in classroom observation techniques, social and emotional screening approaches, the development of individualized action plans, skills necessary for referral and access of community-based services, and effective professional development techniques. Being a social–emotional specialist who is effective in working with young children is essential. Yet, most important, an early childhood classroom consultant must be able to work effectively with other adults so that together they can directly and effectively influence a child's development. This means that cultural competencies and evidence-based early childhood mental health practices are employed on a regular basis. Teamwork, coaching, and extensive documenting of progress monitoring for evidence of effective consultative practices are essential elements of work as a classroom consultant, and skills in these areas are necessary.

EDUCATIONAL REQUIREMENTS

Coursework pertaining to early childhood development, social–emotional health, parenting practices, teacher classroom management, collaborative consultation, caregiver–child relationships, reflective practices, and mental health assessment and intervention is necessary. Typically, an undergraduate degree *and* a master's degree in social work, psychology, counseling, or a related field help to meet the training standards required of these mental health consultants.

EXPERIENCE NECESSARY

Prior work with young children who are developmentally at risk, those with disabilities, and those presenting with mental health issues is important. Experience as an early childhood educator can also provide an effective context for consulting with caregivers.

CERTIFICATION, LICENSURE, AND CONTINUING EDUCATION REQUIREMENTS

Those who are credentialed in their respective fields, such as a certified social worker or a master's licensed psychologist, are desired. Certification as an infant mental health specialist or as a certified mental health professional/associate also can help distinguish an individual from other applicants. Continuing education and a commitment to learning are essential to maintain a high level of knowledge in a rapidly evolving field with an emerging body of knowledge pertaining to early childhood mental health.

SALARY/COMPENSATION

The average salary for an early childhood classroom consultant is between $30,000 and $45,000, depending on location and certification/licensure.

EMPLOYMENT OUTLOOK

The increased focus on early childhood education has created a substantial need for early childhood classroom consultants. Head Start mandates involvement of these mental health specialists in Head Start programs, and school districts that are increasing their early childhood programs appear to be adding these specialists to their staff at a brisk pace, based on a review of job-placement websites.

FURTHER INFORMATION FOR EXPLORATION

One resource of particular value to early childhood classroom consultants is the website of the Center for Early Childhood Mental Health Consultation (www.ecmhc.org). To further explore the field of early childhood mental health and to determine whether your interests align with work performed within this career, also explore the websites of the World Association for Infant Mental Health (www.waimh.org), the Center on Social and Emotional Foundations for Early Learning (www.csefel.edu), and the Technical Assistance Center on Social Emotional Intervention for Young Children (www.challengingbehavior.org).

Career-in-Education Profile
EARLY CHILDHOOD CLASSROOM CONSULTANT
Interview With Kerry Frawley (BA, Sociology; MSW, Social Work)

Describe your educational background.

I majored in sociology with a minor in philosophy. I then earned an advanced degree in social work. As a part of my graduate studies, I provided social work services in the public schools. I also did a field placement at a learning center doing therapy with very young children and their parents. Finally, I earned my social work certification from a public university in the Midwest.

Describe your prior experiences and the path you took to get to this career.

While in high school, I volunteered at a nursing home. In college, I volunteered in the emergency room and was in charge of admissions and check-in. After finishing my sociology degree, I worked in advertising but found that I didn't like that line of work. I then worked at a law firm that specialized in adoption and provided case management services to the birth mothers. Part of my role was to assess the birth mother's thoughts about her decision to give up the baby for adoption. That work was career changing. I then began taking classes in social work and gained experience by working at an adolescent psychiatric hospital.

Describe the work that you do.

Classroom consultants screen classrooms for social, emotional, and behavioral concerns regarding students. Also, part of the job is consulting with teachers and staff regarding concerns about the children in their classes as well as overall classroom management. There are times when classroom consultants are called to make referrals to Child Protective Services. Another piece of the role is supporting staff. Often the staff members are very stressed and overwhelmed and the classroom consultant is one who can support

(continued)

(continued)

them, troubleshoot with them, as well as just listen to their overall stressors. Classroom consultants, also known as early childhood mental health consultants, work on a continuum to support the adults (parents and staff) to understand and respond to each child and/or group of children's needs. Examples include participation in teaching teams, conducting parent/staff meetings, being involved in administrative groups, and working closely with community-based agencies.

What is a typical day like for you in this career?

There is no typical day in this career. One must be flexible because crises always arise. However, in my typical routine, I usually start in the office and then go observe classrooms. I then do home visits to work with parents or observe a child in the home. I consult with teachers regarding behavior plans that have been written and implemented. Documentation and being accountable for my services is an important part of my daily responsibilities.

What is the most challenging part of your career?

The most challenging part of my career is the stress of whether or not the program will be funded each year. Every year there are concerns that Head Start will not receive sufficient federal funding. The second most challenging part of the career is that Head Start standards/policies are always changing and when one thing is learned something new has to be learned very quickly.

What is the most rewarding part of your career?

The most important part of my career is when I see that a child's behavior has changed due to the changes that the family has made as a result of my consultative services. Many of the families that I work with in Head Start have lots of challenges, whether they are social–emotional or financial. These life challenges also create barriers to effective parenting.

(continued)

(continued)

What advice do you have for someone in high school or currently at the undergraduate level who might be interested in this career?

The advice I would give individuals who are interested in going into this career is that I would suggest they have a backup plan. Although the career is very rewarding and fun, it does often have its financial struggles. I would also tell them to be flexible in case they don't like the work they would be doing. They also need to remember that much of the work of a consultant is with adults and not necessarily direct service provision to young children. Working with adults (e.g., parents, teachers) who work with young children is the primary focus of this position.

What advice do you have for someone currently in a different career/field who might be interested in your career?

First, really analyze why you would want to change careers. Next, try to job shadow for a while to see whether or not a position in education is truly what you think it will be. Finally, explore the economic aspect of the career and whether or not the income would be a factor. For example, if you are in a much more lucrative field, explore this career by doing volunteer work in a preschool classroom.

If you decided to advance your career, what steps would you take and what career(s) might you seek out?

In my line of work there are many different careers to choose from. For example, after 13 years as a classroom consultant, I decided I needed a change. My vision was to get additional experience working across the age range of children. I especially wanted to get back to working with teenagers who were struggling with social–emotional issues. I decided to take a position in a local school district as a school social worker. I have also considered seeking out my ultimate career dream: to be in private practice where I might see a variety of clients (ages 3 to 25 years) and control my own work schedule.

4. HOME VISITOR

BASIC DESCRIPTION

Home visitors, also known as family educators or family advocates, are employed in a number of different agencies. Home visiting has a long history in the field of nursing as being an evidence-based approach to meeting the needs of pregnant women and new moms/parents. Typically, in the field of early childhood education, home visitors work with caregivers in the home setting to improve maternal and child health, reduce accidents, prevent child maltreatment, increase school-readiness skills, reduce domestic violence, support families' economic self-sufficiency, and help connect families to community-based services. Developing a positive relationship with participating families and the use of effective family education practices are essential to the success of in-home services.

CORE COMPETENCIES AND SKILLS NEEDED

Home visitors are particularly good at working with caregivers to conduct a needs assessment and identify a plan of action to meet those particular needs. These positions are often directed at low-income families and other families residing in high-risk communities (e.g., high rates of crime, school dropout, and child abuse). The ability to communicate effectively, listen attentively, and keep focused on problem solving are particular attributes of those who work successfully as home visitors. Understanding, empathizing, and appreciating each family's unique economic, developmental, and cultural background is crucial to developing a strong, trusting relationship. A nonjudgmental, respectful, and professional approach to working with families is essential. Specific knowledge pertaining to young children's health, parent education, poverty, special education services, and community-based services aimed at supporting families and young children are particularly helpful within this career. A family-strengths perspective is essential to home visitors given the challenges and stressors faced by families with young children. A family or neighborhood's unique deficits and challenges can be quite substantial and often serve as a barrier to implementing and sustaining an appropriate course of action. In this position it is important to be flexible and receptive to change in the face of crises and challenges. Staying positive and using a family's particular strengths as a part of the treatment plan is important. Good organizational and time-management skills are essential to meeting the diverse and sometimes erratic schedules of the families being served.

EDUCATIONAL REQUIREMENTS

Educational requirements for home visitors vary considerably depending on the employing agency (e.g., public school, child-care program, Head Start, special education). Some positions may only require a high school diploma with appropriate training and experiences. The majority require at least a 2-year degree, such as an associate's degree in child development, education, social sciences, or a related field. Other positions may require a bachelor's degree in early childhood education or a master's degree pertaining to early intervention services, early childhood special education, and social work.

EXPERIENCE NECESSARY

Prior experience working with families concerning issues of health and mental health are important. Successful experience working in high-risk communities is often sought by those hiring home visitors. Individuals who are parents and grandparents may bring a unique and needed perspective to this work.

CERTIFICATION, LICENSURE, AND CONTINUING EDUCATION REQUIREMENTS

State-level credentialing related to home visiting, such as the Child Development Associate credential, the Family Development credential, or an early childhood certification, may be particularly important to obtain prior to working as a home visitor. Continuing education is expected, with a particular emphasis on keeping up to date on home- and family-based interventions that are effective in meeting young children's health and mental health needs.

SALARY/COMPENSATION

Earnings for a home visitor vary widely by state and employing agency. Average hourly pay appears to be in the range of $10 to $20 per hour and will typically vary based on credentials, degree, and years of experience. This hourly rate equates to a salary below $30,000 per year. For those with master's degrees working in certain parts of the country, salaries may approach $40,000. Wages and benefits are typically low within this career given the limited resources that are found within high-risk communities that employ home visitors.

EMPLOYMENT OUTLOOK

Increasing numbers of agencies, including public schools, are now focused on early childhood development and education. The perceived effectiveness (i.e., low cost, high return on investment) of the home visiting programs associated with early childhood education seems to be leading to an increased focus on these positions. The mandate of these services within the federally funded Early Head Start and Head Start programs will likely create a strong demand for high-quality, well-trained home visitors for many years to come. Bilingual home visitors are particularly in demand.

FURTHER INFORMATION FOR EXPLORATION

The Parents as Teachers program (www.parentsasteachers.org) is an approved home visiting model that meets the evidence-based criteria of the federally funded Maternal, Infant, and Early Childhood program. The mission of the nonprofit Parents as Teachers group is to help organizations and professionals work with parents of children ages 0 to 5 years of age.

5. PARENT EDUCATOR

BASIC DESCRIPTION

The primary responsibility of parent educators is to improve a person's parenting skills. They do this through planning, coordinating, and teaching programs that address the well-being of both parents and their children. These strategies can be geared to different stages of parenting, such as those who wish to have a child or those who would like to adopt a child. Parent education can also be delivered to individuals who are going to have a child, such as pregnant women and their partners. Finally, individuals who already have a child might choose to take part in a parenting class in an effort to prevent problems or to help them manage existing parent–child interaction difficulties (e.g., parent management training programs). Parent educators are often employed through early childhood education programs in schools, Head Start programs, or community-based settings. Parent education programs are typically geared to different levels of a child's development, such as infancy, toddlerhood, or the teenage years. To understand what parent educators teach, it is essential to explore what makes parents effective at parenting their children. These details can be gleaned from specific evidence-based parenting training programs that have been identified as being universally effective and are utilized frequently across the world. Such programs include Triple P (Positive Parenting Program; www.triplep.net) and the Incredible Years (www.incredibleyears.com). Reviewing these two parenting programs provides a good overview of the type of knowledge and skills (e.g., the use of parenting practices and strategies that promote children's academic, social, and emotional skills) that are taught by parent educators. These skills include (a) creating a safe, interesting, and responsive environment for children; (b) using assertive discipline; (c) providing realistic expectations; and (d) ensuring that both parents and children experience a positive and healthy relationship. There are various approaches one can use to deliver parenting curriculums, including large-group, small-group, or an individual format.

CORE COMPETENCIES AND SKILLS NEEDED

In order to support parents and help them work toward meeting their needs, parent educators need to be good at self-reflection, especially as it relates to interpersonal interactions. The ability to form secure, trusting relationships with parents is essential. Having skills in planning, marketing, and evaluating parenting programs is also important. Use of effective instructional strategies helps to ensure that parents can access, use, and practice what has been taught. Finally, it is important to be able to consult and a build professional network with other parent educators. Thus, communication skills, conscientiousness, and professionalism are essential for working as a parent educator.

EDUCATIONAL REQUIREMENTS

Coursework pertaining to child and life-span development, family systems, family education, diversity, home–school collaboration, and assessment/evaluation is typical for those who wish to be parent educators. Diverse arrays of degree programs link well to the competencies and skills required of parent educators. Examples of undergraduate and graduate degree programs include parent education, marriage and family counseling, mental health counseling, social work, early childhood education, and early childhood special education.

EXPERIENCE NECESSARY

Prior experience in helping parents to understand and nurture their children's development is necessary. A work history that demonstrates prior success in helping parents to guide, motivate, and advocate on behalf of their children is important.

CERTIFICATION, LICENSURE, AND CONTINUING EDUCATION REQUIREMENTS

Certification and licensure requirements vary by state and the employing agency. The National Council on Family Relations offers a Certified Life Educator (CFLE) professional certification that provides evidence that a parent educator is well trained for the position. This certification requires a minimum of a baccalaureate degree and at least 2 years of experience in a family life education program. In the state of Minnesota, a parent educator license is required for those who wish to work in the public schools, such as within the early childhood family education program.

SALARY/COMPENSATION

The salary range varies by state, employing agency, and the degree held by the employee. Those with a master's degree may earn up to $40,000 per year. Typically, those with a bachelor's degree will earn less than $30,000 when first entering the career. Low pay and minimal benefits have been associated with this position as well as other early childhood education careers.

EMPLOYMENT OUTLOOK

Substantial population increases for children between the ages of 3 and 5 are anticipated. This projected increase combined with a federal- and state-level focus on the importance and value of early childhood education and the important role that parents play in this education suggest that this career field will grow substantially in the coming years.

FURTHER INFORMATION FOR EXPLORATION

A valuable resource used to explore the career of parent educator is the National Parenting Education Network (www.npen.org). In addition, the website of the Parents as Teachers organization that was recommended for those interested in a career as a home visitor is also an excellent resource for those interested in a career as a parent educator (www.parentsasteachers.org).

REFERENCE

Bureau of Labor Statistics, U.S. Department of Labor. (2014). *Occupational outlook handbook, 2014-2015 edition, Preschool Teachers.* Retrieved July 7, 2015, from http://www.bls.gov/ooh/education-training-and-library/preschool-teachers.htm

4 ■ CAREERS WORKING IN K–12 SCHOOLS

6. KINDERGARTEN TEACHER

BASIC DESCRIPTION

Kindergarten teachers prepare 4- to 6-year-old students for future schooling. They teach and refine a number of basic interpersonal skills, such as sharing, playing fair, working with a peer, keeping one's hands to oneself, and using one's words to communicate needs. Kindergarten teachers are instrumental in teaching and promoting basic academic skills such as early literacy (e.g., print concepts, word recognition, phonics, fluency, phonemic awareness), early writing (e.g., text types and purposes), and early numeracy (e.g., number recognition, simple math, story problems). Introductions to age-appropriate lessons in science, art, music, social studies, literature, and other school subjects are also provided. Most teachers at this level teach the same group of children throughout the day. Some may teach a different group if half-day morning and afternoon sessions are available in the school district. Typically, grading of homework is not involved at this grade level; however, parent involvement and close communication with caregivers can take up a substantial amount of time given the developmental nature and needs of children who are entering the formal elementary school setting. Issues pertaining to social–emotional, intellectual, and language development are especially important. For example, separation anxiety from parents/home, diverse levels of academic-readiness skills, a wide range of intellectual and physical development, issues of self-regulation, and behavior management are unique challenges within a kindergarten classroom.

CORE COMPETENCIES AND SKILLS NEEDED

Patience, kindness, caring, and a great respect for both children and parents are essential for this career. A desire to engage children readily in active learning is essential given the varying levels of attention present at this developmental stage. Skills in classroom management and effective use of transitions are essential. Having "eyes in the back of your head" is an especially important quality, as vigilance and keen observation skills are necessary to help keep a group of young people learning and productive throughout the school day.

EDUCATIONAL REQUIREMENTS

A bachelor's degree from a recognized teacher preparation program is required; some states may require an alternative route to certification for those with degrees in other fields. States may also require completion of a general teaching certification test. Background checks are required of all teachers. Coursework in undergraduate elementary education degree programs typically includes multiple professional education courses and courses in elementary mathematics, children's literature, science, history, geography, creative arts, child-centered arts, and physical activity/health.

EXPERIENCE NECESSARY

Student teaching (practicum experience) within degree programs is required, although some degree programs require this internship or student teaching placement to occur in the final year of training or post-degree. This work involves close supervision and collaboration with a mentor teacher within the district. It is through this experience and specialized curriculum (e.g., early childhood, literacy) that teachers show specialization in the early elementary school years.

CERTIFICATION, LICENSURE, AND CONTINUING EDUCATION REQUIREMENTS

Kindergarten teachers must have state-issued certification or licensure to be employed in schools. Teaching certificates may be for grades K–3 or K–5, and preparation in teaching across these grade levels is expected. Most states require additional training and coursework post-certification, and many districts are supportive of teachers who work on advanced degrees, such as a master's degree. Some states now require their teachers to earn a master's degree.

SALARY/COMPENSATION

According to the Bureau of Labor Statistics (2014c), the median pay for a kindergarten teacher is $50,120, yet there is considerable geographical variation, making it important to look closely within states/districts for a more accurate picture of salaries. Employee benefits such as health insurance and retirement matching often create a well-compensated position for kindergarten teachers working under a 9-month contract in public or private schools.

EMPLOYMENT OUTLOOK

Currently, many parts of the country are saturated with a large supply of kindergarten teachers. However, rural and urban areas continue to show great demand for highly qualified individuals who match the racial diversity of the students being served. In addition, bilingual teachers (e.g., English/Spanish) are in significant demand in many parts of the country.

FURTHER INFORMATION FOR EXPLORATION

To learn more about a career as a kindergarten teacher, visit the website of the National Kindergarten Alliance (www.nkateach.org), an organization designed to promote high-quality kindergarten programming. In addition, many states offer their own professional organizations to support kindergarten teachers (e.g., www.njake.org, www.californiakindergartenassociation.org). The National Education Association (www.nea.org) and the National Association for the Education of Young Children (www.naeyc.org) provide many helpful resources covering the latest developments in educating young children.

7.   SECOND-GRADE TEACHER

BASIC DESCRIPTION

Second-grade teachers work with students who are 7 to 9 years of age. Second-grade teachers are instrumental in ensuring that students have the basic academic skills necessary to succeed in later school years. This includes teaching literacy (e.g., reading for comprehension, story elements, character traits), writing (e.g., appropriate use of subjects, verbs, adjectives), and math skills (e.g., computational and measurement skills, introductory geometry). Age-appropriate lessons in science, social studies, and other school subjects are also provided. Teachers at this level may teach different groups of children throughout the day, specializing in reading, math, science, or social studies. Typically, grading of homework becomes a greater responsibility for teachers at this grade level. Parent–teacher conferences, engagement in professional in-service activities, and working closely with other staff are inherent in this career.

CORE COMPETENCIES AND SKILLS NEEDED

Skills in organization and time management are especially important at this grade level. Facilitating, monitoring, mentoring, and teaching are active roles taken throughout the day as children are taught in large groups, as they break out into small groups, as they work with peer partners, and as they work independently at their desks. Classroom management skills are essential given the distractions that can occur and impede the learning of the entire classroom.

EDUCATIONAL REQUIREMENTS

A bachelor's degree from a recognized teacher preparation program is required; some states may require an alternative route to certification for those with degrees in other fields. States may also require completion of a general teaching certification test. Background checks are required of all teachers. Coursework in undergraduate elementary education degree programs typically includes multiple professional education courses, early child development, teaching methods, diversity, elementary mathematics, children's literature, science, history, geography, creative arts, child-centered arts, and physical activity/health. A particular emphasis on one or more of the elementary core content areas may be required, as some districts require second-grade teachers to teach multiple groups on the same subject matter.

EXPERIENCE NECESSARY

Student teaching (practicum experience) within degree programs is typically required, although some degree programs require this internship or student teaching placement to occur in the final year of training or post degree. This work involves close supervision and collaboration with a mentor teacher within the district. It is through this experience and unique curricular electives (e.g., in language arts, math, science, and social studies) that teachers begin to show areas of specialization in the early elementary school years.

CERTIFICATION, LICENSURE, AND CONTINUING EDUCATION REQUIREMENTS

Second-grade teachers must have state-issued certification or licensure to be employed in schools. Teaching certificates may be for grades K–3 or K–5, and preparation in teaching across these grade levels is expected. Most states require additional training and coursework post-certification, and many districts are supportive of teachers who work on advanced degrees, such as a master's degree. Some states now require their teachers to earn a master's degree in the areas in which they serve as a primary instructor.

SALARY/COMPENSATION

According to the Bureau of Labor Statistics (2014c), the median pay for a second-grade teacher is $53,400, yet there is considerable geographical variation, making it important to look closely within states/districts for a more accurate picture of salaries. Employee benefits such as health insurance and retirement matching often create a well-compensated 9-month position for those working in public or private schools.

EMPLOYMENT OUTLOOK

Currently, many parts of the country are saturated with a large supply of second-grade teachers. However, rural and urban areas continue to show great demand for those who are highly qualified and who help to match the racial diversity of the students being served. In addition, bilingual teachers (e.g., English/Spanish) and specialists (e.g., master's degree) are in significant demand in many parts of the country.

FURTHER INFORMATION FOR EXPLORATION

To learn more about a career as a second-grade teacher, the websites of the National Education Association (www.nea.org) and the Association of American Educators (www.aaeteachers.org) can be of assistance. To explore the types of skills that a student is expected to acquire during the second grade, see the helpful webpage and associated resources at www.scholastic.com at the "Parents" page under the "School Success" tab.

Career-in-Education Profile
SECOND-GRADE TEACHER

Interview With Erin DiPerna (BS, Elementary Education;
MS, Educational Psychology)

Describe your educational background.

I graduated with a degree in elementary education and a concentration in social studies. I completed my student teaching in first- and fourth-grade classrooms. During the first part of my teaching career, I worked with an interdisciplinary group of researchers at a large public university. Through this research project, I was able to complete a master's degree in educational psychology with a specialization in cognitive psychology.

Describe your prior experiences and the path you took to get to this career.

When growing up, I always loved working with children. One summer, I coached the "8 and under" swim team and taught hundreds of swim lessons. It was the perfect job for me because I gained experience working with large groups of kids and the "teacher qualities" of patience, optimism, organization, flexibility, and communication with parents. After college, I moved to a small rural town where I took my first teaching job as an alternative education teacher with 6th-through 10th-grade students and learned three very valuable lessons:

1. Do everything possible to never let any of my students "fall through the cracks."
2. Making personal connections with students outweighs any academics taught.
3. Ask more questions in job interviews, as it's better to realize fit before you take a job.

The following year, I spent 1 year teaching second grade in this rural school district and realized that even the smallest, seemingly insignificant things (like a box of tissues or a package of cookies) can mean the world to a child who has little. I also realized that all parents love their children and are committed to seeing them succeed. After

(continued)

(*continued*)

a number of different teaching positions and 10 years away from the classroom given the most important teaching job I have had to date, being a mom to my three children, I am now back in the classroom teaching second grade.

Describe the work that you do.

Currently, I teach in a second-grade classroom in a school district near a large university town in the eastern United States. Each year I have between 18 and 24 second graders. I am responsible for teaching language arts, writing, math, social studies, and science to my students.

What is a typical day like for you in this career?

I typically arrive at school 45 minutes before the students arrive. Making photocopies, e-mailing parents, talking to colleagues, and preparing for activities are tasks that need to be done before the students arrive. When the bell rings, I greet each of my students at the door and help them unpack their homework or notes from home. I take attendance, and might comfort a student whose pet passed away the night before, or listen to a student talk about his baby brother who is going to arrive soon. The Pledge of Allegiance is next. We then all gather for our Morning Meeting, where I go over the schedule and announcements. We end every Morning Meeting with a game or a dance. We then get ready for Snack and Read Aloud. As the kids eat, I read a chapter from such books as *Gooseberry Park*, *James and the Giant Peach*, and *Because of Winn-Dixie*. Next up is language arts. Students work on reading strategies, vocabulary, and writing. Next is math; I teach a whole-group math lesson and then we break into math stations. Then we have 15 minutes for lunch followed by 15 minutes for recess. Then it is Stop Often and Read (SOAR) time, and then a 1-hour block of writing. The focus is on editing and revising. Next is afternoon recess, where I can be found refereeing kickball and wallball games. After recess, my students then go to special classes (art, gym, library, or music) or science and social studies, depending on the day. Finally, students return to the classroom and get packed up

(*continued*)

(continued)

to leave. Each afternoon, I stay at school until 5:00 to get ready for the next day or to attend meetings with staff or parents.

What is the most challenging part of your career?

Year after year, my greatest challenge is with the rare student who has severe behavioral issues. Being an advocate for inclusive practices, I struggle having a student in my classroom whose behavior has a negative effect on not only fellow classmates, but teachers and support staff as well. The emotional strain is indescribable.

What is the most rewarding part of your career?

The most rewarding part of my career is "when a light bulb flicks on in their little heads." Being witness to the social, emotional, behavioral, and academic progress of my students and helping them to become lifelong learners is a fantastic part of the job. When my students have a passion for learning, there is nothing better or more rewarding.

What advice do you have for someone in high school or currently at the undergraduate level who might be interested in this career?

Take the time to shadow elementary school teachers in different grades for at least a week early in your college career. I think that it's important to see the weekly demands and the pros and cons of the teaching profession. Finally, think seriously about your readiness to be a part of a profession that is probably the second hardest job after being a parent, yet equally exciting and fulfilling.

What advice do you have for someone currently in a different career/field who might be interested in your career?

I would want them to be absolutely sure about switching into a profession that may bring less pay and possibly require a few years of substitute teaching before they get a full-time contract.

(continued)

(*continued*)

If you decided to advance your career, what steps would you take and what career(s) might you seek out?

I have considered working toward certification to become a reading specialist, which would require 2 years of classwork (while working full time). Some teachers also broaden their degree by getting certification in special education.

8. FIFTH-GRADE TEACHER

BASIC DESCRIPTION

Fifth-grade teachers work with students who are typically between the ages of 10 and 11. Fifth graders show substantial diversity both physically and academically. Their independent thinking skills can both facilitate and hinder instructional processes. They tend to enjoy being treated as if they are older, yet also appreciate the reassurance, support, and guidance of their teachers as they did when they were younger. Being able to read and decipher the individual needs of students is particularly essential at this grade. Addressing issues such as students' use of humor or lack thereof, their friendship preferences, their learning styles, how they handle success/failure, and their motivations for learning/behaving are key to facilitating successful learning. Peer socialization takes on significantly greater meaning at this age and can serve as a major distraction and barrier to the instructional environment. Small-group learning and peer tutoring are two ways to capitalize on students' desire to be social. Role-playing or modeling appropriate behavior, combined with high expectations for learning and behavior, can be a powerful classroom management tool at this grade level. Teaching fifth graders to modify and adapt their behavior as situationally appropriate is a very important skill. Most fifth-grade teachers instruct different groups of children throughout the day and may specialize in reading, math, science, or social studies. Typically, grading of homework becomes a significantly greater responsibility at this grade level. Parent–teacher conferences, engagement in professional in-service activities, and working as a team are inherent aspects of this career.

CORE COMPETENCIES AND SKILLS NEEDED

Classroom management is especially important at this grade level. Facilitating, monitoring, mentoring, and teaching are active roles taken throughout the day as children are taught in large groups, as they break out into small groups, as they work with peer partners, and as they work independently at their desks. Adaptability and flexibility are essential.

EDUCATIONAL REQUIREMENTS

A bachelor's degree from a recognized teacher preparation program is required; some states may require an alternative route to certification for those with degrees in other fields. States may also require completion of a general teaching certification test. Content tests may also be required at the advanced elementary grades. Background checks are required of all teachers. Coursework in undergraduate elementary education degree programs typically includes multiple professional education courses, teaching methods, diversity, elementary mathematics, children's literature, science, history, geography, and creative arts. A particular emphasis on one or more of the elementary core content areas is typical, as fifth-grade teachers tend to teach multiple groups on the same subject matter across the school day.

EXPERIENCE NECESSARY

Student teaching (practicum experience) within degree programs is typically required, although some degree programs require this internship or student teaching placement to occur in the final year of training or post degree. This work involves close supervision by and collaboration with a mentor teacher within the district. It is through this experience and unique curricular electives (e.g., in language arts, math, science, and social studies) that teachers begin to show areas of specialization in the later elementary school years.

CERTIFICATION, LICENSURE, AND CONTINUING EDUCATION REQUIREMENTS

Fifth-grade teachers must have state-issued certification or licensure to be employed in schools. Teaching certificates are typically granted across the elementary grades of K–5/6, and preparation in teaching across these grade levels is expected. Most states require additional training and coursework post certification, and many districts are supportive of teachers who work on advanced degrees, such as a master's degree.

Some states now require their teachers to earn a master's degree, especially if advanced content is being delivered in math or science.

SALARY/COMPENSATION

According to the Bureau of Labor Statistics (2014c), the median pay for a fifth-grade teacher (and all elementary-grade teachers) is $53,400, yet there is considerable geographical variation, making it important to look closely within states/districts for a more accurate picture of salaries. Employee benefits such as health insurance and retirement matching often create a well-compensated 9-month position for those working in public or private schools.

EMPLOYMENT OUTLOOK

Currently, many parts of the country are saturated with a large supply of fifth-grade teachers. However, rural and urban areas continue to show high demand for those who are highly qualified and who help to match the racial diversity of the students being served. In addition, bilingual teachers (e.g., English/Spanish) and specialists (e.g., master's degree) are in significant demand in many parts of the country.

FURTHER INFORMATION FOR EXPLORATION

To explore the types of skills that a student is expected to acquire during the fifth grade, see www.pbs.org/parents/education/going-to-school/grade-by-grade/fifth/ or the Common Core Curriculum web page at www.corestandards.org/read-the-standards. Most states clearly specify their curriculum standards by grade level on their respective Department of Education home pages.

9.   ELEMENTARY SCHOOL COUNSELOR

BASIC DESCRIPTION

Elementary school counselors are professional educators who focus on meeting the mental health needs of a diverse student body. They help children in grades K–6 to become competent learners by focusing on the development, implementation, and evaluation of a comprehensive school guidance curriculum. This curriculum includes study and test-taking skills, goal setting, interpersonal relationships, communication, problem solving, conflict resolution, and multicultural awareness. Services are typically presented via classroom-based formats. For example, the implementation of social–emotional learning curriculum may be undertaken within all second-grade classrooms. Small-group approaches might also be used, such as a weekly social skills group (e.g., friendship group, anger management) or a loss group (e.g., children who are experiencing substantial family or peer changes). Additionally, an elementary school counselor also works individually with children who are experiencing barriers or challenges to their learning. Working as a part of a team within the school building (e.g., issues of school climate, classroom management) and frequent communication with classroom teachers (e.g., academic support) and parents (e.g., parent education, home-school collaboration) are common responsibilities.

CORE COMPETENCIES AND SKILLS NEEDED

The ability to interact and work effectively with children and adults in either individual or group settings is essential. The ability to demonstrate strong data-based problem-solving skills combined with appropriate documentation of efforts is essential to the work of an elementary school counselor. Teamwork, strong listening and speaking skills, empathy/compassion, appreciation and respect for diversity and individual differences, the ability to work under challenging and sometimes stressful conditions impacting children's development, and a high degree of professional and ethical behavior are all expected characteristics of elementary school counselors.

EDUCATIONAL REQUIREMENTS

Coursework pertaining to children's development and mental health (e.g., social psychology, abnormal psychology, theories of personality, theories of intervention) tends to position one well to go on to obtain an advanced degree in school counseling, which is the entry-level credential in most school districts across the country. Typical undergraduate degrees include counseling, psychology, and social work. Life-span development, theories and applications of counseling approaches, professional ethics, social foundations of development, research, and program evaluation are examples of the type of classes that one would take at the undergraduate level. Advanced or graduate-level offerings of these types of courses are expected, combined with the active engagement in and carrying out of counseling practices under supervision.

EXPERIENCE NECESSARY

Practicum and internship experiences in carrying out the roles and functions of a school counselor under supervision are required. Some states require prior teaching experience to be a school counselor.

CERTIFICATION, LICENSURE, AND CONTINUING EDUCATION REQUIREMENTS

Certification or licensure as a school counselor is required. A criminal background check is usually a part of this process. Check the state's Department of Education website for specific information about certification and credentialing, as it can vary by state.

SALARY/COMPENSATION

The median annual salary for any type of school counselor (elementary through postsecondary) is $53,610 according to the Bureau of Labor Statistics (2014f). When combined with public school district benefits, this is a well-supported 9-month career in the field of education and may have many advantages over similar mental health positions in hospital- or community-based settings.

EMPLOYMENT OUTLOOK

The need for mental health services in schools is receiving considerably greater attention in recent years. Changes in family composition; increased attention to issues of school violence, bullying, and school shootings; and heightened understanding of the role that mental health can play in promoting or hindering academic and developmental success will likely make this field relevant for many years to come. However, a substantial supply of school counselors at the elementary level is evident across many parts of the country, as the advanced degree in school counseling tends to be one of the shorter courses of study (2 years) when compared to other advanced degrees pertaining to school-based mental health (e.g., school psychologist, 3 years).

FURTHER INFORMATION FOR EXPLORATION

For more information not only about elementary school counselors but other careers associated with this profession, see the American School Counselor Association (www.schoolcounselor.org). Most states also have professional associations affiliated with the school counseling profession (e.g., www.gaschoolcounselors.com). Looking closely at the requirements for accredited school counseling programs espoused by the Council for Accreditation of Counseling & Related Educational Programs (CACREP) will give those interested in this career in education an in-depth look at required training, professional competencies, and the credentialing process (www.cacrep.org).

10. ELEMENTARY SCHOOL LIBRARY MEDIA ASSISTANT

BASIC DESCRIPTION

An elementary school library media assistant, sometimes referred to as library instructional assistant, works closely with the school's librarian and school principal to carry forward the mission of the library, which may include a district-prescribed library/media curriculum. These individuals provide access and assistance to students and teachers pertaining to materials provided in the school library media center. This includes managing circulation, reading and sharing literature with students through outreach, coordinating volunteers, planning for book fairs, helping to set up author visits, and other clerical and administrative tasks. Most positions are part time, and many are assumed by parents of children in the district.

CORE COMPETENCIES AND SKILLS NEEDED

Strong organizational skills are necessary. Being detail oriented is essential. The ability to work with groups of students and teachers is important given the customer service nature of this career. Responding appropriately to supervision, direction, and guidance from the library/media director is essential.

EDUCATIONAL REQUIREMENTS

Most typically, those who assume an assistant role will have an associate's or bachelors' degree in an unrelated field, although some who desire only part-time work may have a degree in library science. In some cases, a high school diploma with appropriate work experience might suffice. The primary requirement for this career is a passion for sharing information with others.

EXPERIENCE NECESSARY

Most elementary school library media assistants are well positioned to carry out their roles and responsibilities after short-term on-the-job training. Gaining familiarity with the library system through volunteering is often one way that individuals began work in this position.

CERTIFICATION, LICENSURE, AND CONTINUING EDUCATION REQUIREMENTS

Library certification is not required for this position. A desire to use technology to carry out the mission of the library is often important given the rapid and fast-paced technological changes taking place regarding access to information.

SALARY/COMPENSATION

Most positions are part time and paid on an hourly basis, with limited to no benefits. Those interested in this career might want to check with the district's paraprofessional unions, if they exist, to help to clarify pay and benefits issues. The median hourly wage is $11.27, according to the Bureau of Labor Statistics (2014d). Flexible hours and a 9-month position are positives of the job.

EMPLOYMENT OUTLOOK

Due to continuing advances in technology and use of multimedia, we can expect growth in the need for elementary school library media assistants in the future. Unfortunately, this growth is at the expense of librarians, who are more costly for districts to employ. Districts facing significant budget constraints are especially pressured to reduce costs outside of the typical classroom and may see library-related expenses as one place to make budget cuts through restaffing.

FURTHER INFORMATION FOR EXPLORATION

A number of helpful resources for school librarians and assistants can be found within the publication *School Library Monthly* (www.schoollibrarymonthly.com). For more general information about library sciences and the profession of librarianship, see the website of the American Library Association (www.ala.org).

Career-in-Education Profile
ELEMENTARY SCHOOL LIBRARY MEDIA ASSISTANT

Interview With Cindy Clement (BA, Communication Arts; MA, Communication)

Describe your educational background.

I earned my undergraduate degree in communication arts, with a focus on interpersonal communications, public relations, and corporate communications. I minored in French. My senior project was on college radio. I held a work/study job in the Communication Arts Department during my undergraduate studies and spent a semester abroad in France. My master's thesis topic was on the coverage of the Pennsylvania Ballet in the *Philadelphia Inquirer*, arts coverage versus business coverage. During my graduate studies, I held a work/study job in a fine-arts library.

Describe your prior experiences and the path you took to get to this career.

My career began in health care planning and marketing. I stopped working full time when my first child was 1 year old. Until I returned to the workforce, I volunteered at the YMCA in marketing, at a local hospital in business development, and at local schools in many capacities, including within an elementary school library. After 2 years of volunteering at my children's school library, the head librarian encouraged me to apply for the position of elementary library media assistant (ELMA). The hiring process involved an interview with the head librarian and then a second interview with the head librarian and the building principal.

Describe the work that you do.

I am one of two part-time paraprofessionals in the library. The head librarian is full time (certified library media specialist) and we are part time; together we work a total of 35 hours. My colleague focuses mainly on cataloging and collection management (i.e., keeping nonfiction current, managing donations, cataloging and covering new

(continued)

(continued)

books). My two main foci are circulation (e.g., daily collection, holds, renewals, managing the overdue system) and parent volunteers (e.g., organizing schedule, overseeing work). In addition, we both contribute to planning and coordinating author visits and designing library displays, and participate in statewide reading programs.

What is a typical day like for you in this career?

My work day is usually from 9:00 to 1:00. I have the flexibility (both personal and professional) to use my 20-hour work week as efficiently as possible. For example, if we have an author visiting I may work a long day on the day of the visit, then cut back on another day. On a typical day, I organize the parent volunteers as they arrive for their shifts. After the Pledge of Allegiance, we collect returning books from every class coming to library that day. We assist the head librarian in preparing curriculum for the day. We check in all returned books and manage holds and renewals. When each class arrives we assist with book selection and checkout. My other tasks, such as book repair, fulfilling teacher requests for books, researching new books/series, and so forth, are fit in around this daily framework of book check-in/checkout.

What is the most challenging part of your career?

In schools there is often a divide between the certified staff and the noncertified staff, and that can flare up from time to time. For example, when the head librarian is out (e.g., illness, conference) a certified substitute must be brought in to teach library classes for that day. Even though I may have watched/participated in that exact curriculum earlier in the week, I cannot, as a paraprofessional, teach the class. It can be frustratingly inefficient to spend time bringing a sub up to speed rather than simply stepping in and teaching that day's curriculum. Speaking of curriculum, one other point of frustration is the perception that "library" is simply checking out books. We have a full and challenging curriculum that each class in the building engages with when they come to library each week. In our school, library is one of the unified arts, which also includes art, music, and physical education.

(continued)

(continued)

What is the most rewarding part of your career?

There are very few barriers to innovation and creativity. If I have an idea for a bulletin board, display, or system improvement, I am free to enact it. I also truly enjoy the interaction with my head librarian and fellow paraprofessional. Of course, seeing students work their way through a book series, get excited about new books from the Book Fair, or bring a new author to our attention is fantastic. Truly, an elementary library should be the heart of a grammar school, and as a library worker you have the opportunity and responsibility to advocate for exactly that.

What advice do you have for someone in high school or currently at the undergraduate level who might be interested in this career?

Be aware that technology is a large part of the profession (e.g., e-books, electronic checkout systems, library collection databases, curriculum taught to students on iPads and Google Docs). Be prepared to engage with all of that and champion your library's technological bona fides to administrators or colleagues who may have an outdated view of what occurs in an elementary library. Also, research whether your school district has a full, district-wide library curriculum. I've learned that some schools use their libraries simply for checking out books and don't take advantage of the full skill set of a certified library media specialist who has professional parity with the classroom teachers. Our curriculum includes Internet safety, online research, fiction versus nonfiction, autobiography and biography, and historical nonfiction. The library curriculum supports and complements the Common Core initiative.

What advice do you have for someone currently in a different career/field who might be interested in your career?

Begin as a volunteer. Schools are chronically underfunded and understaffed. A reliable volunteer could learn about and be trusted with so many aspects of elementary library education.

(continued)

(continued)

If you decided to advance your career, what steps would you take and what career(s) might you seek out?

The next step in my career would be to become a certified library media specialist. In my state this involves a master's degree in library science plus a practicum in education. There are some alternate routes to certification if one's master's degree isn't as old as mine or if library media specialist is declared a shortage area.

11. MIDDLE SCHOOL MATH TEACHER

BASIC DESCRIPTION

Middle school math teachers help to prepare students, typically aged 12 to 15, in developing the math skills and competencies that will serve as a foundation for meeting or exceeding high school math requirements. Course preparation, instruction, competency assessment, and grading homework and tests related to the math curriculum (e.g., prealgebra, algebra, intermediate math, geometry) to which they are assigned makes up the majority of their responsibilities. However, serving as a homeroom or study-time supervisor/teacher may also be a part of the day. Many middle school teachers partake in supporting extracurricular activities, which may help to supplement their income. Working with other adults within the middle school environment (e.g., school counselor, special education staff, administration) also takes on a substantial role within these grade levels.

CORE COMPETENCIES AND SKILLS NEEDED

Middle school math teachers need a strong understanding of subject-matter knowledge and effective approaches to teaching math to middle school students. Strong communication skills are necessary. Adapting communication patterns to a diverse group of students, parents, and colleagues is important. An understanding of both typical and atypical adolescent development is especially important. Promoting both academic and social skills in young adolescents should be a priority for those teaching in middle school settings. A high level of professionalism, a commitment to equity, and a strong set of organizational skills are

55

also important. Effective classroom management incorporating a strong focus on academic engaged time takes on an increased emphasis within the middle school years.

EDUCATIONAL REQUIREMENTS
Most states require middle school teachers to be certified and well trained in the area in which they will teach. A bachelor's degree in math or math education combined with certification in K–8 education or 7–12 education is typical. Some teachers have advanced degrees in math and then complete the requirements necessary to become certified to teach in schools.

EXPERIENCE NECESSARY
Student teaching is a part of degree requirements pertaining to middle school teaching. A 1-year placement involving the teaching of multiple math subjects under the supervision of a mentor teacher and a university-based supervisor is typical.

CERTIFICATION, LICENSURE, AND CONTINUING EDUCATION REQUIREMENTS
States have varying certification and license requirements for middle school teachers. Certification to teach middle-school-age students, as well as math content, is required. Continuing education is typically required as a part of maintaining state credentialing but is also one means by which middle school teachers can further advance their training in teaching math.

SALARY/COMPENSATION
According to the Bureau of Labor Statistics (2014e), the median pay for a middle school teacher is $53,430, yet there is considerable geographical variation, making it important to look closely within states/districts for a more accurate picture of salaries. Employee benefits such as health insurance and retirement matching often create a well-compensated 9-month position for those working in public or private schools. Initial pay levels will depend on the location and size of the school district, as well as the fiscal resources available. Additional pay can be received following completion of an advanced degree or by assisting with extracurricular activities (e.g., clubs, sports).

EMPLOYMENT OUTLOOK

A push toward the teaching of advanced math content during middle school has received considerable attention in recent years. This push for math achievement stems from the need to have our country's high school graduates on par with students in other countries regarding math knowledge. A focus on increasing both the quality and quantity of well-trained middle school math teachers has resulted. In addition, teacher attrition can be fairly high among those teaching at the middle school level. Teaching large groups of students who have a diverse array of math preparation skills can be quite challenging. This turnover also means that position openings for middle school teachers are typically more available than those for other grades. Those trained for teaching positions in grades K–8 often find themselves in middle school positions given the limited supply of positions available in the elementary grades. Realization of a poor fit with the unique characteristics of this developmental level only happens after experiencing the demands and challenges associated with this position.

FURTHER INFORMATION FOR EXPLORATION

The National Middle School Association (www.nmsa.org) provides professional support to those committed to meeting the educational needs of middle school students. The National Council for Teachers of Mathematics provides exceptional resources for math teachers at all grade levels (www.nctm.org).

12. MIDDLE SCHOOL SCIENCE TEACHER

BASIC DESCRIPTION

Middle school science teachers instruct students in grades 6 to 8 in science (e.g., physical science, physics, biology). Matching one's lesson plans and teaching to the science curricular guidelines of the district and state is necessary. Instructional practices should be multimodal to meet the diverse needs of middle school students. Lectures, demonstrations, discussions, and laboratory experiences are typical teaching strategies used in teaching science to middle school students. Helping students to explore their world to understand scientific theories and principles through hands-on experiences and activities is an important responsibility within this career. Providing group and individual instruction helps to capitalize on the learning needs of students at this age level. Preparation,

57

administration, scoring, and reporting of homework assignments and tests is an essential role. Coordination of school science fairs and mentoring students for science competitions might also be an important role within some districts. Middle school science teachers typically serve as homeroom or study-period teachers. Working with other adults within the middle school environment (e.g., math teachers, special education staff, counselors) also takes on a substantial role within these grade levels.

CORE COMPETENCIES AND SKILLS NEEDED

Middle school science teachers need a strong understanding of subject-matter knowledge and effective approaches to teaching science to middle school students. Strong communication skills are necessary. Adapting communication patterns to a diverse group of students, parents, and colleagues is important. Promoting both academic and social skills in young adolescents should be a priority for those teaching in middle school settings. A high level of professionalism, a commitment to fairness and equity, and a strong set of organizational skills are also important. Effective classroom management incorporating a strong focus on academic engaged time takes on an increased emphasis within the middle school years.

EDUCATIONAL REQUIREMENTS

To teach science at the middle school level, a bachelor's or master's degree in science education is necessary. An alternative route is to complete a degree in a field of science and to then complete a teacher certification program. Advanced graduate study, such as a master's degree, is common for those teaching at the middle school level.

EXPERIENCE NECESSARY

Teaching experience in the form of student teaching is necessary. Working with a mentor teacher to teach a diverse array of science classes usually occurs in the final year of the teaching certificate training. During this year, student teachers also take part in a student teaching course within their university training program.

CERTIFICATION, LICENSURE, AND CONTINUING EDUCATION REQUIREMENTS

Certification for science education varies by state. Examining the Department of Education website of the state in which you are considering employment is essential. Keeping abreast of the latest technology and science discoveries is essential and is required to maintain credentialing.

SALARY/COMPENSATION

According to the Bureau of Labor Statistics (2014e), the median pay for a middle school teacher is $53,430, yet there is considerable geographical variation, making it important to look closely within states/districts for a more accurate picture of salaries. Employee benefits such as health insurance and retirement matching often create a well-compensated 9-month position for those working in public or private schools. Initial pay levels will depend on the location, size, and fiscal resources available to the school district. Additional pay can be received following completion of an advanced degree or by assisting with extracurricular activities (e.g., clubs, sports).

EMPLOYMENT OUTLOOK

A push toward the teaching of advanced science content during the middle school years has been apparent in recent years. This push for science achievement has come from the need to have our country's high school graduates on par with students in other countries regarding science knowledge and the skills required for postsecondary learning pertaining to the fields of science and math. A focus on increasing both the quality and quantity of well-trained middle school science teachers has resulted. In addition, teacher attrition can be fairly high among those teaching at the middle school level. Teaching large groups of students who have a diverse array of preparation in science and motivation for developing their science skills can be quite challenging. This turnover also means that position openings for middle school teachers are typically more available than those for other grades. Those trained for teaching positions in grades K–8 may find themselves in middle school positions given the limited supply of positions available in the elementary grades. Realization of a poor fit with the unique characteristics of this developmental level only happens after experiencing the demands and challenges associated with this position.

FURTHER INFORMATION FOR EXPLORATION

The National Middle School Association (www.nmsa.org) provides professional support to educators committed to meeting the learning needs of middle school students. The National Science Teachers Association (www.nsta.org) is a professional organization dedicated to improving science instruction and increasing awareness of science education. The association's website provides valuable resources for those teaching science across the life span.

13. MIDDLE SCHOOL LANGUAGE ARTS TEACHER

BASIC DESCRIPTION

Middle school language arts teachers work with students 12 to 15 years of age to further develop their understanding and appreciation of the English language through reading, writing, and speaking. Language arts teachers may spend a considerable amount of time selecting reading material and preparing assignments to meet the curricular expectations of the district and/or state. In addition, the writing process requires considerable time in providing feedback at multiple points as drafts develop. The content, organization, and mechanics of the written product are assessed. Helping students to be critical consumers of what they read is an important lifelong learning skill taught to middle school students. Documentation of student's progress in meeting the core components of the middle school language arts curricular standards is essential. In addition to teaching language arts classes, possibly across multiple grades, responsibilities may include supervising homeroom or study periods. Middle school language arts teachers also communicate regularly with parents and other teachers within the building.

CORE COMPETENCIES AND SKILLS NEEDED

A thorough understanding of language arts and how to teach it to middle school students is essential. Patience, fairness, and respect for diverse ideas are all important characteristics for those who choose to pursue a career at the middle school level. A strong desire to help students think independently and share their original ideas orally and in writing should be present. Being able to establish order within the class and maintain on-task student behavior is important to creating a productive learning environment. Adapting communication patterns to a diverse group of students, parents, and colleague is important.

EDUCATIONAL REQUIREMENTS

Middle school language arts teachers need to possess a bachelor's or master's degree in secondary education or a related field. Specific endorsement or certification in English or language arts is necessary. Individuals with a bachelor's degree in English must further their education to meet requirements for state teaching certification.

EXPERIENCE NECESSARY
Student teaching under the supervision of a mentor teacher is a required component of teacher certification training. This may occur either in the last year of the teaching program or during the first year following graduation. A strong background and set of experiences related to teaching English language arts is necessary.

CERTIFICATION, LICENSURE, AND CONTINUING EDUCATION REQUIREMENTS
Certification for teaching English language arts varies by state. Examining the Department of Education website of the state in which you are considering employment is essential. Continuing education and possibly an advanced graduate degree related to language arts are typical of those in this position.

SALARY/COMPENSATION
According to the Bureau of Labor Statistics (2014e), the median pay for a middle school teacher is $53,430, yet there is considerable geographical variation, making it important to look closely within states/districts for a more accurate picture of salaries. Employee benefits such as health insurance and retirement matching often create a well-compensated 9-month position for those working in public or private schools. Initial pay levels will depend on the location and size of the school district, as well as fiscal resources available. Additional pay can be received following completion of an advanced degree or by assisting with extracurricular activities (e.g., clubs, sports).

EMPLOYMENT OUTLOOK
The outlook for middle school language arts teachers is less robust when compared with the outlook for those who specialize in the areas of science, math, technology, or foreign language at the middle school level. However, middle school teachers, generally speaking, are often especially in demand in school districts with limited resources and/or high rates of attrition (e.g., districts in high-poverty areas).

FURTHER INFORMATION FOR EXPLORATION

The National Council of Teachers of English (www.ncte.org) is a professional association of educators in English studies, literacy, and language arts. The mission of this organization is to improve the teaching and learning of English and the language arts at all levels of education. For a more general focus on literacy, see the website of the International Reading Association at www.reading.org. For those interested in educating students at the middle school level, see the website of the National Middle School Association (www.nmsa.org).

14. MIDDLE SCHOOL FOREIGN LANGUAGE TEACHER

BASIC DESCRIPTION

Middle school foreign language teachers design and implement curriculum to meet the foreign language requirements expected of middle school students, typically grades 6 to 8. At the middle school level, foreign language courses are typically introductory, involving exposure to and experience in speaking, listening, and writing the language. Conversational skills and vocabulary building are typically the primary focus. Exposure to culture and customs is often emphasized. Middle school teachers who are well versed in the specific language being taught often serve other students by teaching at the high school level and sometimes in elementary schools. Classes commonly taught in middle school include Spanish and French. Other foreign languages such as German, Chinese, Japanese, Italian, and Russian are sometimes taught at the middle school level.

CORE COMPETENCIES AND SKILLS NEEDED

Expertise and fluency in the foreign language being taught are essential. Proficiency in reading, writing, and speaking the language is expected. Prior travel to and familiarity with the culture, customs, and countries associated with the language are helpful in creating an environment in which students can learn effectively. The personality characteristics commonly associated with this career in education include a high level of patience, a strong sense of creativity, an appreciation of and talent for using technology, and a desire to share both the language and the culture associated with the foreign language to a diverse group of adolescents, many of whom have limited to no experience with the language being taught. Being able to establish order within the class and maintain student on-task behavior is important to creating a productive learning environment. Adapting communication patterns to a diverse group of students, parents, and colleagues is important.

EDUCATIONAL REQUIREMENTS

A bachelor's degree in foreign language, linguistics, or a related field is necessary. In addition, meeting requirements for teacher certification at the middle and high school levels is common.

EXPERIENCE NECESSARY

Student teaching under the supervision of a mentor teacher is a required component of teacher certification training. This may occur either in the last year of the teaching program or during the first year following graduation. Unique to this teaching career are advantages in hiring associated with extensive experiences with the language and culture via study or living abroad.

CERTIFICATION, LICENSURE, AND CONTINUING EDUCATION REQUIREMENTS

Certification to teach at the middle and high school levels is a typical requirement. In some cases the teaching certificate might be for grades K–8. Specialization in the foreign language to be taught is expected but may vary by state. A desire for engaging in continuing professional development concerning the language and the methods of instruction that are best suited to teach the foreign language is essential.

SALARY/COMPENSATION

The median salary for foreign language teachers at the middle school level is $53,430, according to the Bureau of Labor Statistics (2014e). Initial pay levels will depend on the location and size of the school district, as well as the fiscal resources available. Combined with typically strong health/retirement packages from school districts, total compensation for this teaching position is attractive, especially for those who are passionate about sharing the language and culture of another country with young people.

EMPLOYMENT OUTLOOK

There is currently a great demand for teachers and other professionals who are well qualified to teach a foreign language. As our society continues to expand globally and becomes more diverse, foreign language teachers will continue to be in great demand.

FURTHER INFORMATION FOR EXPLORATION

The American Council on the Teaching of Foreign Languages (www .actfl.org) is focused on the improvement of teaching and learning of foreign languages across the life span. Each language also is typically associated with a national professional organization, such as the American Association of Teachers of Spanish and Portuguese (www.aatsp.org) or the American Association of Teachers of French (www.frenchteachers .org). Other professional organizations of potential interest to future foreign language teachers include the National Council of State Supervisors for Languages (www.ncssfl.org) and the National Foreign Language Center (www.nflc.org). Both organizations promote the teaching of foreign language and have a number of interesting links related to policy and advocacy for teaching foreign language courses to our nation's school-age population.

Career-in-Education Profile
MIDDLE SCHOOL FOREIGN LANGUAGE TEACHER
Interview With Karen Wallace (BS, French; MA, Educational Psychology)

Describe your educational background.

I majored in French and was fortunate to have been able to study abroad at a university in France. After moving to a different state to teach middle school, I decided to continue my graduate studies in educational psychology.

Describe your prior experiences and the path you took to get to this career.

As a senior in high school I knew for certain that I was passionate about learning the French language. I had ambitions of traveling and working in a career of international business. It all seemed so glamourous. During my sophomore year of undergraduate studies, I came to the realization that the "cut-throat" world of business was not for me. I then spent a semester just focusing on what I loved—French! My advisor suggested I take a few education courses to explore the world of teaching. I did, but with many reservations. Teaching was not something I had ever envisioned myself doing. However, I enjoyed my high school students immensely during my student teaching, and, voilá, I was hooked!

Describe the work that you do.

My days are exhausting but so fulfilling. I spend half a day teaching French I and II to middle school students and the other half teaching French III to high school freshmen, sophomores, juniors, and seniors. I get the privilege of watching my students grow and develop across multiple years. The relationships that develop are unique and special. The middle school curriculum is the same as the high school curriculum in my district, thus being very rigorous, so I have to move my students along at a good pace while still making it fun and motivating. I spend hours on detailed lesson plans that involve movement, and,

(continued)

(continued)

most of all, using the target language. It's not just about listening to me speak French; the students must get as much or more practice speaking French daily. I conduct all of my classes, whether it is French I, II, or III, in French for at least 90% of the class time. Consequently, I must use visual aids and do a lot of modeling and gesturing to get students to understand the meanings of words and phrases.

What is a typical day like for you in this career?

Although I spend most Sundays working 2 to 3 hours to plan for the week, I still arrive at school by 6:30 a.m. to review and set up. Although I have already prepared the daily lesson, I print out a copy for my lesson plan book and get my "Warm-Up" ready to go on the project. The lesson objective is posted on the whiteboard at the front of the classroom. Partner activities and any other handouts are stacked in the order I'll be using them so there is less transition time between activities. Visual aids and/or manipulatives (e.g., individual clocks when learning how to tell time in French) are set out on my prep table, homework is posted on the bulletin board as well as posted online, and any audio is readied to be able to hit "play" at a moment's notice. From the minute the students enter the class, the lesson is active and language centered.

What is the most challenging part of your career?

Getting students and parents to overcome the notion that not all students can learn another language is more challenging than I ever could have imagined.

What is the most rewarding part of your career?

Observing students using the target language both in and out of the classroom, whether it's perfectly spoken or riddled with errors—it's incredibly rewarding seeing the students excited about learning another language and about other cultures, and opening their eyes to the world around them. I have had the opportunity to take high school students to both Canada and France, which were extremely rewarding teaching experiences.

(continued)

(continued)

What advice do you have for someone in high school or currently at the undergraduate level who might be interested in this career?

You must study abroad and really learn the language and culture. I often see university students who say they can speak another language, yet have never spent time in another country. They have taken years of coursework in the target language and may even be able to write decently. However, one cannot truly speak the language unless one has spent a good amount of time being surrounded by the language and culture.

What advice do you have for someone currently in a different career/field who might be interested in your career?

Spend some considerable time in schools volunteering and/or observing in a variety of classrooms and other school settings so you can see how students best learn.

If you decided to advance your career, what steps would you take and what career(s) might you seek out?

Related to my work as a French teacher, I would love to teach language methodology courses at the university level to help future students be better prepared to teach a world language. I enjoy interviewing new language teachers, and have had the privilege to mentor some of them throughout my career. I love to share invaluable ideas, techniques, activities, and methods with others. Recently, I decided to pursue a master's degree in educational psychology, and, following completion of that training, was hired as a school counselor. That change was the result of having worked with middle school students for several years in my role as teacher, and seeing the reward in connecting and forming relationships with them. This change in roles with the population that I love will be a wonderful new adventure.

15. MIDDLE SCHOOL TECHNOLOGY TEACHER

BASIC DESCRIPTION

Middle school technology teachers, also known as computer teachers or career/technical education teachers, provide students in grades 6–8 with instruction pertaining to computers and use of technology within the classroom. Exposure and experience with computer hardware, software, and other tools of educational technology are provided to students. This may include specific instruction in word processing, writing computer code, working with spreadsheets and databases, creating presentations, engaging in video editing, developing websites, and ethics/legal aspects of technology use. This content is especially well suited to middle school students given their love of engaging in active learning and working with their peers. Course material is aligned with districts' and/or states' curricular expectations related to technology. Development of assignments, creation of rubrics for grading, and overall evaluation of student class performance is necessary. It is important to work with other school district personnel to ensure that adequate/appropriate technology and equipment are available for instruction. Formal use of an agreement to ensure students are engaged in "appropriate technology use" is necessary. Monitoring for inappropriate downloading, file sharing, or other legal/ethical issues is an important responsibility within this teaching position. Consulting opportunities with other teachers in the building or district pertaining to effective use of technology in the classroom may be available. Middle school technology teachers may teach a homeroom or study-period class. In addition, computer technology clubs or after-school programs may be another responsibility of a middle school technology teacher.

CORE COMPETENCIES AND SKILLS NEEDED

Specific competencies related to computers and technology are necessary. In addition, familiarity with best practices in instructing middle school students on the use of these tools is essential. It is important for a middle school technology teacher to recognize that computer use is closely linked to higher order thinking and problem solving. Strong organization and management of student behavior within the classroom are additional skills needed within this position. Excellent communication skills and the ability to adapt those communications to students, parents, and other teachers are required. Patience, guidance, and frequent individual feedback are especially important given the varying levels of computer/technology skills that might be present within the classroom.

EDUCATIONAL REQUIREMENTS

A bachelor's degree in education, computer science, or a related field is required. Certification to teach at the middle school level is also required, and each state provides guidelines for those training expectations. Seek out credentialing information on the website of the Department of Education of the state in which you are looking for employment.

EXPERIENCE NECESSARY

Student teaching is required as a part of the certification process. Working under the supervision of a mentor teacher, student teachers in technology gain experience in developing and carrying out instructional goals, objectives, and methods. Having experience in the use of computers and technology in the private sector could help individuals distinguish themselves from others seeking a career in this field of education.

CERTIFICATION, LICENSURE, AND CONTINUING EDUCATION REQUIREMENTS

Certification to teach at the middle school level and the specific area of computer technology is necessary. Given the fast-paced changes in technology, an advanced degree or continuing education related to computers and technology in the classroom is likely necessary to maintain credentialing.

SALARY/COMPENSATION

The median annual salary for a middle school technology teacher (i.e., career and technical education teachers) is $54,220, according to the Bureau of Labor Statistics (2014a), but characteristics of the employing school district can influence the rate of pay.

EMPLOYMENT OUTLOOK

The outlook for middle school technology teachers is currently less robust when compared with the outlook for those who specialize in the areas of science, math, or foreign language at the middle school level. The push for advanced education in technology has yet to spread to middle and high schools, although we can anticipate that this will change in future years as recognition of the importance of additional training in this content area is realized.

FURTHER INFORMATION FOR EXPLORATION

Numerous professional organizations support teaching and learning associated with the field of technology. These include the International Technology and Engineering Educators Association (www.iteaconnect. org), the International Society for Technology in Education (www.iste. org), the Society for Information Technology and Teacher Education (www.site.aace.org), and the Association for Career & Technical Education (www.acteonline.org). For those generally interested in educating students at the middle school level, see the website of the National Middle School Association (www.nmsa.org).

16.   ADVANCED PLACEMENT CALCULUS TEACHER

BASIC DESCRIPTION

Advanced Placement (AP) calculus teachers adhere to a standardized curriculum (e.g., textbook, course description guide) that helps to position high school students to take a national exam offered by the College Board (www.collegeboard.org). Passing that national exam with high scores allows high school students to be granted placement and college credits for that work. To teach a class in calculus that has the AP designation means that the course has been audited by the College Board to ensure that it meets the curricular and instructional standards expected. Two levels of AP calculus are typically taught by an AP calculus teacher, Calculus AB and Calculus BC. These courses help students understand the concepts, application, and methods associated with calculus. Specific goals and objectives are prescribed. Examples include (a) the ability to work with functions and their many representations; (b) an understanding of the meaning of definite integrals; and (c) the ability to model a physical situation with a function, a differential equation, or an integral. A high level of content knowledge pertaining to advanced math skills and competencies is expected. In addition, the use of effective instructional approaches to teach calculus to high school students is necessary. Finally, a high degree of organization, accountability, and frequent monitoring of student's progress within the course is expected. Public disclosure of AP exam results creates a sense of "high-stakes teaching" that other high school courses may not possess. High school AP calculus teachers also typically will teach other advanced math courses (e.g., AP statistics) and may provide guidance to clubs or study groups associated with taking the AP exam.

CORE COMPETENCIES AND SKILLS NEEDED

Expertise in advanced mathematical concepts is necessary. Competencies associated with both content and instruction of precalculus, calculus AB, calculus BC, and other higher level math classes are expected. AP teachers help students get a jump start on their college education, and a strong desire for a position involving advisement, mentorship, guidance, and support of high-achieving adolescents fits well with this career in education.

EDUCATIONAL REQUIREMENTS

A bachelor's degree in math education, math, or some other related field is required. Most likely an advanced degree in math or math education is necessary for those interested in teaching at the highest math level within high schools. Certification to teach at the high school level is necessary, and requirements vary by state. A close review of these requirements via the Department of Education website of the state in which you would like to be employed is essential.

EXPERIENCE NECESSARY

Student teaching is a requirement of teaching certification programs. In addition, teachers interested in teaching AP calculus at the high school level typically will have many years of experience in successfully teaching advanced math courses. Evidence of successfully teaching calculus at the high school level is typically necessary.

CERTIFICATION, LICENSURE, AND CONTINUING EDUCATION REQUIREMENTS

A teacher certificate in secondary education is required. Endorsement or specialization in advanced math content (i.e., calculus) is expected. Continuous improvement through engagement in the annual audit process with the College Board ensures that national standards are being met. Continuing education requirements are also associated with renewing teaching certificates.

SALARY/COMPENSATION

The median salary for an AP calculus teacher is $55,050 (all high school teachers), according to the Bureau of Labor Statistics (2014b). It is important to note that an advanced degree, years of experience, and characteristics of the employing school district may result in significant variation in salaries. It is interesting to note that high school teachers who hold advanced degrees, albeit in different fields, will ultimately start at the same pay scale despite different areas of expertise. However, some districts are turning to a market-based policy (e.g., pay based on supply and demand) for setting teacher salaries, meaning that advanced math and science teachers (i.e., disciplines in high demand) would earn more than art, physical education, or English teachers.

EMPLOYMENT OUTLOOK

There is a substantial push for additional science, technology, engineering, and math teachers who can meet the needs of our nation's students in these important areas of study. Demand for high-quality teachers in the area of advanced math is likely to continue for years to come given the recent push toward higher rates of college degrees in the math field. This public pressure to increase the competencies and skills of our future workforce means more and more students will need to demonstrate their competencies in calculus and other advanced math courses in the future.

FURTHER INFORMATION FOR EXPLORATION

For additional information about requirements and expectations for an AP calculus course, please see www.collegeboard.org. For additional information about teaching math, there are two professional organization websites that should be of interest: the Mathematical Association of America (www.maa.org) and the National Council of Teachers of Mathematics (www.nctm.org).

17.   ECONOMICS TEACHER

BASIC DESCRIPTION

Economics teachers work with students in grades 9 to 12. Content may include topics such as trade, markets, competition, money, inflation, and unemployment. Providing a basic foundation in the field of economics can help prepare students for coursework at the college level. The primary purpose of a high school economics curriculum is to teach students about how goods and services operate within a global economy. Economics courses are typically electives within the high school curriculum. This means that diverse levels of interest and motivation will be apparent in the students who enroll in the course. Creating relevant activities and lessons through use of real-world economics problems is especially important for teaching high school students. Teaching responsibilities may be spread to other courses such as civics, history, business, or social studies, depending on the high school and the teacher's educational background and training. Economics teachers might also work part time or be employed to teach economics courses in multiple school districts given the focused nature of the subject. Two Advanced Placement (AP) courses pertaining to economics may be taught to high school students: AP Macroeconomics and AP Microeconomics.

CORE COMPETENCIES AND SKILLS NEEDED

Economics teachers need a strong understanding of the economics curriculum (e.g., macroeconomics, accounting, finance) as well as expertise in teaching the content to high school students. Good communication skills are necessary and must be adapted to the students, parents, and teachers with whom economics teachers come into contact. Problem-solving skills, critical thinking skills, and excellent organizational skills are also important for a high school economics teacher.

EDUCATIONAL REQUIREMENTS

Teaching economics at the high school level requires a bachelor's or master's degree in economics, secondary education, or a closely related field. A teaching certificate is also required from the state in which you will be employed. Look closely at the Department of Education website of the state in which you would like to work for additional information pertaining to certification requirements.

EXPERIENCE NECESSARY

Student teaching is a requirement of all teaching certification programs. Working under a mentor teacher to develop and carry out the economics curriculum is necessary. Experience working in a field of business may help to position one with the real-world skills and competencies necessary to teach economics to high school students.

CERTIFICATION, LICENSURE, AND CONTINUING EDUCATION REQUIREMENTS

Secondary education certification is required. Specialization or an endorsement in the field of economics is expected. Continuing education is necessary to maintain a teaching certificate.

SALARY/COMPENSATION

The median pay for economics teachers is $55,050 (all high school teachers), according to the Bureau of Labor Statistics (2014b). It is important to note that an advanced degree, years of experience, and characteristics of the employing school district may result in significant variation in salaries.

EMPLOYMENT OUTLOOK

The employment outlook for economics teachers is anticipated to be similar to that for other high school teaching positions (i.e., just under 10% growth in the next 10 years, according to the Bureau of Labor Statistics, 2014b) not directly related to science, technology, engineering, and math. Geographic variations may also be apparent, as some school districts shift their resources to teaching core requirements of language arts, math, and science. Other districts that are preparing the majority of their graduates for college would be likely to offer an economics curriculum, including AP economics courses, to prepare students for postsecondary education opportunities.

FURTHER INFORMATION FOR EXPLORATION

Two professional organizations are particularly focused on economics education and provide excellent resources for those interested in a career teaching economics: the Council for Economics Education (www.councilforeconed.org) and the Foundation for Teaching Economics (www.fte.org). For a review of particular online K–12 lessons and resources pertaining to educating students in economics, see www.econedlink.org. For additional information related to the content of AP courses in macroeconomics and microeconomics, see apstudent .collegeboard.org/apcourse.

18. HIGH SCHOOL ART TEACHER

BASIC DESCRIPTION

High school art teachers provide students in grades 9 to 12 with the knowledge and skills pertaining to an array of art curriculum topics, including drawing, painting, and making ceramics. Art history, theory, and concepts are typically a part of these course offerings. Planning and implementing a comprehensive art curriculum will vary by the type of course taught and the curricular standards of the school district. Ordering the inventory and supplies necessary to allow students to meet the course objectives is a significant responsibility of the high school art teacher.

Maintaining a clean, safe, and productive environment in which students can create is also necessary. Modeling and reinforcing the proper use and care of art supplies, including tools and equipment, is important. Students typically will be evaluated on their artistic performance and their understanding of aesthetics, yet a clear rubric for grading will be important to convey to students. Four Advanced Placement (AP) art classes are widely available in high schools: AP Art History, AP Studio Art: 2-D Design, AP Studio Art: 3-D Design, and AP Studio Art: Drawing. More advanced skill sets and a high level of organization and accountability are necessary to teach AP classes. High school art teachers might also support extracurricular activities or clubs.

CORE COMPETENCIES AND SKILLS NEEDED

A strong interest in art and a passion for teaching it to others are important. The ability to teach a diverse group of learners, including beginning art students, will require patience, feedback, and a supportive instructional approach. Modeling, provision of feedback, and reinforcement of students' effort and products are essential. Excellent communication skills are necessary. Allowing students the opportunity to practice and make mistakes is an essential component of this teaching position. Being open to a student's unique creativity, having a diverse perspective regarding the definition of creativity or artistic talent, and creating a supportive environment are important competencies for a high school art teacher to possess. In addition to being able to teach the content effectively, having artistic talents that can be used to model and demonstrate for students is an important skill.

EDUCATIONAL REQUIREMENTS

A bachelor's or master's degree in education, art, or a related field is necessary. Teacher certification at the high school level is necessary. Certification requirements to be a high school art teacher will vary depending on the state of employment. A close review of the credentialing requirements noted on the Department of Education website of the state in which you wish to work is important.

EXPERIENCE NECESSARY

Many years of experience in creating, evaluating, and working with others on artistic endeavors are important for this career. Experience working with adolescents and young adults via hands-on activities is generally preferred in those hired to teach art. Student teaching is a requirement of all teaching certification programs. Working under a mentor teacher to develop and carry out the arts curriculum is necessary.

CERTIFICATION, LICENSURE, AND CONTINUING EDUCATION REQUIREMENTS
Secondary education certification is required. Specialization in art is expected. Continuing education is necessary to maintain a teaching certificate.

SALARY/COMPENSATION
The median pay for art teachers is $55,050 (all high school teachers), according to the Bureau of Labor Statistics (2014b). It is important to note that an advanced degree, years of experience, and characteristics of the employing school district may result in significant variation in salaries.

EMPLOYMENT OUTLOOK
The employment outlook for high school art teachers is anticipated to be a bit less robust than that for other high school teaching positions (i.e., just under 10% growth in the next 10 years, according to the Bureau of Labor Statistics, 2014b) that are not directly related to science, technology, engineering, and math. Jobs for art teachers at the elementary and middle school levels are anticipated to be more available than those at the high school level. Geographic variations may also be apparent as some school districts shift their resources to teaching core requirements of language arts, math, and science. Other districts that are preparing the majority of their graduates for college may offer an extensive arts curriculum, including AP arts courses, to prepare them for postsecondary education opportunities.

FURTHER INFORMATION FOR EXPLORATION
For additional information on art education, please see the website of the National Art Education Association (www.arteducators.org) or the Association of Teaching Artists (www.teachingartists.com). For a review of resources and materials pertaining to educating students in the arts in grades K–12, see the helpful webpage from the Museum of Modern Art at www.moma.org/learn/teachers/index. For additional information related to the content of AP art courses, see apstudent.collegeboard .org/apcourse.

Career-in-Education Profile
HIGH SCHOOL ART TEACHER

Interview With Derek J. Carlson (BA, Studio Art;
MEd, Art Education)

Describe your educational background.

I received my undergraduate degree in studio art with a minor in Asian studies. I took a nontraditional route into teaching by enrolling in a master's degree program in art education within a large public university. The initial 15 months of the program were designed for those who had an undergraduate degree outside of a teacher education program (but related to teaching) but were interested in pursuing a teaching certificate/license. As a part of that advanced degree training, I completed three student teaching experiences that involved four settings (K–12 program, elementary school, middle school, high school). To become licensed in the state in which I am now working, I had to take two additional courses via a correspondent program with an out-of-state university. I found it a bit ironic and sort of humorous to have to take those courses out-of-state to become licensed within the state that I teach.

Describe your prior experiences and the path you took to get to this career.

I believe my reckoning to become a teacher happened the summer of my junior year in college. I received the unique opportunity to work at a camp in the Montana Rocky Mountains. At this camp we would take kids, from the ages of 12 to 18, on overnight treks into the Rocky Mountains. Older kids usually went on longer excursions across multiple nights, whereas the younger teens would typically go out for one night. My job, as counselor, was to guide them on various trails, set up camp, make dinner, and be nature's facilitator. What really inspired me was the appreciation and change so many of these kids experienced. Still not convinced education was the career path for me, I decided to spend a year teaching English in China. Once again, the positive connections I had with students and the overall appreciation they conveyed convinced me this was my calling.

(continued)

(*continued*)

Describe the work that you do.

I teach middle and high school art. The middle school classes consist of a 6-week rotation for each of the sixth, seventh, and eighth grades. I share my high school duties with another full-time art teacher. At the high school level, for the most part, the curriculum for our classes revolves around a particular medium. For example, I am responsible for the drawing and painting subjects and teach a total of four classes.

What is a typical day like for you in this career?

My morning starts out teaching four classes at a high school, which includes drawing, painting, or design class (an art class focused on color theory, balance, and overall public perception of art). My last 3 hours of the day are devoted to my middle school classes in a separate building located across the parking lot. In each building I also have 20 minutes of homeroom where students can receive special help from various teachers or simply use the time for needed work.

What is the most challenging part of your career?

In the past 10 years or so, public perception has changed considerably toward public education and public employees. Much of that perception has a negative tone to it for those of us in the schools. One recent challenge that has emerged is the greater focus being placed on teacher effectiveness and learner outcomes. Although I firmly agree with this concept, there are now substantial responsibilities placed on schools and teachers to record, collect, analyze, and present data to show the growth of student knowledge and educator effectiveness. Carrying forward this mission is very time-consuming and unfortunately takes away from curricular flexibility. At times, it also seems to serve as a sort of barrier to affording individual levels of depth and breadth in learning that would more typically be seen within a classroom of diverse students.

What is the most rewarding part of your career?

The most rewarding part is making that special connection with a student. Watching students develop a sense of pride and confidence

(*continued*)

(continued)

in their abilities is awesome. Being able to share that connection with students and feeling like I had an influence on their learning and development is very gratifying.

What advice do you have for someone in high school or currently at the undergraduate level who might be interested in this career?

Being a teacher has many ups and downs. You may have a day in which all of your lessons are intriguing, your students find you interesting, and you can feel a great level of respect from those in your classroom. The next day, the complete opposite can happen—don't let this get you down or discouraged.

What advice do you have for someone currently in a different career/field who might be interested in your career?

Be sure you enjoy working with teenagers and have a lot of patience, not only with others but with yourself. Teaching can be very rewarding, but don't expect instant gratification every day from your students. In fact, it may be years before students acknowledge their appreciation for what they learned in your classroom.

If you decided to advance your career, what steps would you take and what career(s) might you seek out?

In the world of education it would be fun to teach older students, such as college students or adult learners, to paint and draw. I also have been very interested in and am pursuing my own personal art career. My use of a webpage (www.djcarlson.weebly.com) to feature my own work has been both an enjoyable hobby but also a connection to other artists and art teachers whose work I sometimes bring into my lessons in the classroom. This independent artwork outside of the classroom not only allows me to pursue my own interests but also helps me brush up (no pun intended) on my artistic skills and abilities and learn new techniques and mediums.

19. HIGH SCHOOL PHYSICS TEACHER

BASIC DESCRIPTION

Physics teachers work with students in grades 9 to 12. Content may include topics such as matter, energy, space, time, and force. Providing a basic foundation in the field of physics can help prepare students for future science coursework (e.g., biology, chemistry, earth science, advanced physics) at the college level. The primary purpose of a high school physics curriculum is to teach students about how our universe works and help them to appreciate their daily functioning within the physical world. Teaching the process of research, including hypothesis formation, testing, experimentation, and results reporting, also is a significant role of a physics teacher. Creating relevant activities and lessons through use of real-world physics problems is especially important for teaching high school students. Physics teachers might also provide support to club or extracurricular activities related to the sciences. Many Advanced Placement (AP) courses pertaining to physics exist, including AP Physics B, AP Physics C: Electricity and Magnetism, AP Physics C: Mechanics, AP Physics 1, and AP Physics 2.

CORE COMPETENCIES AND SKILLS NEEDED

Physics teachers need a strong understanding of the science curriculum as well as expertise in teaching the content to high school students. Good communication skills are necessary and must be adapted to the students, parents, and teachers with whom these teachers come into contact. The ability to explain, model, and reinforce complex concepts in ways that a diverse group of learners is able to understand and apply is essential for physics teachers. Problem-solving skills, critical thinking skills, and excellent organizational skills are also important for a high school physics teacher.

EDUCATIONAL REQUIREMENTS

Teaching physics at the high school level requires a bachelor's or master's degree in science education, secondary education, physics, or a closely related field. A teaching certificate is also required from the state in which you will be employed. Look closely at the Department of Education website of the state in which you would like to work for additional information pertaining to certification requirements.

EXPERIENCE NECESSARY

Student teaching is a requirement of all teaching certification programs. Working under a mentor teacher to develop and carry out the physics and other high school science curriculum is necessary. Experience working as a researcher or scientist may help to position one with the real-world skills and competencies necessary to effectively teach physics to high school students.

CERTIFICATION, LICENSURE, AND CONTINUING EDUCATION REQUIREMENTS

Secondary education certification is required. Specialization or an endorsement in the field of science/physics is expected. Continuing education is necessary to maintain a teaching certificate.

SALARY/COMPENSATION

The median pay for physics teachers is $55,050 (all high school teachers), according to the Bureau of Labor Statistics (2014b). It is important to note that an advanced degree, years of experience, and characteristics of the employing school district may result in significant variation in salaries.

EMPLOYMENT OUTLOOK

The employment outlook for physics teachers is anticipated to be strong given the recent push for well-qualified teachers in the areas of science, technology, engineering, and math. Districts that are preparing the majority of their graduates for college would be likely to offer an extensive physics curriculum, including multiple AP physics courses, to prepare them for a multitude of postsecondary education opportunities in the area of science and engineering.

FURTHER INFORMATION FOR EXPLORATION

Three professional organizations are particularly focused on physics education and provide excellent resources for those interested in a career teaching science: the American Association of Physics Teachers (www .aapt.org), the Association for Science Teacher Education (www.theaste .org), and the National Science Teachers Association (www.nsta.org). For informational resources pertaining to science, see www.billnye.com/blog, www.nsf.gov/news/classroom/phyics.jsp, or www.discoveryeducation.com. For additional information related to the content of AP physics courses, see apstudent.collegeboard.org/apcourse.

20. HIGH SCHOOL PHYSICAL EDUCATION TEACHER

BASIC DESCRIPTION

High school physical education teachers organize activities, competitions, and games that promote the physical activity of students in grades 9 to 12. Learning occurs through activities and movement. The purpose of physical education classes is to promote health, wellness, and fitness. Development of skills and competencies such as the following are targeted: good hygiene habits; social and emotional adjustment; strength, agility, and coordination; and familiarity with both team and individual athletic achievement. Knowledge of the rules and customs of an array of sports is provided. Coursework in proper exercise and healthy eating is emphasized. Inclusion of students with all abilities and a diverse array of fitness levels creates unique challenges for instructional planning. High school physical education teachers may also teach health and wellness courses offered within the district. Examples of other duties may include supervisory responsibilities of weight-lifting programs, management of intramural sports programs, or involvement in other athletic events at the high school level. In some districts, if appropriately credentialed, physical education teachers may also be responsible for middle school or elementary school physical education classes. Finally, many physical education teachers take part in coaching sports teams and hold endorsements in those specific sports.

CORE COMPETENCIES AND SKILLS NEEDED

Effective communication skills are essential for physical education teachers. Excellent speaking, listening, and modeling skills are expected. Close monitoring of students' behaviors and activities is necessary to allow sufficient feedback, observation, and evaluation of practice opportunities. Organization of space, students, and equipment is essential to allow for efficient use of instructional time and time involved in physical activity. Leading by example is a unique skill required of physical education teachers. Sensitivity toward, awareness of, and respect for individual differences in gross and fine motor skills and athleticism are expected.

EDUCATIONAL REQUIREMENTS

Teaching physical education at the high school level requires a bachelor's or master's degree in secondary education, kinesiology, physical education, or a closely related field. A teaching certificate is also required from the state in which you will be employed. Look closely at the Department of Education website of the state in which you would like to work for additional information pertaining to certification requirements.

EXPERIENCE NECESSARY

Student teaching is a requirement of all teaching certification programs. Working under a mentor teacher to develop and carry out a physical education curriculum is necessary. Experience in playing and competing in an array of sports or exercise routines (i.e., being physically fit) may be helpful for modeling and guiding students' physical activity during class.

CERTIFICATION, LICENSURE, AND CONTINUING EDUCATION REQUIREMENTS

Secondary education certification is required. Specialization in physical education is required. If also engaged in coaching, an endorsement or coaching credential in that particular sport is required. Continuing education is necessary to maintain a teaching or coaching certificate.

SALARY/COMPENSATION

The median pay for physical education teachers is $55,050 (all high school teachers), according to the Bureau of Labor Statistics (2014b). It is important to note that an advanced degree, years of experience, and characteristics of the employing school district may result in significant variation in salaries.

EMPLOYMENT OUTLOOK

The employment outlook for physical education teachers is anticipated to be similar to that for other high school teaching positions, not including those related to science, technology, engineering, or math. Higher rates of openings for physical education teachers are expected at the elementary and middle school levels in the near future.

FURTHER INFORMATION FOR EXPLORATION

Two professional organizations are particularly focused on supporting teachers of physical and health education and provide excellent resources for those interested in this career: the Society of Health and Physical Educators (www.shapeamerica.org) and the American School Health Association (www.ashaweb.org). For additional general information and

other resources pertaining to adolescent and school health, see www
.cdc.gov and www.fitness.gov.

21. HIGH SCHOOL PSYCHOLOGY TEACHER

BASIC DESCRIPTION

Psychology teachers work with students in grades K–12. Common
introductory topics or units taught pertaining to human behavior and
mental processes include emotion, learning, motivation, personality,
psychological disorders, life-span development, and mental health
treatments. Seven domains of training are recommended within the
American Psychological Association's *National Standards for High
School Psychology Curricula* (2011). These domains include scientific
inquiry, biopsychological development/learning, sociocultural context,
cognition, individual variation, and applications of psychological science. Issues of diversity are specifically recommended to be infused
throughout the teaching of these seven curricular domains. Practical,
real-life application of psychological principles and concepts is an
essential component of a high school psychology curriculum. Helping
students get excited about this field of study so that they are interested in further exploration of the social sciences, especially within
a college curriculum, is the primary focus of this position at the high
school level. Psychology teachers usually are trained in social sciences
and are often responsible for other curriculum in this area of study.
Some school districts may offer an Advanced Placement (AP) course
in psychology.

CORE COMPETENCIES AND SKILLS NEEDED

In addition to content knowledge pertaining to psychology, it is also
expected that high school psychology teachers have demonstrated strong
competencies related to instructional effectiveness. Strong communication skills are necessary. The ability to present complex psychological
theories and principles in easy-to-understand language is important.
Helping students to apply what they are learning to the world around
them is an important skill expected of high school psychology teachers.
A high level of motivation and enthusiasm is sought in those who teach
high school electives like psychology. A data-based problem-solving
approach to instruction and discussion can help model the importance of
observable information within the field of psychology. Problem-solving

skills, critical thinking skills, and excellent organizational skills are also important for a high school psychology teacher.

EDUCATIONAL REQUIREMENTS

Teaching psychology at the high school level requires a bachelor's or master's degree in social sciences, psychology, secondary education, or a closely related field. A teaching certificate is also required from the state in which you will be employed. Look closely at the Department of Education website of the state in which you would like to work for additional information pertaining to certification requirements, as the field of psychology is a bit unique when compared to other specialty areas within the high school curriculum.

EXPERIENCE NECESSARY

Student teaching is a requirement of all teaching certification programs. Working under a mentor teacher to develop and carry out a psychology curriculum is necessary. Experience working in a field of psychology (e.g., mental health provider, researcher, college instructor) may help to position one with the real-world skills and competencies necessary to teach psychology to high school students.

CERTIFICATION, LICENSURE, AND CONTINUING EDUCATION REQUIREMENTS

Secondary education certification is required. Specialization or an endorsement in the field of psychology or social sciences is expected. Continuing education is necessary to maintain a teaching certificate.

SALARY/COMPENSATION

The median pay for psychology teachers is $55,050 (all high school teachers), according to the Bureau of Labor Statistics (2014b). It is important to note that an advanced degree, years of experience, and characteristics of the employing school district may result in significant variation in salaries.

EMPLOYMENT OUTLOOK

The employment outlook for psychology teachers is anticipated to be similar to that for other high school teaching positions (i.e., just under 10% growth in the next 10 years, according to the Bureau of Labor

Statistics, 2014b) not directly related to science, technology, engineering, and math. Geographic variations may also be apparent as some school districts shift their resources to teaching core requirements of language arts, math, and science. Other districts that are preparing the majority of their graduates for college would be likely to offer a psychology curriculum, including an AP Psychology course, to prepare students for postsecondary education opportunities.

FURTHER INFORMATION FOR EXPLORATION

A professional organization that is particularly involved in the teaching of psychology to high school students is the American Psychological Association (APA; www.apa.org). Specifically, a subgroup within the APA called Teachers of Psychology in Secondary Schools (TOPSS; www.apa.org/ed/precollege/topss/index.aspx) provides resources, lessons, and supporting documents for use by high school psychology teachers. One particular reference that would be useful for those interested in teaching psychology at the high school level is the *Resource Manual for New Teachers of High School Psychology* (APA, 2014), recently revised in January 2014, which can be downloaded for free on the APA's website. For additional information related to the content of the AP Psychology course, see apstudent.collegeboard.org/apcourse.

22. ADVANCED PLACEMENT ENGLISH LITERATURE TEACHER

BASIC DESCRIPTION

Advanced Placement (AP) literature (i.e., English literature and composition) teachers adhere to a standardized curriculum (e.g., textbook, course description guide) that helps to position high school students to take a national exam offered by the College Board (www.collegeboard.org). Passing that national exam with high scores allows high school students to be granted placement and college credits for that work. To teach a class in literature that has the AP designation means that the course has been audited by the College Board to ensure that it meets the curricular and instructional standards expected. Two AP areas, English literature and composition, are available for testing, and schools may offer one or both of these courses. Specific goals and objectives are prescribed. Examples include (a) to learn to read college-level texts critically; (b) to explore literary elements such as imagery, tone, and symbolism; and (c) to express one's ideas in writing via expository, analytical, and argumentative essays. A high level of content knowledge pertaining to reading and writing competencies is expected of AP literature teachers. In addition, the use of effective instructional approaches to teach English and literature to high school students is necessary. Finally, a high degree of organization, accountability, and frequent monitoring of student's progress within the course is expected. Public disclosure of AP exam results creates a sense of "high-stakes teaching" that other high school courses may not possess. High school AP literature teachers also typically teach other levels of English and composition. They may also provide guidance to essay contest participants, reading groups, or study groups associated with taking the AP exam in English literature and composition.

CORE COMPETENCIES AND SKILLS NEEDED

The ability to meet the demands and expectations of the College Board is essential for AP literature teachers. Skills in critical thinking, oral communication, written communication, and editing are needed. A passion for helping high school students prepare for college-level literature and writing courses is essential. Considerable time and organizational skills are needed for the intensive demands of reviewing, evaluating, and grading multiple drafts of students' work. Close attention to detail and persistence with the feedback necessary to help students revise and rewrite their assignments are also necessary.

EDUCATIONAL REQUIREMENTS

A bachelor's degree in English, literature, secondary education, or related field is required. Most likely, an advanced degree in English or literature is necessary for those interested in teaching at the highest level within high schools. Certification to teach at the high school level is necessary, and requirements vary by state. A close review of these via the Department of Education website of the state in which you would like to be employed is essential.

EXPERIENCE NECESSARY

Student teaching is a requirement of teaching certification programs. In addition, teachers interested in teaching AP literature at the high school level typically will have many years of experience in successfully teaching English and writing courses. Evidence of successfully teaching these courses to high school students is typically necessary.

CERTIFICATION, LICENSURE, AND CONTINUING EDUCATION REQUIREMENTS

A teacher certificate in secondary education is required. Specialization in literature and composition is expected. Continuous improvement through engagement in the annual audit process with the College Board ensures that national standards are being met. Continuing education requirements are also associated with renewing teaching certificates.

SALARY/COMPENSATION

The median salary for an AP literature teacher is $55,050 (all high school teachers), according to the Bureau of Labor Statistics (2014b). It is important to note that an advanced degree, years of experience, and characteristics of the employing school district may result in significant variation in salaries. Interestingly, high school teachers who hold advanced degrees, albeit in different fields, would ultimately start on the same pay scale despite different areas of expertise.

EMPLOYMENT OUTLOOK

Demand for high-quality AP literature and composition teachers will continue to increase in the coming years, yet at a lower rate as compared with science, technology, engineering, and math teacher openings. School districts are increasingly preparing the majority of their graduates for postsecondary education, and the opportunities to teach AP literature will follow this trend.

FURTHER INFORMATION FOR EXPLORATION

For additional information about requirements and expectations for an AP literature and composition course, please see www.collegeboard.org. For additional information about teaching English, please see the website of the National Council of Teachers of English (www.ncte.org) and the associated website at www.readwritethink.org.

Career-in-Education Profile
ADVANCED PLACEMENT ENGLISH LITERATURE TEACHER

Interview With Marianne Forman (BA, English Education;
MA, Reading Specialist)

Describe your educational background.

I went to high school in a town that was very blue collar, largely dependent on the auto industry. I was not expected or encouraged to go to college, as my father was hoping I would work the assembly line at General Motors. I ended up going to college anyway, starting as a music major (flute). I did some work in theater but ended up graduating as an English education major. Later, I earned a master's degree as a reading specialist.

Describe your prior experiences and the path you took to get to this career.

I'd always wanted to be a teacher. I remember "playing school" in the garage as a young girl. I had originally wanted to be a professional musician, or possibly even a music educator, but I found that my very minimal background in piano was a difficult hurdle to overcome. I dabbled with some theater courses and even some courses in special education, finally realizing I would love to teach literature and writing. This is the place I could bring all my "loves" together and share them with students in a truly humanities-centered classroom. For example, I could read literature, write poetry, dance, sing, act, and share my love of other cultures and anthropology.

Describe the work that you do.

I teach Advanced Placement (AP) Literature and Composition, largely to high school seniors. I read along with my students, even though I've read these novels/plays numerous times. I create writing assignments that help students deeply examine and closely read the literature—helping to prep them for the AP exam held in May of each year. I have students study and write poetry, too, in the hopes that they will become forever poets.

(continued)

(continued)

What is a typical day like for you in this career?

I get up at 5 a.m. every morning and do a series of Qigong and Tai Chi routines. I review what I am going to be working on with students, accompanied by a morning cup of tea. I arrive at work about an hour before students arrive, giving me time to run off materials and get ready for the day. During the school day, I teach both American Literature and AP Literature and Composition. I teach five class periods every day, plus an Excel study period twice a week. I also am the facilitator for the Gay/Straight Alliance Club at school, which meets every Monday right after school. I typically have meetings after school about 3 days each week, which keep me until about 5 p.m. At about 9 p.m., I begin planning for the next day of teaching. I plan and grade papers every evening, usually for about 3 hours a night.

What is the most challenging part of your career?

The most challenging part of my career is dealing with the "powers that be"—administrators, governors, and others. Many times decisions are made that negatively affect students. The folks making the decisions are often so removed from the classroom that they have lost perspective on what it is really like to "be in the trenches." I am the kind of person who always speaks truth to power. The powers that be often don't like to be even peacefully confronted.

What is the most rewarding part of your career?

Working directly with students, every day, is the most rewarding part of career. There has never been a day, in 32 years, in which I did not look forward to going to school. Every day is different, as people change, even over the course of a single day, depending on what is happening in their lives. I have treasured the personal relationships I've established with students over the years.

(continued)

(continued)

What advice do you have for someone in high school or currently at the undergraduate level who might be interested in this career?

Think very carefully about this decision. Teachers just entering the field are being trained to prepare students for assessments and standardized tests. The pressure is real, and teacher evaluations are now largely based on student performance. I had tremendous freedom to be creative these last 32 years. I would also advise a person considering a career in education to actually get in classrooms—observe, volunteer, and, ultimately, find a mentor who is willing to work with you. Further, I would advise a person considering being a teacher to think about the fact that this is not a "job," at least not if you want to do it well. I have found that teaching has consumed me; I'm always on the watch for new ways I can engage my students.

What advice do you have for someone currently in a different career/field who might be interested in your career?

Consider that working this closely with individual human beings is probably one of the most personally satisfying and fulfilling careers you will ever encounter. If you want a career in which you can see every day that you are indeed making a positive difference in a young person's life, this is the path for you. This is a deeply moving and memorable career.

If you decided to advance your career, what steps would you take and what career(s) might you seek out?

If I were to advance my career, I would like to teach at the university level, which would mean pursuing a PhD. Currently, with my master's degree, I can teach at the community college level. However, I love the daily contact I have with students at the high school and their willingness to create a classroom community with me. At the college level, I would teach in a multipurpose classroom that was not my own. No art. No Nepalese prayer flags. No drums and recorders to grab when the spirit moves me. I think that would be a sterile environment for me.

23. HIGH SCHOOL PERFORMING ARTS DIRECTOR

BASIC DESCRIPTION

High school performing arts directors (i.e., directors of visual and performing arts) are responsible for the planning, development, implementation, and evaluation of performing arts curriculum and instructional practices in grades 9 to 12. They are also responsible for organizing performances, drama clubs, and other extracurricular activities that utilize the performing arts facilities. This administrative role also means that leadership within the district and community will be expected. This may mean that budgeting, advertising, and creating school–community partnerships are all priorities for the performing arts director. Close communication with other staff, administrators, parents, and students is expected. This director position may also involve typical duties expected of a drama teacher. These duties include training students in how to act, sing, dance, and/or perform. Lesson plans associated with the drama curriculum, such as drama history, drama theory, acting styles, acting techniques, lighting/sound, and the reading of popular plays/musicals, may be included. Overseeing rehearsal, creating stage designs, directing the cast, and evaluating students' performance are tasks commonly associated with the work of a performing arts director.

CORE COMPETENCIES AND SKILLS NEEDED

Strong communication skills are needed to be both effective and efficient in this leadership role. The ability to work with a diverse array of stakeholders is important. The ability to handle stress while under pressure is an excellent quality to have as a director. Flexibility, determination, and effective organizational skills are needed given the multitude of responsibilities associated with this position. A passion for theater and a commitment to excellence are important qualities sought in a performing arts director.

EDUCATIONAL REQUIREMENTS

A bachelor's degree in the performing arts or theater and a certificate to teach at the secondary education level are required. A master's degree in drama education is the typical route taken to teaching the performing arts within the schools. Prior coursework and training in acting, voice, drama theory, and the history of theater would be expected for this teaching career. In addition, coursework in effective instructional practices and teaching at the high school level is necessary.

EXPERIENCE NECESSARY

Student teaching is a requirement of teaching certification programs. In addition, teachers interested in teaching drama at the high school level typically will have many years of experience in the performing arts through community theater or other venues. Evidence of successful involvement in theater and teaching theater to others is typically necessary for a high school performing arts director.

CERTIFICATION, LICENSURE, AND CONTINUING EDUCATION REQUIREMENTS

A teacher certificate in secondary education is required and usually would be a built-in component of a master's degree program in drama education. Specialization in performing arts, drama, or musical theater is expected. Continuing education requirements are associated with renewing teaching certificates.

SALARY/COMPENSATION

The median salary for a drama teacher is $55,050 (all high school teachers), according to the Bureau of Labor Statistics (2014b). However, this director position would likely provide a salary that would be higher. An advanced degree, years of experience, and characteristics of the employing school district would all be taken into account when establishing the salary support for this director position.

EMPLOYMENT OUTLOOK

Demand for highly qualified performing arts directors will continue to increase in the coming years. Drama teacher positions also are expected to increase, yet at a lower rate than science, technology, engineering, and math teacher openings. School districts realize that the performing arts help students to build self-confidence, communication skills, and presentation skills, all of which are essential for job interviews and future careers. As more and more high school students look to additional post-secondary educational opportunities, it is anticipated that backgrounds in the performing arts will continue to be one way that students can distinguish their talents, skills, and involvement in extracurricular activities when compared with other college applicants.

FURTHER INFORMATION FOR EXPLORATION

For additional information about art education, please see the following professional organizations via their websites: the Educational Theatre

Association (www.schooltheatre.org), the American Alliance for Theatre and Education (www.aate.org), the Arts Education Partnership (www.aep-arts. com), and the National Art Education Association (www.arteducators.org).

24. HIGH SCHOOL BAND/ORCHESTRA DIRECTOR

BASIC DESCRIPTION
High school band/orchestra directors (i.e., music directors) are responsible for the planning, development, implementation, and evaluation of a music curriculum and instructional practices in grades 9 to 12. They are also responsible for organizing concerts, orchestra, jazz band, marching band, soloists, ensembles, and other extracurricular activities that carry forward the mission of the music program. This administrative role also means that leadership within the district and community will be expected. This may mean that budgeting, advertising, and creating school–community partnerships are all priorities for the band/orchestra director. Close communication with other staff, administrators, parents, and students is expected, especially when out-of-town events are coordinated. This director position may also involve typical duties expected of a music teacher. These duties include instrumental music training and establishing a classroom environment that promotes musical learning and success with public performances. The band/orchestra director creates lesson plans associated with the music curriculum, such as music history, music theory, percussion, and the study of famous musicians/bands. Overseeing rehearsals, directing performances, and evaluating students' performance are commonly associated with the work of a high school band/orchestra director. The hiring and supervision of an assistant band director may also be involved in this position, depending on the school district.

CORE COMPETENCIES AND SKILLS NEEDED
Strong communication skills are needed to be both effective and efficient in this leadership role. The ability to work with a diverse array of stakeholders is important. The ability to handle stress while under pressure is an excellent quality to have as a director. Flexibility, determination, and effective organizational skills are needed given the multitude of responsibilities associated with this position. A passion for teaching music to others and a commitment to excellence are important qualities sought in a music director. A willingness to travel for out-of-town performances and the flexibility necessary to put in long hours outside of the regular school day are expected. Fund-raising and working closely with a booster club may also be required.

EDUCATIONAL REQUIREMENTS

A bachelor's degree in music and a certificate to teach at the secondary education level are required. A master's degree in music education is preferred. Familiarity with a diverse music curriculum and multiple musical instruments is essential in this position. In addition, coursework in effective instructional practices and teaching music education at the high school level is necessary.

EXPERIENCE NECESSARY

Student teaching is a requirement of all teaching certification programs. In addition, teachers interested in teaching music at the high school level typically will have many years of experience as a musician, in instructing other musicians, or in serving in a leadership role related to youth musical performances. Evidence of leadership, management, and administration is expected for a music teacher who is applying to be the high school band/orchestra director.

CERTIFICATION, LICENSURE, AND CONTINUING EDUCATION REQUIREMENTS

A teacher certificate in secondary education is required and usually would be a built-in component of a master's degree program in music education. Continuing education requirements are associated with renewing teaching certificates.

SALARY/COMPENSATION

The median salary for a music teacher is $55,050 (all high school teachers), according to the Bureau of Labor Statistics (2014b). However, this director position would likely provide a salary that would be higher. It may include both a salary and additional pay for overseeing the extracurricular activities associated with musical performances (e.g., marching band or orchestra performances at school or in the community). An advanced degree, years of experience, and characteristics of the employing school district would all be taken into account when establishing the salary support for this director position.

EMPLOYMENT OUTLOOK

Demand for highly qualified band/orchestra directors will continue to increase in the coming years as the population of students in grades 9 to 12 increases. School districts realize that the performing arts help students to build self-confidence, communication skills, and presentation skills, all of which are essential for job interviews and future careers. As more and more high school students look to additional postsecondary educational opportunities, it is anticipated that backgrounds in music performance will continue to be a way that students can distinguish their talents, skills, and involvement in extracurricular activities when compared with other college applicants.

FURTHER INFORMATION FOR EXPLORATION

For additional information about music education, please see the following professional organizations via their websites: the American String Teachers Association (www.astaweb.com), the Music Teachers National Association (www.mtna.org), the American School Band Directors Association (www. asbda.com), the National Band Association (www.nationalbandassociation. org), and the National Association of Music Education (www.nafme.org).

REFERENCES

American Psychological Association. (2011). *National standards for high school psychology curricula*. Retrieved from http://www.apa.org/education/k12/psychology-curricula.pdf

American Psychological Association. (2014). *Resource manual for new teachers of high school psychology*. Washington, DC: Author.

Bureau of Labor Statistics, U.S. Department of Labor. (2014a). *Occupational outlook handbook, 2014–2015 edition, Career and Technical Education Teachers*. Retrieved July 10, 2015, from http://www.bls.gov/ooh/education-training-and-library/career-and-technical-education-teachers.htm

Bureau of Labor Statistics, U.S. Department of Labor. (2014b). *Occupational outlook handbook, 2014–2015 edition, High School Teachers*. Retrieved July 7, 2015, from http://www.bls.gov/ooh/education-training-and-library/high-school-teachers.htm

Bureau of Labor Statistics, U.S. Department of Labor. (2014c). *Occupational outlook handbook, 2014–2015 edition, Kindergarten and Elementary School Teachers*. Retrieved July 7, 2015, from http://www.bls.gov/ooh/education-training-and-library/kindergarten-and-elementary-school-teachers.htm

Bureau of Labor Statistics, U.S. Department of Labor. (2014d). *Occupational outlook handbook, 2014–2015 edition, Library Technicians and Assistants*. Retrieved July 9, 2015, from http://www.bls.gov/ooh/education-training-and-library/library-technicians-and-assistants.htm

Bureau of Labor Statistics, U.S. Department of Labor. (2014e). *Occupational outlook handbook, 2014–2015 edition, Middle School Teachers*. Retrieved July 8, 2015, from http://www.bls.gov/ooh/education-training-and-library/middle-school-teachers.htm

Bureau of Labor Statistics, U.S. Department of Labor. (2014f). *Occupational outlook handbook, 2014–2015 edition, School and Career Counselors*. Retrieved July 5, 2015, from http://www.bls.gov/ooh/community-and-social-service/school-and-career-counselors.htm

5 ■ CAREERS WORKING IN POSTSECONDARY EDUCATION

25. TEACHING ASSISTANT, COLLEGE OF EDUCATION

BASIC DESCRIPTION

Teaching assistants (TAs) hired within a college of education typically provide instructional support to faculty who teach either undergraduate or graduate students in education-related content. TAs provide students who are enrolled in a course with an additional contact pertaining to course material. This support may be in the form of grading, meeting one-on-one, running breakout sessions, proctoring exams, preparing supplemental lecture materials, maintaining an online course management system, or lecturing. The level of instructional independence afforded to TAs is dependent on the nature or content of the course. Some introductory education courses may involve considerable use of a TA during class time. Other courses may only involve a TA as a grader of assignments or projects. Teaching assistantship positions are typically 10-hour-per-week (25% time TA) or 20-hour-per-week (50% time TA) appointments. These appointments are generally for one semester or one academic year. However, excellent TAs may be hired across many years or up through completion of their graduate education. Being a TA provides one with excellent experience and skills that are required to become a university professor, often a goal for many who work toward an advanced graduate degree.

CORE COMPETENCIES AND SKILLS NEEDED

One must be enrolled at the university in order to become a TA. Typically, teaching assistantship positions are held by graduate students in the field of study or a related field. Some teaching assistantships can also be held by undergraduate students who may have excelled in the course in the past. Strong written and oral communication skills are necessary. Prior course content knowledge or the ability to quickly learn the material is required. Supervisors of teaching assistantships often look to hire those who demonstrate excellent organizational skills, a high level of initiative, strong interpersonal skills, and the ability to work effectively within a team. It is essential for a TA to work effectively with his or her supervisor. In addition, the ability to respond effectively to critical feedback is essential. Ultimately, strong communication skills are necessary to develop and maintain a good working relationship with both students and supervisors. The need to be highly accessible through phone, in-person, or electronic communications is imperative while performing the teaching assistantship duties. A high level of preparation and practice are often required to be an effective lecturer/presenter.

EDUCATIONAL REQUIREMENTS

An undergraduate degree or an advanced graduate degree is required for this position in higher education. The degree is typically in the field of the course being taught or a closely related field. TAs typically are provided training at the beginning of each semester and the support necessary to successfully fulfill their responsibilities during the semester is given. TA training might include effective and innovative teaching methods, use of technology in the classroom, ethical and legal issues, methods of evaluation, conflict resolution, and accommodations for those with disabilities. For those TAs who are international students, training would also likely focus on English communication skills and the culture of American university classroom practices.

EXPERIENCE NECESSARY

Knowledge and experience with the course material are typically required. Prior experience in public speaking or leading small groups would link well to this position. Many universities have a center for teaching and learning that provides seminars or training to help ready a student for a TA position. Taking seminars or learning from those centers is often a way to distinguish one's preparation from that of other graduate students. Graduate students who are offered admission into an advanced degree program often will be provided with a funding package (i.e., teaching assistantship) in order to increase the likelihood of acceptance of the admission offer.

CERTIFICATION, LICENSURE, AND CONTINUING EDUCATION REQUIREMENTS

Some universities require students to obtain certification or training to become a teaching assistant. Specific markers for English communication skills are typically a requirement for international students. Most universities provide credit and consideration to TAs who teach across multiple years.

SALARY/COMPENSATION

Teaching assistantships are highly sought, given that an appointment provides tuition support (e.g., credit waivers, full tuition coverage) and a modest living stipend. Stipends ($18,000 to $50,000 depending on the appointment terms) and benefits for teaching assistantships can vary across universities and colleges within universities. Examples of benefits include medical leave, bereavement leave, adoption/parental leave, health insurance, prescription drug coverage, dependent health coverage, and dental options.

EMPLOYMENT OUTLOOK

The demand for TAs typically links closely to university funding and is directly tied to demand for undergraduate education programs. As graduate programs ebb and flow, so too does the need for TAs. Teaching assistantships are expected to grow at a strong pace in the next decade.

FURTHER INFORMATION FOR EXPLORATION

Numerous universities across the country have seen their graduate teaching assistants unionize in recent years. For example, the United Auto, Aerospace and Agricultural Implement Workers of America represents groups of TAs at a number of universities, including New York University, the University of California teaching campuses, and the University of Washington. An example of the mission and purpose of teaching assistant unions can be seen at the www.tauaft.org website. The American Federation of Teachers: Higher Education division often represents both faculty and graduate employees in public, private, 2-year, and 4-year institutions of higher education (www.aft.org/highered). Its mission is to help give voice to its members related to issues of employment and collective bargaining (e.g., pay, benefits, work responsibilities, work conditions).

Career-in-Education Profile
TEACHING ASSISTANT
Interview With Erin Seif (MA, PhD, School Psychology)

Describe your educational background.

I majored in psychology and then joined Teach for America. After 4 years of teaching, I decided to go to graduate school to earn an advanced degree in school psychology.

Describe your prior experiences and the path you took to get to this career.

I had several volunteer experiences involving both children's educational programming and leadership development. As a part of graduate school, I had the opportunity to work as a teaching assistant for undergraduate students considering teaching as a career. I have also been a teaching assistant for a graduate-level course in the school psychology program.

Describe the work that you do.

My teaching assistant position is a 50% appointment and I spend 20 hours per work related to my duties. I am responsible for teaching a course using lesson plans that were designed by the university course instructor. I am responsible for managing the day-to-day logistics of the course, such as creating a syllabus, maintaining an electronic gradebook, and grading papers. I also spent time reviewing the literature for recently published peer-reviewed articles related to course content. I also frequently scanned popular press articles to find relevant and current content to add to the scripted lesson plans.

What is a typical day like for you in this career?

I typically taught 2 days a week for 90 minutes each day. The course could also be one 3-hour weekly block. I spent time prepping a day or two before the class and a few minutes prior to the beginning of

(continued)

(continued)

class, and stayed a few minutes after class to speak with students. I held weekly office hours and spent time each day grading papers and responding to e-mails. As a teaching assistant, I think it is more accurate to think of a typical semester as opposed to a typical day because the workload varies. Although the class meeting schedule remained consistent across the semester, essays and projects were typically due at the mid point and the end of the semester and the number of weekly working hours required during these time points increased substantially.

What is the most challenging part of your career?

Two aspects of being a teaching assistant are particularly challenging. The first is engaging all students in the classroom. Students have varying interest in the course content and varying ability levels, and designing activities to meet the needs of all students in a 90-minute class period is difficult. The second challenge is having realistic expectations of the amount of time necessary for general classroom preparation. Typically, a teaching assistant will spend approximately three to four times as long working outside of the classroom as inside of the classroom. The activities completed outside of the classroom, such as creating and editing PowerPoint presentations, staying abreast of new technology to use as part of classroom activities, providing feedback, meeting with students and faculty, managing the course website, and preparing for each lesson, all take a substantial amount of time.

What is the most rewarding part of your career?

The most rewarding part of this career is the opportunity to interact with such a diverse group of students and play a small role in shaping their career identity. I also enjoy watching students' growth and development related to the course content through evaluating their work over the course of the semester.

(continued)

(continued)

What advice do you have for someone in high school or currently at the undergraduate level who might be interested in this career?

I think it's important to volunteer in activities that are directly related to teaching as well as activities that that are not related to teaching. A unique aspect of teaching is that, unlike other careers, most people are surrounded by teachers from toddlerhood through young adulthood and are familiar with the role of teaching due to the extensive amount of time they have spent in schools themselves.

What advice do you have for someone currently in a different career/field who might be interested in your career?

I think it is important to consider the practical aspects of a career change and carefully consider the opportunity cost that a career change might involve. For example, having an accurate understanding of the career opportunities available in the area you would like to live, the projected growth or decline of the career, average salary and benefits, and what costs you might incur by leaving your current career are all important considerations. For some people, finding outlets to teach others through volunteer or other community-based activities in addition to their current career may be a better fit than changing careers altogether.

If you decided to advance your career, what steps would you take and what career(s) might you seek out?

I think understanding what you enjoy most about the role of a teaching assistant is essential prior to deciding what steps to take prior to advancing your career. If it is the particular content knowledge that you enjoy, pursuing an advanced career in that particular field may be the most appropriate course of action. If the act of teaching is what you enjoy most, pursuing a degree in education and teaching at either the secondary, undergraduate, or graduate level would all be viable ways to advance one's career. I chose to go into the field of school psychology to gain specialized skills that would allow me

(continued)

(*continued*)

to engage in school-wide initiatives related to curriculum planning and development and bringing psychology into schools. My teaching assistant work is directly linked to my aspiration to become a school psychologist/licensed psychologist. I am also well positioned to enter a career as a university professor or a clinical assistant professor given the background and experiences I have had as a TA.

26. GRADUATE ASSISTANT, COLLEGE OF EDUCATION

BASIC DESCRIPTION

Graduate assistants (GAs; also referred to as research assistants) hired within a college of education do not provide instructional support and instead support faculty with their research, special projects, or program administration (e.g., recruitment, retention, program development). This support may be in the form of data collection, data analysis, data dissemination, or other research/administrative support. The level of independence afforded to GAs is dependent on the nature or content of the GA assignment. Graduate assistantship positions are typically 10-hour-per-week (25% time TA) or 20-hour-per-week (50% time TA) appointments. These appointments are generally for an academic year. However, excellent GAs may be hired across many years or up through their completion of a graduate degree. Being a GA provides one with excellent experience in the area of research and service, which is often required to become a university professor, a goal for many who work toward an advanced graduate degree.

CORE COMPETENCIES AND SKILLS NEEDED

Graduate assistantship positions are held by graduate students in the field of study or a related field. Strong written and oral communication skills are necessary. Prior research or program content knowledge is required. Supervisors of graduate assistants often look to hire those who demonstrate excellent organizational skills, a high level of initiative/independence, strong interpersonal skills, and the ability to work effectively with others. The ability to work well under deadlines is important. Exceeding a supervisor's expectations for effective and efficient completion of tasks is important given the role that these individuals can play in providing future mentorship and letters of support. It is also essential for a GA to work effectively with his or her supervisor. In addition, the ability to respond effectively to critical feedback is essential. The need to be highly accessible through phone, in-person, or electronic communications is imperative while performing graduate assistantship responsibilities.

EDUCATIONAL REQUIREMENTS
An advanced graduate degree (MA or MS) is typically required for this position in higher education. The degree is typically in the field or a closely related field linked to the assistantship responsibilities. An intrinsic interest in the assistantship responsibilities is important, and past education or training can help ready one for a graduate assistantship.

EXPERIENCE NECESSARY
Graduate students who are offered admission into an advanced degree program often will be provided with a funding package (i.e., graduate assistantship) in order to increase the likelihood of acceptance of the admission offer. Graduate assistantships can often be associated with externally funded research projects and provide students with authentic experiences in what it is like to work as a faculty member within a university.

CERTIFICATION, LICENSURE, AND CONTINUING EDUCATION REQUIREMENTS
No certification or licensure requirements are necessary to be a GA. Being highly motivated and having a strong desire for learning, a focus on details, a commitment to excellence, and an interest in continuous improvement are the most important characteristics necessary to succeed in this position.

SALARY/COMPENSATION
Graduate assistantships are highly sought, given that an appointment provides tuition support (e.g., credit waivers, full tuition coverage) and a modest living stipend. Stipends ($18,000 to $50,000 depending on the appointment terms) and benefits for graduate assistantships can vary across universities and colleges within universities. Examples of benefits include medical leave, bereavement leave, adoption/parental leave, health insurance, prescription drug coverage, dependent health coverage, and dental options.

EMPLOYMENT OUTLOOK

The demand for GAs typically links closely to university funding and is directly tied to the demand within the program of study. As graduate programs ebb and flow, so too does the need for GAs. Graduate assistantships are expected to grow at a strong pace in the next decade given the increase in postsecondary enrollments that is expected.

FURTHER INFORMATION FOR EXPLORATION

Numerous universities across the country have seen their graduate assistants unionize in recent years. The American Federation of Teachers: Higher Education division often represents both faculty and graduate employees in public, private, 2-year, and 4-year institutions of higher education (www.aft.org/highered). Its mission is to help give voice to its members related to issues of employment and collective bargaining (e.g., pay, benefits, work responsibilities, work conditions).

27. LECTURER

BASIC DESCRIPTION

Lecturers within a university setting are responsible for providing students with the knowledge and skills necessary to master course content. Providing lectures, seminars, tutorials, and supervision are all instructional approaches associated with being a lecturer. In addition to being responsible for the delivery of course content, the role of a lecturer involves the creation and administration of assessments of students' learning. This includes the use of quizzes, exams, assignments, and other formal methods of student evaluation. Lecturers are often responsible for a small number of courses (e.g., one to four) each semester; they typically are fixed-term, part-time members of the faculty; and sometimes they may be supervised by another faculty member. Lecturers in the United States are not responsible for carrying forward programs of research or providing service to the university through departmental, college, or university committee work. In other countries, the term *lecturer* is synonymous with the title *assistant professor*, and teaching, research, and service are expected of individuals in this position. Lecturers in the United States are typically employed in colleges, universities, law schools, or business schools as untenured members of the faculty. The title *guest lecturer* is associated with a speaker who is brought in to deliver a single lecture or one aspect of the course curriculum. The title *honorary lecturer* (i.e., a substantial record of service or achievement) is used for persons with great distinction within a field with no affiliation to the university who might present lectures or seminars not necessarily associated with a specific university course.

CORE COMPETENCIES AND SKILLS NEEDED

Strong teaching skills are required. Effective delivery of course content and other responsibilities associated with teaching duties are expected. Strong rapport with students and the ability to provide constructive feedback on student assignments, essays, quizzes, tests, or final exams are important.

EDUCATIONAL REQUIREMENTS

Lecturers typically have a PhD in the field of study in which they teach. That contrasts with the term *instructor*, which designates those who do not hold the doctoral degree.

EXPERIENCE NECESSARY

Prior teaching experience is preferred. Typically, work experience with the content associated with the course is expected. In many situations, educators who have retired from their positions within the field of education serve in the role of lecturer.

CERTIFICATION, LICENSURE, AND CONTINUING EDUCATION REQUIREMENTS

Licensure or certification credentials associated with the content of the course being taught are expected. There are no formal requirements for continuing education to hold the position of lecturer.

SALARY/COMPENSATION

Part-time salary or a stipend for each course taught may be typical for those holding lecturer positions. Salaries vary substantially by university, college, program, and region of the country. Full-time lecturer salaries are lower than salaries for those holding positions at the assistant, associate, or full professor levels. Typical full-time pay ranges might be from $35,000 to $55,000, with even higher rates for visiting lecturers at prestigious universities.

EMPLOYMENT OUTLOOK

Universities and colleges appear to be increasingly using nontenured faculty to teach courses. As postsecondary educational opportunities expand and grow, so too will lecturer positions.

FURTHER INFORMATION FOR EXPLORATION

The employment of part-time faculty within university settings has grown tremendously. As a result, advocacy groups have sprung up to lobby on behalf of lecturers and other part-time faculty (e.g., the California Part-time Faculty Association; www.cpfa.org). An excellent overview of the status of nontenure-track faculty within university settings can be found on the website of the American Association of University Professors (AAUP), whose purpose is to advance academic freedom and emphasize the importance of shared governance (www.aaup.org/report/status-non-tenure-track-faculty).

28. TECHNICAL COLLEGE INSTRUCTOR

BASIC DESCRIPTION

Technical college instructors teach courses that help to prepare students for a range of professional technical (i.e., vocational) careers in fields such as engineering, health, medicine, agriculture, manufacturing, construction, and technology. These instructor positions may be found at a technical college, a community college, or a junior college. Technical college instructors engage in both the teaching and evaluation of the skill sets required within a specific technical career. In addition to being responsible for the delivery of course content, the role of the instructor involves the creation and administration of assessments of students' learning. This includes the use of simulations, exams, assignments, and other methods of student evaluation acceptable to the technical skills being taught. Positions may be part time (3 to 6 credits per semester of teaching) or full time (12 credits per semester). Teaching requirements are substantially higher in technical or community colleges when compared to research universities.

CORE COMPETENCIES AND SKILLS NEEDED

The ability to relate well to adult learners is essential given the role of supervision/evaluation of students' technical skills. The effective use of instructional techniques associated with the course to be taught is necessary. Specifically, the ability to identify the knowledge, skills, and abilities an individual needs to succeed in the technical career of interest is essential. In many cases the instructor will use instructional techniques such as modeling and repeated practice. Strong organizational skills and effective time management are important within this teaching career. Promoting and recruiting students to enter the technical field may also be a part of the job. Less frequently, technical college instructors may also be involved in program development and program review/ accreditation efforts. In sum, foundational skills and abilities, in addition to technical skills that are industry specific, are required.

EDUCATIONAL REQUIREMENTS

Educational requirements will vary based on the technical skills being taught. At a minimum an associate's degree in the area being taught (plus extensive years of experience) is required, but more typically a bachelor's degree associated with the professional technical career (plus 1 to 2 years of experience) is expected.

EXPERIENCE NECESSARY

To garner an understanding of the technical skills expected within an industry, many years of experience in that industry or closely related industries is typically necessary.

CERTIFICATION, LICENSURE, AND CONTINUING EDUCATION REQUIREMENTS

Appropriate credentialing is required within the professional technical career being taught. Credentialing, certification, or licensure requirements vary by the technical career field. Many technical colleges will require instructors to be certified to teach, which is achieved through completion of a number of education-related courses (e.g., teaching methods, educational evaluation, curriculum development, diversity within the classroom). In addition, recertification through completion of additional professional development activities may be expected.

SALARY/COMPENSATION

Salary and compensation vary based on the technical field, years of experience, and the location of the college. Full-time salaries may range from $40,000 to $70,000.

EMPLOYMENT OUTLOOK

Employment for postsecondary teachers, such as technical college instructors, is expected to grow substantially in the coming years. Many of these jobs, however, might be for part-time positions.

FURTHER INFORMATION FOR EXPLORATION

The Association for Career and Technical Education (www.acteonline .org) is an educational organization dedicated to technical careers and professional development. Its website provides a helpful overview of careers and technical education (CTE) associated with a number of careers that are presently experiencing a high demand for additional well-trained employees.

29. ADJUNCT PROFESSOR

BASIC DESCRIPTION

Adjunct professors are hired to teach within a university setting but are not full members of the faculty. They typically teach part time and are not guaranteed work across multiple years. Instead, they are typically hired by course or semester. In addition to being responsible for the delivery of course content, the role of an adjunct involves the creation and administration of assessments of students' learning. Meeting with students individually or in small groups may be required. In addition, providing timely, critical, and constructive feedback to students about their performance on class assignments is essential. Many adjuncts hold full-time positions outside of the university setting and may teach a course or two each year to supplement their income. Both resources and space may be minimal for adjunct faculty, which may influence the ability to conduct office hours or to engage in professional development activities (e.g., conference attendance) that could help to improve their work. Adjunct professors do not typically provide professional services to programs, departments, or the college as a part of their responsibilities. In addition, no expectation for engagement in scholarship or research exists for adjuncts.

CORE COMPETENCIES AND SKILLS NEEDED

Like other postsecondary educators, competencies and skills pertaining to the course being taught or the field of study associated with the course are required. Adjunct professors must be exceptional instructors. They also must be well organized, exhibit strong time-management skills, and be available to students on a regular basis.

EDUCATIONAL REQUIREMENTS
A doctoral degree is required to hold the title of adjunct professor within a university setting. In some disciplines, an advanced degree (master's degree) may be sufficient to serve as an adjunct, but the individual's title would be *adjunct instructor* to reflect that the individual does not have a doctoral degree.

EXPERIENCE NECESSARY
Adjuncts are often hired to teach a course given the familiarity they have with the application of that course content and knowledge within the real-world demands of communities, schools, or industry. Thus, years of experience within a career related to the course will likely be important. Excellent teaching skills and a background in supervision or training may be required.

CERTIFICATION, LICENSURE, AND CONTINUING EDUCATION REQUIREMENTS
Credentialing, certification, or licensure requirements will vary by course of study being taught. For example, a practicing doctoral-level school psychologist might serve as an adjunct professor within a school psychology training program. This adjunct professor might teach a class related to assessment, consultation, or intervention with school-age populations.

SALARY/COMPENSATION
Adjunct professors typically receive a stipend for each course taught. The amount will vary based on discipline, type of university, and geographic region. Typical stipends at a 4-year university may range from $4000 to $7000 per course. Average salaries for adjuncts who teach multiple courses per semester have been estimated to be about $20,000. No benefits or other types of compensation are typically provided to adjuncts, making it difficult not to hold another job.

EMPLOYMENT OUTLOOK
Employment for postsecondary teachers, such as adjunct professors, is expected to grow substantially in the coming years. A recent increase in the use of adjuncts, especially during recent troubled economic times, has

Career-in-Education Profile
ADJUNCT PROFESSOR
Interview With My Lien (BA, Psychology;
PhD, School Psychology)

Describe your educational background.

I completed my bachelor's degree with a psychology major at a private small liberal arts college. I went directly into a school psychology doctoral program after undergrad. My full-time internship the last year of my doctoral program included rotations within school psychology and child clinical psychology. After receiving my PhD, I completed a 1-year postdoctoral fellowship in child clinical psychology in a department of psychiatry at a major teaching hospital followed by a 1-year postdoctoral fellowship in pediatric/chronic illness psychology in the department of pediatrics at a different children's hospital. I have a full psychology license and hold the National Certification in School Psychology.

Describe your prior experiences and the path you took to get to this career.

Following my postdoctoral training, I worked briefly at a group psychology practice engaged in assessment and therapy. I then opened my own private practice and have maintained that since. I began teaching as an adjunct professor shortly after opening my private practice as a way to take part in training future psychologists who work with school-age children and to remain up to date and engaged with the field.

Describe the work that you do.

I have taught a variety of courses as an adjunct professor, typically filling in for another faculty member who is on sabbatical or who has bought out of teaching as a part of a grant. My role as an adjunct professor includes planning classes, teaching, and grading. The courses I have taught range from theory-based to practice-based courses. I provide supervision to students in the practice-based courses. I also work closely with the program faculty to ensure that students

(continued)

111

(continued)

are making adequate progress in their skill development to become future psychologists.

What is a typical day like for you in this career?

There is a lot of flexibility with adjunct teaching. My typical day is commuting to campus, teaching class, and leaving once class is completed. Most of my preparation for class and grading can be completed off campus at home. I meet with students who need additional support at a prearranged time, often by phone or Skype.

What is the most challenging part of your career?

The most challenging part of being an adjunct professor is trying to make connections with students and the program while only being on campus for a short time for class. Another challenge has been with the commute! Living an hour away has posed some difficulties, particularly in inclement weather.

What is the most rewarding part of your career?

The most rewarding part of my career is taking part in training future psychologists.

What advice do you have for someone in high school or currently at the undergraduate level who might be interested in this career?

My advice would be to major in psychology at the undergraduate level and complete graduate-level training in a psychology-related program. Seek out opportunities in teaching/training when you can to give yourself experience.

What advice do you have for someone currently in a different career/field who might be interested in your career?

My advice would be to complete the necessary prerequisites (i.e., graduate-level program in a psychology-related field) and network

(continued)

(continued)

with programs that might be in need of adjunct professors. If you are in private practice, consider offering your clinic as a place where advanced students can complete practica or internships. This can be one way to become familiar with the training program and allow those program faculty to see you work successfully as a clinical supervisor.

If you decided to advance your career, what steps would you take and what career(s) might you seek out?

Advancement in my career would likely mean seeking full-time teaching or a tenure-track professorship at a local college or university. The steps I would seek out are networking with psychology and/or school psychology programs. For a tenure-track position, I would need to become more active in research (i.e., publishing) and grant writing.

been viewed critically by many who are concerned that universities are taking advantage of the skills and competencies of a workforce that requires little capital/resources. The increase in the use of adjuncts is likely to continue given the long-term costs associated with hiring tenure-track faculty.

FURTHER INFORMATION FOR EXPLORATION

To read about the advocacy work being done on behalf of adjunct faculty, see the website www.adjunctnation.com. Additionally, www.newfacultymajority.info is an organization that is dedicated to advancing the standing of adjunct faculty members within postsecondary educational settings. An Internet search for "adjunct faculty" will likely yield a number of resources that discourage professionals from assuming such positions in university settings, and it is important to balance those ideas with the intrinsic motivation and exciting challenges associated with teaching others.

30. TENURE-TRACK PROFESSOR

BASIC DESCRIPTION

Tenure is a college professor's job security. It typically is earned after 6 to 7 years of high-quality scholarship in teaching, research, and service as an assistant professor. The tenure process is an intensive yearly evaluation of one's readiness to be a contributor to his or her field of study. It culminates in what is referred to as a tenure review, which involves peer evaluation of one's work at the department, college, university, and national levels. With promotion to the associate professor level, a faculty member typically receives tenure. Following an additional period of 6 to 7 years of high-quality scholarship, faculty can request a review for promotion to become a full professor. Tenure-track professors contribute substantially to their profession through their teaching of students; engagement in research that is fundable or recognized by others as being meritorious; and engagement in service to their colleagues at the university, state, and national levels.

CORE COMPETENCIES AND SKILLS NEEDED

Exceptional communication skills are necessary. Both oral and written communication skills are required to perform professorial responsibilities at a high level. The ability to work well under stressful conditions, including the ability to meet deadlines, juggle multiple responsibilities, handle challenging legal and ethical situations that arise in teaching and research, and deal with an assortment of personalities (faculty/administrators/students) is paramount. The job of a professor never ends, and working nights/weekends is typical. Completing responsibilities in a professional and timely manner is essential. Frequent communication with colleagues and students is expected during the academic year. Summertime often allows professors to manage or write grants, work on special projects, and complete an assortment of writing projects (e.g., peer-reviewed journal articles, chapters for edited books, books, grant reports). Some professors might also teach or supervise students during the summer months. Being skilled in teaching, research, *and* service responsibilities requires a diverse set of skills and competencies. Most important, it requires a high level of knowledge within the discipline in which one is working and the ability to effectively share it with others.

EDUCATIONAL REQUIREMENTS

A doctoral degree is required in the field in which one becomes a tenure-track professor. Specific specialization or emphasis within a discipline is also expected and is typically referred to as one's line of research or inquiry. Expertise in particular areas within a field typically helps to determine what courses a faculty member will be assigned to teach.

EXPERIENCE NECESSARY

Prior experience as a practitioner, researcher, or teacher is often required to be hired into a tenure-track position. Having completed a postdoctoral fellowship position might also be necessary to compete successfully for a university faculty position.

CERTIFICATION, LICENSURE, AND CONTINUING EDUCATION REQUIREMENTS

Being accountable for one's learning and competencies is expected. Certification and licensure would be expected in those disciplines that require it. Renewal of these credentials often requires additional training and education. Being a lifelong learner is one of the greatest attributes that a tenure-track professor might possess. Through research, teaching, practice, and conference attendance, one can stay abreast of the latest knowledge in one's discipline.

SALARY/COMPENSATION

Salary and compensation vary considerably by university and discipline. For example, professors in business colleges, law schools, and medical schools often earn substantially more compared to those in other disciplines. In addition, the level at which one holds a professorial position (assistant, associate, full professor, distinguished professor) will greatly affect yearly earnings. For example, a 9-month salary for an assistant professor might be between $50,000 and $75,000. A salary for a full professor might be $80,000 and $150,000. A distinguished professor might make $250,000 or more. Additional money can be earned through summer earnings (e.g., teaching, grants), consulting, or book royalties.

EMPLOYMENT OUTLOOK

The job outlook for university faculty depends substantially on the field of study. Many disciplines are currently experiencing faculty shortages due to a limited supply of well-trained doctoral graduates. Other disciplines might receive over 100 applications for a faculty opening given the ample supply of PhDs in that field. Pending retirements of a large segment of professors will create supply–demand issues within universities in the years ahead.

FURTHER INFORMATION FOR EXPLORATION

Discipline-specific professional organizations for faculty members should be consulted for additional information. For example, the American

Educational Research Association (AERA; www.aera.net) represents a number of disciplines within colleges of education. The American Association of University Professors (www.aaup.org) and *The Chronicle of Higher Education* (www.chronicle.com) are additional resources to explore pertaining to work as a university faculty member.

31. CAREER COUNSELOR

BASIC DESCRIPTION

Career counselors in a postsecondary setting help individuals with the process of making a choice in careers and/or postsecondary educational programs. They serve as mentors, teachers, and advisors by helping individuals examine and better understand their interests, personality, and abilities. Making a connection between individual characteristics and potential career choices is the primary function of a career counselor. Finding a career for an individual that is both satisfying and an excellent way to support oneself financially is ideal. Often career and personality inventories are completed and analyzed as a part of the counseling relationship. Interpreting the results and making connections between those inventories and the educational paths leading to a specific career are essential within this career. Helping to evaluate one's background, experience, skills, and readiness for an occupational path is also an essential part of the counseling process. Specifically, individuals can be either counseled into or out of an educational or career path. Dealing with others' stress and anxiety about having an ill-defined path toward a career can be both challenging and rewarding. Career counselors may work in a variety of settings, including government agencies, career centers, and private practice.

CORE COMPETENCIES AND SKILLS NEEDED

The ability to develop a strong working relationship with students or others seeking assistance is essential. Working with individuals experiencing significant occupation-related stress requires great patience and care on the part of the counselor. Empathy, a focus on goal-directed behavior, and an emphasis on action plans within the counseling relationship are essential for being an effective career counselor. Strong oral and written communication skills are also very important. A working knowledge of a range of career options within multiple fields of study is essential in this line of work.

EDUCATIONAL REQUIREMENTS

Typically, a master's degree in counseling with a specialization in career counseling or adult psychology/adjustment is required.

EXPERIENCE NECESSARY

Prior work experience is typically required and is usually a part of one's training program to become a career counselor. Experience working across the life span or with the specific population to be served is expected. Having exposure to a wide variety of assessment tools (inventories) and their use in making career decisions is required.

CERTIFICATION, LICENSURE, AND CONTINUING EDUCATION REQUIREMENTS

Credentialing will vary by state and place of employment. Most career counselors will hold certification or licensure as a counselor in the state in which they are employed, with a specialization in career counseling. Professional development via continuing education is expected within this service field given the ever-changing nature of assessment instruments, emerging research, and refinement of best practices within the discipline.

SALARY/COMPENSATION

Salaries for career counselors will vary based on employment setting and geographic location. Average pay for work within a postsecondary setting may range from $40,000 to $50,000.

EMPLOYMENT OUTLOOK

Demand for career counselors is expected to grow as the rate of individuals seeking postsecondary education continues to increase. Career counselors are essential within university settings and within communities, as vocational uncertainty, a job change, or a loss of one's job may create a need for career counseling and support.

FURTHER INFORMATION FOR EXPLORATION

The National Career Development Association's motto of "Inspiring Careers . . . Empowering Lives!" (www.ncda.org) is an important one to explore for those interested in becoming a career counselor. The American Counseling Association (www.counseling.org) and the National Employment Counseling Association (www.employmentcounseling.org) are additional sources of information.

32.   UNIVERSITY LIBRARIAN

BASIC DESCRIPTION

University librarians help to select and organize text and electronic resources that can be of use to students and faculty. Management and dissemination of library materials is a substantial part of this career. Providing individual support to students who are working on assignments or conducting research is typically expected. Engaging in clerical work and supervising other library staff members are other common responsibilities of the librarian. Different departments exist within the library. These include the reference department, circulation, collection development, historical collections, and online library resources. An array of libraries exists on college campuses and may range from a law library to a medical library to the main campus library. Specialized knowledge will be necessary within discipline-specific libraries.

CORE COMPETENCIES AND SKILLS NEEDED

Given the frequent interaction with students and faculty, strong written/oral communication and interpersonal skills are essential for this career. The ability to think critically, collaboratively solve problems with others, and exhibit a high level of curiosity will bode well for those interested in becoming a university librarian. A vast knowledge about a diverse array of topics and subjects or an extensive understanding of a specific discipline is also needed depending on the type of library where one works.

EDUCATIONAL REQUIREMENTS

Those holding a bachelor's degree will need to earn a master's degree in library science (MLS) from a program that is accredited by the American Library Association to become a university librarian. Courses such as library management, cataloging, research methods, library collections, and reference materials are required. A second master's degree in a subject area is often required in academic libraries. A doctoral degree in library science may allow an individual to hold administrative or teaching privileges within a university or research institution. University librarians who hold faculty privileges will often have promotion and tenure requirements similar to those of other professors.

EXPERIENCE NECESSARY

Prior experience associated with an internship or practicum in a university library will help to distinguish oneself from other applicants. Work as volunteer or paraprofessional within a university library may lead to an interest in additional education and work toward a master's degree in library science.

CERTIFICATION, LICENSURE, AND CONTINUING EDUCATION REQUIREMENTS

Credential requirements vary by state and place of employment. A graduate certificate and state certification are typically required. To renew these certificates it is often necessary to engage in continuing education.

SALARY/COMPENSATION

The salary for a university librarian varies by institution, region of the country, and specialty area. In addition, years of experience affect the rate of pay. A range of salaries between $45,000 and $60,000 may be seen within academic libraries. Librarians working within government agencies have yearly salaries considerably higher than those of librarians in school or university settings.

EMPLOYMENT OUTLOOK

As college enrollments increase in future years, so too will the need for librarians and resource staff within universities. Advancements in technology and online resources may move some library responsibilities to a virtual environment. This movement could emerge more quickly if university budgets remain constrained or become diminished.

FURTHER INFORMATION FOR EXPLORATION

The website of the American Library Association (ALA; www.ala .org) provides valuable information, news, and resources related to the field of library science. In addition, a subdivision of the ALA called the Association of College and Research Libraries (www.ala.org/acrl) is important to explore for those specifically interested in a career as a university librarian. This professional organization is specifically dedicated to improving the library services being offered within institutions of higher education.

Career-in-Education Profile
UNIVERSITY LIBRARIAN

Interview With Julie Fricke (BA, Communication Processes, Humanistic Studies; Master of Library and Information Sciences [MLIS])

Describe your educational background.

I majored in communication processes with a minor in humanistic studies. As a part of my undergraduate degree, I did a project with students about their likes and dislikes of the campus library. This independent study work allowed me to closely examine issues around customer service within the university's library. That project was the beginning of my interest in library science and my pursuit of an advanced degree.

Describe your prior experiences and the path you took to get to this career.

I always knew that I wanted to be a part of higher education. My dad was a professor and university administrator and I knew that a university career was right for me. The more difficult thing for me was the type of university career I wished to pursue. While in graduate school, I had the opportunity to work at a 2-year university campus library that allowed me to learn about the state university's library system. As the night monitor, the "library bouncer," I enforced time limits on the Internet, assured appropriate web-surfing behavior, and helped patrons remember the library rules, such as to keep quiet. As a part of my training, I had to complete an internship in library systems.

Describe the work that you do.

My responsibilities involve serving as a reference (online/in person); consulting with students about their research; serving as the webmaster; collaborating with other staff, including meeting monthly; completing special projects/campaigns; engaging in public service; and engaging in decision making by committee.

(continued)

(*continued*)

What is a typical day like for you in this career?

In a given typical week I might work three day shifts (8 a.m. to 5 p.m.) and one night shift (1 p.m. to 10 p.m.). I also usually work one weekend day per month (e.g., Sundays, 1 p.m. to 10 p.m.). A typical day would include the following: a 2-hour reference shift, working on the website, exploring technologies for use in the library, supervising my student worker, consulting with students who have editing needs, and cleaning and maintenance of technology (e.g., iPads).

What is the most challenging part of your career?

The most challenging part of my work includes working within an "emotionally charged" environment while trying to complete the mundane tasks required within the library, such as filling the paper trays or tracking down staples. When students are feeling time crunches with their assignments and display limited patience or social skills, it can be quite challenging to perform my work in a customer-friendly manner.

What is the most rewarding part of your career?

I absolutely love working with college students given their ability to take responsibility and initiative for their own learning. They also catch on quickly. Working in reference is also great fun given the unknown nature of what issues or challenges might arise.

What advice do you have for someone in high school or currently at the undergraduate level who might be interested in this career?

No matter what you might have majored in as a part of your undergraduate degree, you could definitely find a way to use that knowledge as a university librarian. My best advice is for you to find your passion. Then, follow that passion as an undergraduate and, ultimately, you could then use that if you go into library science.

(*continued*)

(continued)

What advice do you have for someone currently in a different career/field who might be interested in your career?

Check out where library schools are offered. Some schools do offer distance education options. I would also encourage you to consider getting a part-time job to get immersed in the library culture, explore interests, and consider likes/dislikes associated with working in the library.

If you decided to advance your career, what steps would you take and what career(s) might you seek out?

A PhD in library science is only beneficial if you want to be a director at a research university. Ultimately, it doesn't really advance your career within most universities. Sometimes getting a second master's degree in an area of specialization can help to advance one's career.

6 ■ PART-TIME CAREERS IN EDUCATION

33. SUBSTITUTE TEACHER

BASIC DESCRIPTION

Substitute teachers are those who fill in to teach a classroom when the regular classroom teacher is unavailable (e.g., on leave, out with an illness, attending professional development activities). Long-term substitutes or day substitutes exist. Almost all of these positions are very time limited (i.e., day substitutes), and instability in grade level, hours, and location typifies this career. In a few instances, long-term substitute teachers may take over a classroom for an extended period of time, such as when a teacher goes on maternity leave or following an illness/accident. Substitute teachers often receive their assignments early in the morning and then must respond immediately with their availability. The primary role of this position is to help students learn their course material in the absence of their regular teacher. This may involve the presentation of classroom lessons, management of individual seatwork, working with small groups, or any other instructional technique deemed appropriate for the content of the course being taught. Basically, the substitute teacher carries out the lesson plan prescribed by the classroom teacher and documents how well things went. Taking attendance and managing an effective learning environment are also carried out. Consultation with other teachers or administrations is expected.

CORE COMPETENCIES AND SKILLS NEEDED

To be a substitute teacher, one must first be highly adaptable in terms of work schedule and able to respond immediately for requests to teach. Substitute teachers need to be well trained in effective instructional methods, familiar with a diverse array of curriculum, knowledgeable about a wide variety of academic subject matter, and competent in classroom management techniques. Being able to work with a diverse group of students is especially essential for this highly transitory role. Effective communication skills are particularly important when leading a classroom full of students through their lesson plans. Finally, the ability to think critically and solve problems efficiently and effectively is essential for this position.

EDUCATIONAL REQUIREMENTS

Qualifications vary by state, with some requiring substitute teachers to meet the same level of training as certified teachers (e.g., Iowa). Others require a minimum of a bachelor's degree (e.g., Wisconsin). Other states require the completion of some college education (e.g., Michigan) or a high school diploma (e.g., Utah). Many states do require at least a substitute teacher certificate.

EXPERIENCE NECESSARY

Prior experience working with groups of students is important. A background in teaching or prior training in an education-related field is expected.

CERTIFICATION, LICENSURE, AND CONTINUING EDUCATION REQUIREMENTS

All substitute teachers will go through the same hiring process as regular teachers, including a criminal background check. Certification and licensure requirements vary by state, and Department of Education websites should be consulted for specifics. Many states require individuals to possess a substitute teacher certificate.

SALARY/COMPENSATION

Pay for substitute teaching varies by location, district, and state. Daily stipends are typically in the range of $75 to $80 for those without certificates and slightly higher ($100+) for those with a teaching certificate.

EMPLOYMENT OUTLOOK

There is currently a shortage of substitute teachers, and this need is anticipated for the foreseeable future given the part-time, low-wage nature of this position.

FURTHER INFORMATION FOR EXPLORATION

A web page devoted to substitute teachers (www.stedi.org) provides a state-by-state summary of credential requirements and the status of substitute teaching across the United States.

34. HIGH SCHOOL COACH

BASIC DESCRIPTION

High school coaches work with students interested in a diverse array of sports (e.g., soccer, softball, gymnastics, swimming, football) through practice, support, advice, and direct instruction. They must observe and assess players' skills. Making decisions about rosters and playing time can be very challenging. Coaches assign positions, implement drills, and organize game strategies. Coaches must be familiar with the rules and regulations of any sport they coach. Sometimes schools hire coaches on a full-time basis; at other times the coaching duties are considered part time because the coach also serves as a full-time teacher in the district. Working nights, holidays, evenings, and weekends may be necessary. In addition, many coaches work across the fall, winter, and spring seasons because they may teach up to three sports in any given academic year.

CORE COMPETENCIES AND SKILLS NEEDED

Effective communication and the ability to motivate young adults are essential in this career. Coaches must be highly organized, demonstrate strong time-management skills, be very knowledgeable about the sport, and must be able to utilize effective instructional methods. The ability to motivate youth to perform at their highest level is a quality seen in excellent coaches. Possessing leadership qualities and being able to understand players' motivations, interests, and performances are necessary to compete at a high level. The ability to work well with district administrators and the athletic director is essential.

EDUCATIONAL REQUIREMENTS

Coaches most typically have a minimum of a bachelor's degree, although many have pursued advanced graduate study. The majority have a background in teacher education, physiology, nutrition, kinesiology, or leadership training. State certification requirements for coaches vary by state. Cardiopulmonary resuscitation (CPR) training and certification in sport fundamentals/safety are often required.

EXPERIENCE NECESSARY

Experience as a player of the game or having a background as an assistant coach is typical for those seeking a career in coaching. To become a head coach in a larger school district, it is typically necessary to have many years of effective coaching experience.

CERTIFICATION, LICENSURE, AND CONTINUING EDUCATION REQUIREMENTS

Research state-level requirements to be a high school coach on state-specific Department of Education websites. Most states have multiple levels of state certification, and continuing education is typically required.

SALARY/COMPENSATION

Those who teach in the district in which they coach typically receive a set percentage of their salary to take on the extracurricular activities associated with coaching. These salaries will vary by sport and years of experience. Supplemental income to be a coach may range from $2,000 to $20,000. Sometimes booster clubs supplement the district's pay for coaches or they help to defray costs associated with hiring assistant coaches.

EMPLOYMENT OUTLOOK

Pending retirements are expected to result in growth in coaching positions in the near future. Despite budget challenges, school districts appear to see the benefit of promoting high school athletics.

FURTHER INFORMATION FOR EXPLORATION

The National High School Coaches Association (www.nhsca.com) serves as a professional organization for coaches, coaching programs, and administrators.

Career-in-Education Profile
COACH

Interview With Mike Van Antwerp (BS, Wildlife Biology; BS, Biology; MA, Curriculum and Teaching)

Describe your educational background.

I attended a private all-boys' school that has been very influential in my adult life. The school's motto of "Men for Others" perseverates through what I do as an adult, especially in my roles as boys' varsity lacrosse coach and high school science teacher.

Describe your prior experiences and the path you took to get to this career.

Having played lacrosse in high school and college, I had developed a passion for the game. When working as a counselor on some wilderness canoe trips, I realized that I enjoyed working with high school-age students. Combining teaching and lacrosse into coaching was a natural progression for me. I currently teach 10th-grade biology and 11th- and 12th-grade physics. I have found coaching and teaching in the classroom very similar. You set goals, design a curriculum/practice plan to meet those goals, and work toward them. All students want to succeed in the classroom, just like all players want to succeed on the field. Since I started coaching, I've thought about coaching other sports as I've realized that the tactical knowledge isn't necessarily the number one strength of a coach, but interacting and building relationships with the kids is. In order to get my coaching job, I first responded to the school's job posting. I then interviewed with the school's athletic director. Many schools also have applicants interview with a booster club.

Describe the work that you do.

I coordinate all aspects of our varsity and junior varsity programs. This includes ordering apparel, creating a schedule, finding coaches and volunteers, running out-of-season conditioning programs, and creating practice plans. Our school pays for my position as head coach,

(continued)

(*continued*)

but our club funded the pay for assistant and junior varsity coaches. As head coach, I have supervised up to nine adults, depending on the year. I have also started my own lacrosse training program (www .atomiclacrosse.com), which gives players from our region of the state a chance to play competitive lacrosse. This summer program also supports the development of fundamental skills of lacrosse in youth from local school districts in the area. My program has grown from offering high school and adult leagues in the evenings to running summer youth travel teams and instructional clinics for youth.

What is a typical day like for you in this career?

In season, it means responding to parent and coach e-mails, creating a practice plan or game plan during "free time" at lunch, e-mailing parents about any last-minute details, and then either running practice after work or traveling to a game. If it's a game night, I typically get home around 10:30. If it's a practice night, I typically go from our high school practice to my son's team's practice and then get home about 7:30.

What is the most challenging part of your career?

The most challenging part is juggling the multiple roles as a husband, father, teacher, and coach. The time demands of each means that none gets your complete attention. I really enjoy having players in the classroom, but am also aware of the dual relationship that I have with them. I have found that in almost all cases, my players' classroom performance was better than normal because of the relationship we already had built outside the classroom. Yet, I have had a few challenges arise. It can be hard for my players to see me as laid-back and joking in the classroom to being the same guy who pulled them out of the game for underperforming, or didn't play them as much due to them not earning a spot on the field. On the other hand, I've seen many students (not on my team) in my classes who struggle with this dual role, as I have been accused of favoritism of kids on my team. One additional interesting challenge in this dual role involves my colleague teachers. In a few instances, other teachers have felt it was important for me to help them with students (my players) who may be struggling.

(*continued*)

(continued)

If a minor situation, my awareness of the situation can result in almost immediate changes. When major situations arise, I encourage these teachers to handle things independently, as the dual relationship that exists has the chance to be quite problematic for many people involved.

What is the most rewarding part of your career?

There are multiple things that are rewarding: seeing a player achieve something through hard work and sacrifice is extremely rewarding, seeing a player sacrifice some personal glory for his team as a whole is rewarding for its immediate value and also for the long-term lesson it teaches, and seeing kids create memories that they'll cherish for a lifetime is probably the best part.

What advice do you have for someone in high school or currently at the undergraduate level who might be interested in this career?

You have to have a passion for the game and for teaching it. There are also multiple aspects of coaching that can interfere with your goals, such as parents and other coaches, so you have to be careful to navigate your way through those challenges.

What advice do you have for someone currently in a different career/field who might be interested in your career?

I think someone can always start a career in coaching. Depending on the individual's level of game knowledge, he or she can start out at different levels. The ability to motivate players and teach values that are greater than the game is the most important quality for a coach to possess.

If you decided to advance your career, what steps would you take and what career(s) might you seek out?

Coaching in a respected club program or at a small college would be the next step. Coaching at a college typically means sacrificing a lot of free time as you are on the road recruiting. Oftentimes, you have to be prepared to volunteer your time in order to get a foot in the door.

35. ACTIVITIES DIRECTOR

BASIC DESCRIPTION

Activities directors are usually found within high school settings and work under the supervision of the building principal. Their primary responsibility is to plan and oversee student government, organizations, and extracurricular activities. A focus of this position is on student leadership development through involvement in extracurricular activities. This will include scheduling clubs/activities, supervising fund-raisers, and hiring/training/evaluating additional staff. Overseeing budgeting and budget reports is also expected in this position. Oversight of the use of district buildings and meeting spaces for activities is required. Serving as faculty advisor for student organizations may also be involved. This role requires a great deal of communication with parents, teachers, and administrators pertaining to events and activities.

CORE COMPETENCIES AND SKILLS NEEDED

A high level of organization and independence is required for this leadership position. Strong oral and written communication skills are needed. Working well with others, especially students, is expected. The ability to make decisions under stressful conditions or with consideration to limited resources is needed. Knowledge about student government and student development is an essential competency needed within this position. Skills in planning and implementation fit well within this career in education.

EDUCATIONAL REQUIREMENTS

A minimum of a bachelor's degree is required. Most activities directors have completed teacher education programs and may have also completed advanced graduate training. Education in public administration, student development, or leadership development is often found in individuals who are selected for these positions.

EXPERIENCE NECESSARY

Prior experience as a teacher or administrator allows for a high degree of leadership in organizing events and activities within the schools. Prior supervision of students or staff is also expected for those who become activities coordinators. Background and experience in running student organizations is necessary.

CERTIFICATION, LICENSURE, AND CONTINUING EDUCATION REQUIREMENTS

Most often, teachers within the district are hired to become activities directors given their knowledge, background, and success in working with other school staff. Teacher certification is often a requirement for these positions. Specific certification and continuing education requirements vary across districts, communities, and states.

SALARY/COMPENSATION

Positions may be either part time or full time. Part-time activities directors will often receive an additional percentage in their teaching salaries (i.e., an additional 20%–30% pay). Full-time activities directors might receive pay consistent with the schedule of an administrator. Pay may range from $60,000 to $70,000. Factors associated with the school district, such as resources available and geographic location, will influence compensation levels. In addition, years of experience will also play a role in determining salary.

EMPLOYMENT OUTLOOK

Demand for highly organized and interpersonally talented individuals to provide leadership within high schools through this position is expected to grow in the years ahead.

FURTHER INFORMATION FOR EXPLORATION

Many states have professional organizations devoted to the work of activities directors (e.g., www.cada1.org and www.uhsaa.org). Also, you are encouraged to seek out the position description for an activities director in your local high school for additional information about the roles and responsibilities assumed by individuals in this career in education.

36. STUDENT COUNCIL ADVISOR

BASIC DESCRIPTION

A student council advisor assists student leaders (e.g., president, vice president, secretary, treasurer) in planning events and making decisions. At the beginning of the year, it is important for the advisor to help carry forward the processes associated with selection of student body representatives and to help the student council establish its mission, procedures, and activities. Setting up an environment of trust, respect, and confidentiality is essential within the student council, and the advisor can play an important role in making that happen. Advisors can help evaluate the effectiveness of the council through a close examination of the processes and products that arise from council decision making. Providing leadership in maintaining financial records and helping the council with fund-raising ideas and efforts are also important. Finally, a strong student council advisor serves as a cheerleader for the group (i.e., promotes school identity/pride). This means that in the advisor role it is essential to advocate to the rest of the school for the need for a strong and active student council.

CORE COMPETENCIES AND SKILLS NEEDED

Communication skills are essential for this role. The ability to listen well and to reflect accurately the needs and wishes of the council are important. Strong organizational skills, the ability to work well within a group setting, and effective time-management strategies are needed. Developing relationships with both students and teachers is important given the roles that advisors play in serving as a consultant, advisor, and advocate. A willingness to work both before and after school is necessary.

EDUCATIONAL REQUIREMENTS

Most typically, a bachelor's degree with a teaching certificate is necessary, as teachers within the district often will assume this part-time, after-school position. In some cases, elementary or middle school buildings will establish student councils. In those cases, it may be that leaders within the community assume those extracurricular responsibilities.

EXPERIENCE NECESSARY

Prior experience in student government is needed. Evidence of prior leadership of student or teacher groups is also important. A background that demonstrates the ability to effectively engage in problem solving is necessary for this advisory position.

CERTIFICATION, LICENSURE, AND CONTINUING EDUCATION REQUIREMENTS

Most typically, teachers within the building serve in this part-time capacity. A degree in teacher education or a closely related field is required. Student council advisors are encouraged to focus their efforts on continuous improvement, and engagement in continuing education related to student governance and leadership is expected.

SALARY/COMPENSATION
Teachers who assume the role of student council advisor will often receive a salary or stipend that represents an additional percentage of their teaching salaries (i.e., an additional 20%–30% pay). Salary is likely to vary based on district. This part-time position typically does not provide benefits or other compensation.

EMPLOYMENT OUTLOOK
Demand for highly organized and interpersonally talented individuals to provide leadership within high schools through this position is expected to grow in the years ahead.

FURTHER INFORMATION FOR EXPLORATION
The National Association of Student Councils (www.nasc.us) provides a number of helpful resources that may be of use to student council advisors, especially the adviser resources section (www.nasc.us/adviser-resources.aspx).

37. GRANT WRITER

BASIC DESCRIPTION
Grant writers develop funding proposals for various agencies. This type of work within schools tends to be part time and may focus on specific targeted grant competitions. Close collaboration with school administrators is needed to identify areas in need of grant funding. Grant writers typically are funded through soft money (i.e., grant funding that is obtained) or through a small stipend.

CORE COMPETENCIES AND SKILLS NEEDED
Strong writing skills are needed to be a grant writer. Good computer research skills are also essential for both looking for possible grant competitions and putting together a well-supported grant proposal. Being very detail oriented and highly organized is essential for this position.

A good understanding of the grant proposal process and how to develop budget proposals is necessary.

EDUCATIONAL REQUIREMENTS

Grant writers typically are required to have a bachelor's degree. Undergraduate majors in communication, journalism, or English might be particularly well suited for this position in schools.

EXPERIENCE NECESSARY

Prior grant writing experience is necessary. A history of effective collaboration with others to secure grant funds is often sought in those selected as grant writers.

CERTIFICATION, LICENSURE, AND CONTINUING EDUCATION REQUIREMENTS

There are no certification or licensure requirements for this position. However, engagement in professional development in topics such as advanced proposal writing, developing grant budgets, and writing effective annual grant reports is expected.

SALARY/COMPENSATION

Salary is typically contingent on receipt of funded grant proposals. In some instances a small stipend might be available to support the grant writer's efforts to secure additional funding for the school district.

EMPLOYMENT OUTLOOK

As resources in schools continue to be limited, it is likely that grant writers will be sought in greater numbers to help school administrators address important unfunded needs within their districts.

FURTHER INFORMATION FOR EXPLORATION

The American Grant Writers' Association (AGWA; www.agwa.us) is a national association of professional grant researchers, grant writers, and grant administrators. The AGWA website provides a number of resources and links helpful to those who assume grant writer positions in educational settings. In addition, an Internet search will yield numerous resources to help in the grant-writing process.

38. TUTOR

BASIC DESCRIPTION

A tutor is a teacher who assists individual students or small groups of students to succeed in a specific subject area. Tutors can assist individuals in better understanding their academic struggles through the use of a number of assessment practices. Most important, tutors work with students to make improvements in their areas of academic deficits. Study strategies, effective instructional practices, and intensive practice are common techniques used within the tutoring process.

CORE COMPETENCIES AND SKILLS NEEDED

A strong understanding of the subject matter being taught is needed. Moreover, the ability to effectively communicate that knowledge to others is paramount. The ability to work well with both children and their families is essential. This includes being a good listener and having strong presentation skills.

EDUCATIONAL REQUIREMENTS

It is important to have a degree and/or teacher certificate in the area being tutored. Subject-matter knowledge and the ability to effectively teach academic content are required to be a tutor.

EXPERIENCE NECESSARY

Prior teaching experience in the subject matter being tutored is important. A history of working effectively with students and their parents is expected.

CERTIFICATION, LICENSURE, AND CONTINUING EDUCATION REQUIREMENTS

Subject-matter certification is often sought in those who are hired to be tutors. However, it is common for subject-matter content to be taught by experts who may not necessarily be certified as a teacher. Instead, they may hold credentials that demonstrate their ability to provide that subject matter within a tutoring relationship.

SALARY/COMPENSATION

Wages for well-qualified tutors in private agencies may be between $20 and $30 per hour. Typically, those who tutor are part-time employees and hold other jobs during the workday. Tutoring can provide certified teachers the opportunity to earn additional wages at night or during weekends.

EMPLOYMENT OUTLOOK

Private tutors are in high demand as students strive for academic success. It is anticipated that tutoring services in both schools and communities will continue to grow in the years ahead. In addition, it is anticipated that educational technology will be utilized more frequently to assist students with the learning of academic content (e.g., reading, math, science, social studies).

FURTHER INFORMATION FOR EXPLORATION

Additional information about the tutoring profession can be found at the National Tutoring Association website (www.ntatutor.com) or the American Tutoring Association website (www.americantutoringassociation.org). For specific resources that might be helpful in the tutoring process, take a close look at www.tutor.com.

III ■ CAREERS IN SCHOOLS: SERVING SPECIAL POPULATIONS

7 ■ CAREERS WORKING WITH STUDENTS WITH SPECIAL NEEDS

39. EARLY INTERVENTION SPECIALIST

BASIC DESCRIPTION

Early intervention specialists work directly with young children who present with developmental delays. They carry out individual and small-group interventions in a preschool classroom or center-based program. Home visits or classroom-based assessment might be required depending on the specific nature of the position and/or one's background and training. Early intervention specialists work as a part of an interdisciplinary group of professionals to meet the needs of infants and toddlers who have developmental delays, physical impairments, or some other type of disability. They work closely with families and school staff to implement and monitor the effectiveness of interventions. Promoting the developmental success of young children is the primary goal of this specialist position.

CORE COMPETENCIES AND SKILLS NEEDED

Extensive knowledge in child development and its application within the classroom setting is important. The ability to work well with a diverse group of young children and their families is necessary. A high degree of patience, empathy, compassion, and optimism are important for working with young children with developmental delays. It is important to work well as a member of a team. Being highly organized and possessing good time-management skills are essential.

EDUCATIONAL REQUIREMENTS

A credential in early intervention services is required. Typically, this means the completion of a bachelor's degree in special education with an endorsement for working as an early intervention specialist. Some states allow for an associate's degree along with many years of experience in early intervention services. No matter what degree is completed, coursework would include educating young children, infant mental health, developmental disabilities, early childhood curriculum, preschool instructional practices, and classroom-based interventions. Extensive knowledge in child development (e.g., communication, cognitive, physical, social–emotional, adaptive) is expected within this career.

EXPERIENCE NECESSARY

Prior experience working with young children (ages 0–5) is necessary. This may be in a day care or other early childhood settings. A history of delivering early intervention services to young children is required and will likely be a part of degree-required practica and internship experiences in the schools.

CERTIFICATION, LICENSURE, AND CONTINUING EDUCATION REQUIREMENTS

Certification requirements vary by state, and it is important to look closely at the Department of Education website of the state in which you would like to work for specific details.

SALARY/COMPENSATION

Pay for early intervention specialists tends to be quite low compared with other teaching professions. Median annual salary is estimated to be between $35,000 and $50,000 depending on geographic location. Years of experience and type of undergraduate degree/credentials will also influence one's salary within this career.

EMPLOYMENT OUTLOOK

The current demand for early childhood intervention specialists is high. A focus on prevention and early childhood populations has led to recent increases in funding for providing services to children at risk for disabilities or those already identified as having disabilities. Intervening early is viewed as an effective use of resources in an effort to reduce future costs associated with educating individuals with disabilities.

FURTHER INFORMATION FOR EXPLORATION

For additional information about a career as an early intervention specialist, the following professional organizations should be consulted: the National Association for the Education of Young Children (www.naeyc.org) and

Zero to Three, The National Center for Infants, Toddlers, and Families (www.zerotothree.org).

40. EARLY CHILDHOOD SPECIAL EDUCATION TEACHER

BASIC DESCRIPTION

Early childhood special education teachers work in a special education classroom or are engaged in team teaching with preschool teachers. They work with young children, typically ages 3 to 8 years, who have been identified as having met criteria for a special education disability. Being skilled in effective instructional practices for those with disabilities is an important part of this career. The ability to work well with a diverse group of young children and their families is necessary. Conducting home visits or classroom-based assessment might be a part of this position. Early childhood special education teachers work as a part of an interdisciplinary group of school-based professionals. Planning, implementing, monitoring, and documenting the effectiveness of special education interventions is a major responsibility of this position. Promoting the developmental success and meeting the needs of young children with disabilities is the primary goal of this career in education.

CORE COMPETENCIES AND SKILLS NEEDED

Extensive knowledge in special education, disability law, and evidence-based instructional strategies is needed. The application of this knowledge and the ability to work well with a diverse group of young children and their families are necessary. A high degree of patience, compassion, and optimism are important for working with young children with disabilities. Being highly organized and possessing good time-management skills are essential.

EDUCATIONAL REQUIREMENTS

A bachelor's degree in special education with an endorsement for working in early childhood is required. Coursework would include classes in educating young children, developmental disabilities, screening and assessment, early childhood special education programming, preschool instructional practices, and individualized education planning. Extensive knowledge in child development (e.g., communication, cognitive, physical, social–emotional, adaptive) is needed with this career. A master's degree in early childhood intervention is an alternative option to achieve state special education teacher licensing for work with young children.

EXPERIENCE NECESSARY

Prior experience working with young children (ages 0–5) is expected. This may be in a day care or other early childhood setting. A history of delivering assessment and special education services to young children is necessary and will likely be a part of degree-required practica and internship experiences in the schools.

CERTIFICATION, LICENSURE, AND CONTINUING EDUCATION REQUIREMENTS

Certification requirements vary by state; it is important to look closely at the Department of Education website of the state in which you would like to work for specific details.

SALARY/COMPENSATION

Pay for early childhood special education teachers is similar to that for other teaching careers. Median annual salary is estimated to be between $50,000 and $60,000 depending on geographic location. Years of experience and possession of a master's degree will also influence one's salary within this career.

EMPLOYMENT OUTLOOK

The current demand for special educators is high, especially in the area of early childhood. A focus on prevention and early childhood populations has led to recent increases in funding for providing services to children at risk for disabilities or those already identified as having disabilities.

FURTHER INFORMATION FOR EXPLORATION

For additional information about a career as an early childhood special education teacher, the following professional organizations should be consulted: the Council for Exceptional Children (www.cec.sped.org), the Division for Early Childhood (ww.dec-sped.org), and the National Association of Special Education Teachers (www.naset.org).

41. PARAPROFESSIONAL—AUTISM SPECTRUM DISORDER

BASIC DESCRIPTION

A paraprofessional provides specialized assistance within the school setting to students identified as having disabilities. Those who provide services to children with autism spectrum disorder will assist special education teachers in carrying out the child's individualized education plan (IEP). This may include providing assistance or guidance within the classroom setting, supervising the student while he or she is outside of the classroom setting (e.g., playground, at lunch, transitioning to the bus, on field trips), and supporting the teacher in completion of administrative activities associated with teaching a student with disabilities (e.g., monitoring the effectiveness of the child's IEP). The specific duties to be completed by a paraprofessional will depend on the specific individual needs of the student as identified by the multidisciplinary evaluation team. Some examples might include helping the child to be independent, assisting the teacher in the presentation of instructional materials, applying instructional strategies to foster social skills, using positive reinforcement and other principles of applied behavior analysis to promote children's appropriate behavior in the classroom, and maintaining an orderly and safe learning environment. The paraprofessional is supervised by the special education teacher who is responsible for instructing the student with autism.

CORE COMPETENCIES AND SKILLS NEEDED

Extensive knowledge of child development, learning, and behavior is needed. In addition, the application of these principles within the classroom setting is essential. Good communication skills and the ability to work well under supervision are also needed. Astute observational skills, an appreciation of human diversity, and detailed record keeping are important. Assisting in basic care and promoting acceptable social behaviors in the classroom are expected.

EDUCATIONAL REQUIREMENTS

At a minimum, it is expected that the paraprofessional will have completed requirements for a high school diploma or an associate's degree. Many paraprofessionals have bachelor's degrees, although sometimes not related to the field of education. Courses in child care, psychology, education, special education, and autism would be typical for this position.

EXPERIENCE NECESSARY

Prior experience working with individuals with disabilities and, specifically, autism spectrum disorder would be preferred. Familiarity with the special education classroom and instructing students with disabilities is ideal. A history of work experience that clearly demonstrates the ability to work well under supervision and/or as a member of a team is necessary.

CERTIFICATION, LICENSURE, AND CONTINUING EDUCATION REQUIREMENTS

No formal state-level certification consistently exists for paraprofessionals in the United States. Some positions require a driver's license, participation in training to become a paraprofessional, cardiopulmonary resuscitation (CPR) or first-aid certification, and a high level of English proficiency. Paraprofessionals are involved in regular professional development activities that are targeted at training special education staff.

SALARY/COMPENSATION

Hourly rates ranging from $10 to $20 are usually provided to paraprofessionals. Benefits or other forms of compensation are not typical in this career, which is usually considered part time (i.e., less than 32 hours per week).

EMPLOYMENT OUTLOOK

The field of paraprofessionals has increased substantially in recent years. Providing additional supports to students with disabilities so they may be able to benefit from their IEPs is the primary reason for this increase. Additionally, the identification of autism spectrum disorder has increased substantially in recent years, resulting in the need for additional service providers in this area of special education.

FURTHER INFORMATION FOR EXPLORATION

Exploration of www.paraelink.org, a resource providing education to paraprofessionals, is highly recommended for those interested in this career. This website provides training in nine specific competencies expected of paraprofessionals: foundations of special education, student characteristics, diagnosis and evaluation, instructional practices, supporting the learning environment, managing student behavior, communication and collaboration, professionalism and ethics, and

Career-in-Education Profile
PARAPROFESSIONAL—AUTISM SPECTRUM DISORDER

Interview With Michelle Carlson (BA, Spanish; MPA, Public Administration)

Describe your educational background.

I attended public high school in a large urban city and then went to a public 4-year university where I earned my BA in Spanish. I then completed 1 year of teacher education at a private college, as I wanted to become a teacher. I was thinking maybe a Spanish or bilingual teacher at the time. Then life happened. After decades of being out of the university setting and unable to reach that initial career goal, I just completed my master's degree in public administration within a part-time graduate study program. This arrangement allowed me to hold my current employment as a city events planner while going back to school to someday be a director of a nonprofit agency or seek a leadership position in city government.

Describe your prior experiences and the path you took to get to this career.

I had always wanted to be a teacher. I began a teacher certification program when I finished college but was unable to finish. My husband's career moved our family around the country for several years, and I was able to find employment working with kids at each of the places we lived. I worked as a part-time elementary school Spanish teacher (not certified) in an after-school program and then as a preschool classroom teacher's assistant. After another move across the country, I had an opportunity to work as a paraprofessional in an autism spectrum disorder (ASD) classroom. I thought this would be a good opportunity to see whether I would like working in this type of classroom and whether I might be more interested in providing services on an individual level to those presenting with significant needs.

(continued)

(continued)

Describe the work that you do.

As a paraprofessional in an ASD classroom, I was responsible for one child throughout the entire day. My assignment would change weekly or daily, depending on need. I would help the children with all of their daily tasks, from taking off their coats to having a snack, and accompany them to a mainstream classroom. I was supervised by the lead special education teacher and often shared my observations and experiences with her.

What is a typical day like for you in this career?

I helped the kids get off their buses and move them to the classroom. Supporting transitions was a big part of my responsibilities. I assisted children with their daily routines, including lessons, assignments, snacks, and lunch, and helped them to participate in a mainstream classroom for half of the day.

What is the most challenging part of your career?

The most challenging part of working within this classroom was communicating with the kids. Many of the kids I worked with were nonverbal. They each had a different tool used to communicate, and sometimes you had to figure something out that would work, such as a picture board. It was also challenging to keep each child on his or her own individual plan and schedule. Some kids had to eat at a certain time and had special foods; others were capable of staying in a mainstream classroom for long periods of time, whereas others only could be in a classroom for 15 minutes.

What is the most rewarding part of your career?

The most rewarding part of this work was seeing a child's progress with a new task, or learning how to communicate his or her needs and to interact with other kids in the school. It was very powerful to be in that position to see such impressive growth given the significant challenges that each child faced in the classroom.

(continued)

(continued)

What advice do you have for someone in high school or currently at the undergraduate level who might be interested in this career?

I would tell them that working within a special education classroom can be a very rewarding career. You get to work with incredible educators and the kids are amazing. Despite significant disabilities and barriers to learning, these children can do many things with a little positive guidance and support. It is hard and emotional work but it is also rewarding. It was a wonderful part-time position for me while I was raising my own children. It allowed me flexibility in work hours while also meeting my need to support my own children's educational schedules. Finally, it afforded me the opportunity to further explore my interests in the field of special education.

What advice do you have for someone currently in a different career/field who might be interested in your career?

I would tell them to weigh their options and make sure it is a permanent position. Funding can be very uncertain for paraprofessional services. Yet, continuity of the paraprofessional–child relationship is very important for those students receiving special education services. Think hard about the group of students you are most interested in working with, in terms of their challenges and uniqueness. Remember that there are paraprofessionals for many types of learning challenges facing students. You will receive a lot of on-the-job training as well as being able to benefit from preservice training offered by the school district. You need to be willing to work closely with the child's lead special education teacher and also be quite flexible, yet consistent in carrying out a child's individualized education plan.

If you decided to advance your career, what steps would you take and what career(s) might you seek out?

If I were to advance my career I would have gone back to school to get an advanced degree in special education and become a full-time

(continued)

(*continued*)

special education teacher rather than a paraprofessional. Instead, my career path has led me to pursue work in community event planning. My focus on educating others has moved from the classroom/school setting to a more global one of working at the community level.

academic instruction. The National Resource Center for Paraeducators (www.nrcpara.org) and the following two websites specific to autism spectrum disorder might also be of interest: www.autismspeaks.org and www.autismaction.org.

42. READING SPECIALIST

BASIC DESCRIPTION

Reading specialists work to improve reading skills and reading achievement through teaching, coaching, and providing leadership in selecting reading curriculum. Reading specialists provide expertise in reading assessment and reading instruction. Their primary responsibility is to those students who have been screened or identified as being struggling readers. Close collaboration with other teachers (e.g., literacy coach) to implement strong reading programs is an important part of this career in education. This collaboration also extends to other school staff concerning interpretation and dissemination of reading assessment results. Reading specialists provide a high degree of leadership to the school and community regarding issues of literacy, given their expertise and knowledge.

CORE COMPETENCIES AND SKILLS NEEDED

Reading specialists must be able to work well with a diverse array of children and adults. They must be able to work well in both one-on-one situations and in small or large groups. Efficient and effective written and oral communication skills are needed. Specialized knowledge pertaining to research-based reading assessment and intervention is essential for this position. Applying that research within school-based practices is critical for this career in education.

EDUCATIONAL REQUIREMENTS

A master's degree in education with a focus on reading, literacy, and writing is required. Coursework will include topics such as foundational knowledge in reading and writing, literacy development, curriculum/instruction, assessment/evaluation, intervention, and professional development.

EXPERIENCE NECESSARY

Advanced graduate programs aimed at training reading specialists will include practicum and/or internship experiences in the schools. Experience working with students with reading challenges is expected. In addition, prior collaboration with and coaching of teachers in carrying out evidence-based reading curriculum or interventions are necessary. Prior teaching experience is also common.

CERTIFICATION, LICENSURE, AND CONTINUING EDUCATION REQUIREMENTS

State-level certification as a teacher is required. An endorsement to be a reading specialist is also expected. Requirements vary by state, and the Department of Education website of the state in which you wish to work should be consulted for additional information about specific certification requirements. Engagement in continuing education and professional development are essential to remain informed about the latest research and innovations within the reading discipline.

SALARY/COMPENSATION

The average salary for a reading specialist is quite variable ($45,000 to $72,000), as discovered in a review of current position openings found through an Internet search. Payscale.com lists the average salary as $50,345 per year. Factors such as geographic location, years of experience, and the degree held will influence one's pay.

EMPLOYMENT OUTLOOK

The employment outlook for reading specialists is particularly strong given recent changes in how schools address state standards and the increased focus on literacy assessment. Specifically, the Response-to-Intervention (RtI) movement has focused extensively on school-wide data collection, increased use of evidence-based reading curricula within the classroom, and an emphasis on data-based decision making (e.g., reading assessment data) for those students found to be at risk for later reading challenges.

FURTHER INFORMATION FOR EXPLORATION

A number of reading careers and a host of resources pertaining to literacy can be found at www.reading.org, the website of the International Reading Association. For additional information about the importance of literacy and reading interventions, see the Reading Is Fundamental site (www.rif.org) or the Center on Response to Intervention website (www.rti4success.org).

43. SPECIAL EDUCATION TEACHER—AUTISM SPECTRUM DISORDER

BASIC DESCRIPTION

Special education teachers provide adapted instruction and support to students who meet criteria for one or more special education diagnoses (e.g., autism; deaf–blindness; deafness; hearing impairment; mental retardation; multiple disabilities; orthopedic impairment; other health impairment; serious emotional disturbance; specific learning disability; speech or language impairment; traumatic brain injury; visual impairment, including blindness). Those who specialize in the education of children diagnosed with an autism spectrum disorder (ASD) work to carry forward the individualized education plan (IEP) that has been determined by the child's multidisciplinary team to have the best chance to improve learning for that child. The term *autism* encompasses a number of developmental conditions. Children diagnosed with ASD have particular challenges with social communication, repetitive/restrictive behaviors, language, and/or social relationships. Each child with ASD is unique and may display a varied level of dysfunction. This may mean that a child presents with little to no language and serious adaptive behavior challenges. It could also mean that a child only has mild symptoms affecting social relations and minimal signs of dysfunction at home or school.

CORE COMPETENCIES AND SKILLS NEEDED

Substantial knowledge is needed related to the education of students with disabilities. Familiarity with legal, ethical, and professional standards associated with regular and special education is important. A special education teacher must be able to create a positive, safe, and nurturing teaching environment. Teaching those with autism spectrum disorder requires extensive foundational knowledge pertaining to developmental disabilities. It also requires the effective use of positive behavioral supports and behavior management techniques. Given the issues with communication, being a special education teacher specializing in ASD requires familiarity with assistive technology that can help make learning easier. Knowledge and expertise with sign language or picture boards can also be essential when working with students with ASD. Working collaboratively with other adults in the school building is important. Effective oral and written communication is especially needed given the importance of documentation and progress monitoring within the delivery of special education services.

EDUCATIONAL REQUIREMENTS

An undergraduate degree in special education is needed. In addition, an endorsement in autism spectrum disorder or specialized training in applied behavior analysis is required. Coursework typically will include the following topics: characteristics and etiology of autism, assessment for instructional planning, evidence-based instructional techniques across the life span (0–21 years), and collaborative consultation.

EXPERIENCE NECESSARY

Experience in teaching children with diverse needs is necessary to specialize in educating those with ASD. A specific number of hours engaged in educational and behavioral programming for students with autism is expected.

CERTIFICATION, LICENSURE, AND CONTINUING EDUCATION REQUIREMENTS

A teaching certificate or license is required to teach in public schools. An undergraduate degree from a teacher education program that specializes in training in special education and autism provides the most direct route into this education career. Some states may require a master's degree or advanced training/specialization in the area of autism spectrum disorder. Given the increased attention given to ASD populations in recent years, many universities are adding autism teaching endorsements or specialized training in applied behavioral analysis.

SALARY/COMPENSATION

The median pay for special education teachers is $55,060, according to the Bureau of Labor Statistics (2014). Salaries vary substantially across the country. In addition, years of teaching experience and the level of one's graduate education will influence pay.

EMPLOYMENT OUTLOOK

There is currently a shortage of special education teachers across many parts of the country. This is especially true for ASD given the substantial increases in educational service needs seen in recent years within this population of students.

FURTHER INFORMATION FOR EXPLORATION

The Council for Exceptional Children (www.cec.org) and the National Association of Special Education Teachers (www.naset.org) provide important information for those interested in a career in special education—autism spectrum disorder. For more information about ASD, see the website of the autism advocacy organization Autism Speaks (www.autismspeaks.org).

44. SPECIAL EDUCATION TEACHER—HIGH-INCIDENCE DISABILITIES: RESOURCE/INCLUSION

BASIC DESCRIPTION

Special education teachers provide instruction and support to students who meet criteria for one or more special education diagnoses (e.g., autism; deaf–blindness; deafness; hearing impairment; mental retardation; multiple disabilities; orthopedic impairment; other health impairment; serious emotional disturbance; specific learning disability; speech or language impairment; traumatic brain injury; visual impairment, including blindness). Teaching those with high-incidence disabilities (e.g., specific learning disability, mild/moderate mental retardation, communication disorders) requires adaption of curriculum and instruction to meet the diverse academic challenges of those considered to have mild/moderate disabilities. Special education teachers who specialize in high-incidence disabilities may teach part of the day within inclusive classrooms, meeting the needs of their students with disabilities within the regular education classroom. For the remainder of the day they may teach math, reading, or writing within a resource room where small groups of students with mild disabilities are educated.

CORE COMPETENCIES AND SKILLS NEEDED

Substantial knowledge is needed related to the education of students with disabilities. Familiarity with the legal, ethical, and professional standards associated with regular and special education is important. A special education teacher must be able to create a positive, safe, and nurturing teaching environment for students. Teaching those with high-incidence disabilities requires extensive foundational knowledge pertaining to learning disabilities/mental retardation/communication disorders/behavior disorders, effective accommodations for students with disabilities, and core academic subject areas. It also requires the effective use of evidence-based instructional methods and classroom management techniques. Working collaboratively with a team of special educators or related services personnel within the district is important. Effective oral and written communication is especially needed given the importance of documentation and progress monitoring within the delivery of special education services. Patience, empathy, and good listening skills also fit well within this education career.

EDUCATIONAL REQUIREMENTS

A bachelor's degree in special education is required from a state-recognized teacher preparation program. Some states require the completion of a master's degree, and the website of the Department of Education of the state in which you are looking to work should be consulted. Coursework to teach in this area of special education typically involves special education disabilities (i.e., mild, moderate, severe), assessment, identification, collaboration, effective instruction, math/reading/writing curricula, and special education law/ethics/professional standards. In addition, coursework pertaining to working with diverse learners is typically required.

EXPERIENCE NECESSARY

Student teaching experience with individuals presenting with high-incidence disabilities is required within special education degree programs. Prior work or experience with students with special needs is often desired in applicants to undergraduate special education degree programs.

CERTIFICATION, LICENSURE, AND CONTINUING EDUCATION REQUIREMENTS

All states require special education teachers to be certified. Special education teachers who specialize in high-incidence disabilities might have completed a typical teaching degree (e.g., early childhood, elementary, secondary education), but all special educators must be endorsed (e.g., high-incidence, mild disabilities) in the area of special education for which they are providing education.

SALARY/COMPENSATION

The median pay for special education teachers is $55,060, according to the Bureau of Labor Statistics (2014). Salaries vary substantially across the country. In addition, years of teaching experience and the level of one's graduate education will influence pay.

EMPLOYMENT OUTLOOK

There is currently a shortage of highly qualified special education teachers across many parts of the country. Specifically, more teachers who are well trained to work with high-incidence populations in both resource and inclusion settings are needed.

FURTHER INFORMATION FOR EXPLORATION

The Council for Exceptional Children (www.cec.org) and the National Association of Special Education Teachers (www.naset.org) provide important information for those interested in a career in special education with a focus on high-incidence disabilities. For more information about high-incidence disabilities, see the Learning Disabilities Association of America (www.ldaamerica.org), the American Association on Intellectual and Developmental Disabilities (www.aaidd.org), or other websites of professional organizations typically associated with high-incidence disabilities (e.g., national authority on attention deficit hyperactivity disorder [ADHD]; www.chadd.org).

45.　SPECIAL EDUCATION TEACHER—LOW-INCIDENCE DISABILITIES

BASIC DESCRIPTION

Special education teachers who specialize in low-incidence disabilities provide instruction and support to students who meet criteria for one or more low-incidence (<1 % of the school-age population) special education diagnoses (e.g., deaf–blindness, low vision, deafness, hearing impairment, mental retardation, multiple disabilities, orthopedic impairment, other health impairment, significant developmental delay, complex health issues, multiple disability). Teachers who work with students presenting significant physical, sensory, or developmental needs that interfere with academic functioning typically work in self-contained classrooms with the support of a teaching assistant. Instructional priorities will depend on the individual needs of the student but may link to issues of communication, social–emotional functioning, basic literacy and other academic skills, adaptive skill development, and community functioning. Teaching functional skills pertaining to daily living is a primary focus of this career. Instruction is often modified to merge standard curricular objectives with functional skill development.

CORE COMPETENCIES AND SKILLS NEEDED
Substantial knowledge is needed related to the education of students with disabilities. Familiarity with the legal, ethical, and professional standards associated with regular and special education is important. Effective oral and written communication is especially needed given the importance of documentation and progress monitoring within the special education service-delivery system. Patience, strong organizational skills, and the ability to work as a part of a special education team are essential for this position. An appreciation of individual differences and a "can-do" attitude bode well for what at times can be a very physically and emotionally challenging teaching career.

EDUCATIONAL REQUIREMENTS
Background and training in special education and teacher education are required. A bachelor's or master's degree in special education and specialized training to become certified or licensed in disability (e.g., low incidence) and severity-based (e.g., mild, moderate, severe) special education teaching are expected.

EXPERIENCE NECESSARY
Degree programs will require supervised teaching experience through the completion of an internship pre- or postdegree. Background and

training within populations presenting with severe disabilities are necessary.

CERTIFICATION, LICENSURE, AND CONTINUING EDUCATION REQUIREMENTS

All special education teachers are required to have a bachelor's degree and a state-issued teaching certificate or license (e.g., early childhood, elementary, secondary). A specific endorsement in the area of low-incidence disabilities is also required. In some states, emergency certification may be granted within communities where the demand for special education teachers with the specialized skill set necessary to meet the special needs of their students far exceeds the supply of appropriately credentialed personnel.

SALARY/COMPENSATION

Salaries vary based on years of experience, location, and other community-based variables. Typically, the average salary falls between $50,000 and $60,000.

EMPLOYMENT OUTLOOK

The relative rarity of low-incidence disabilities in public schools and the specialized skills needed to teach in this area often create challenges to meeting the specialized needs of the low-incidence-disability student population. A shortage currently exists for special education teachers, and this need is anticipated to continue into the future.

FURTHER INFORMATION FOR EXPLORATION

The Council for Exceptional Children (www.cec.org), the National Association of Special Education Teachers (www.naset.org), the Center for Parent Information and Resources (www.parentcenterhub .org), and the National Center on Accessible Instructional Materials (www.aim.cast.org) provide important information for those interested in a teaching career in special education with a focus on low-incidence disabilities. Specific disability professional associations can also be an excellent source of information for those working within this specialized special education career (e.g., American Association of Intellectual and Developmental Disabilities, www.aamr.org; United Cerebral Palsy, www.ucp.org).

46. SPECIAL EDUCATION TEACHER—EMOTIONAL IMPAIRMENT

BASIC DESCRIPTION

Special education teachers who specialize in emotional impairment (emotional disturbance) provide instruction and support to students who struggle academically due to emotional and/or behavioral challenges. These challenges may include the presence of a diagnosed childhood mental health disorder such as anxiety disorders (e.g., obsessive-compulsive disorder), bipolar disorder (e.g., manic-depression), conduct disorders (e.g., oppositional, defiant), eating disorders (e.g., anorexia), or thought disorders (e.g., schizophrenia). Special education instruction must address a child's unique educational and emotional needs that are the direct result of the child's disability. Teachers of children receiving services for an emotional impairment adapt their instructional and evaluative methods to the individualized education plans (IEPs) developed by the school's multidisciplinary team that oversees the special education service-delivery process. Coordination of services across home, school, and community settings is essential. Teachers must be adept at relating effectively to students who present with a diverse array of needs and personalities. They must also possess effective classroom management techniques. This teaching role requires considerable case coordination due to the potential impact of student challenges in multiple settings within the school. Special education teachers who specialize in emotional impairment must be able to work closely with other school staff, the child's parent(s), and other mental health personnel who may be working with the student within the community.

CORE COMPETENCIES AND SKILLS NEEDED

Substantial knowledge is needed related to the education of students with disabilities and specifically in the area of instructional practices for students with emotional impairments. Familiarity with the legal, ethical, and professional standards associated with regular and special education is important. A special education teacher who specializes in emotional impairment must be able to create a positive, safe, and nurturing teaching environment. Teaching those with emotional or behavioral disorders requires extensive foundational knowledge pertaining to developmental disabilities. It also requires the effective use of positive behavioral supports and behavior management techniques. Patience, the ability to

157

motivate others, strong problem-solving skills, and the ability to think quickly to defuse interpersonal conflict are essential. Working collaboratively with others in the school building is important. Effective oral and written communication is especially needed given the importance of documentation and progress monitoring.

EDUCATIONAL REQUIREMENTS

A bachelor's degree from an accredited teacher preparation program is required to teach in public school settings. A master's degree focused on emotional and behavioral disorders is highly desired. An additional endorsement or specialization related to emotional impairment/disturbance may be required, and state requirements should be consulted.

EXPERIENCE NECESSARY

Prior student teaching experience via practica and internship placements in classrooms serving students with emotional and behavioral challenges is essential. Working closely with a master teacher in the area of emotional impairment can be especially important for those just entering this teaching career.

CERTIFICATION, LICENSURE, AND CONTINUING EDUCATION REQUIREMENTS

An endorsement in the area of emotional impairment is typically required above and beyond a typical teaching or special education teaching degree/certificate. This endorsement will require additional coursework and clinical experience with the population of interest. Given the potential for job burnout in this highly challenging teaching career, it is essential to engage in additional training and professional development. In addition, turning to colleagues and peer mentor teachers for guidance and support is important when first starting out in the field.

SALARY/COMPENSATION

Salaries vary considerably based on years of experience, the grade level taught, and the community in which the teacher is employed. Typical salaries for special education teachers tend to average between $50,000 and $60,000. However, the low range may extend down to the low $30,000 range, and higher salaries may extend up to $80,000.

EMPLOYMENT OUTLOOK

The current need for special education teachers has been recognized for more than a decade. Highly qualified teachers who are exceptional teachers of students with emotional impairments are highly sought. The job outlook for those careers looks very positive in the years ahead.

FURTHER INFORMATION FOR EXPLORATION

The Council for Exceptional Children (www.cec.org) and the emotional and behavioral disorders section of the website of the National Association of Special Education Teachers (www.naset.org) provide important information for those interested in a career in special education with a focus on emotional impairment. State organizations such as the Michigan Association of Teachers of Children with Emotional Impairments (MATCEI; www.matcei.org) can also be consulted for additional information. Professional associations that advocate on behalf of individuals with emotional and behavioral disorders also provide information important to explore (e.g., National Alliance on Mental Illness; www.nami.org).

Career-in-Education Profile
SPECIAL EDUCATION TEACHER—EMOTIONAL IMPAIRMENT

Interview With Sheila Nash (BA, Elementary Education/Emotional Impairment; MA, Special Education—Secondary Learning Disabilities)

Describe your educational background.

I completed my undergraduate degree in elementary education, with certification in the special education area of emotional impairment. I also completed an advanced degree in special education pertaining to learning disabilities.

Describe your prior experiences and the path you took to get to this career.

I grew up in a community with a strong network of support for people with disabilities. I grew up knowing that people of all abilities played important roles in our community. I realized as I got older that special education programs were geared toward people with severe problems. People I knew with more subtle issues were treated pretty harshly in schools and often fell through the cracks. I realized that if I ever became a teacher I would want to work with kids with uneven levels of development and growth. Long story short, I knew that I wanted to teach either gifted students or struggling students. The world of students receiving services under the category of emotional impairment gives me the opportunity to do both.

Describe the work that you do.

Throughout most of my career I have taught in self-contained programs for students with emotional impairments. I typically work with a full-time classroom assistant. Most of the students placed in the class receive special education services due to an emotional impairment and have behavioral issues that prevent them from being successful in a typical classroom. There are also students placed in the program because of a combination of disabilities. I generally

(continued)

(continued)

teach five subjects (math, reading, English, science, social studies), and the students attend a general education elective. The lessons are differentiated to meet each individual student's skill levels. The lessons also reflect the grade-level curriculum being taught in the general education classes. In addition to academic programming, individual behavior plans are developed and incorporated into the class-wide behavior support system. Developing, monitoring, and modifying the behavior system are a major part of the program. Advocating for the students and collaborating with teachers and administrators to provide appropriate programming are a big part of the job.

What is a typical day like for you in this career?

There are no typical days. Each day brings something unexpected. Transitions are the most volatile times of the day. Some students are escorted into class from their buses, whereas others arrive on their own. Monitoring the students in the hallway as they arrive and getting them into the classroom is the first challenge of the day. The students eat breakfast (and lunch) in the classroom. The cafeteria is an unpredictable environment where a fight or other extreme outburst involving students outside of the behavior program is most likely to occur. Earning privileges associated with having time in the cafeteria is part of the classroom behavior system. Getting students started on their work and engaging them in learning is another challenge during the day. Several minor behavior problems (e.g., name-calling, refusal to work, refusal to follow directions) will arise, and some will escalate into major issues (e.g., threatening language, trying to start a fight, insubordination, other aggressive behaviors). The major issues will involve a temporary removal from the classroom, a conference with the student, and possibly a conference with the principal. Extreme incidents may require physical restraint of the student. Some incidents result in suspension or, in extremely rare cases, expulsion from school (i.e., harm to a teacher, bringing weapons to school). Positive reinforcement, rewarding behaviors, and monitoring the behavior system are ongoing throughout the day.

(continued)

(*continued*)

What is the most challenging part of your career?

Collaborating with other staff and administration has been a continuous challenge. People have difficulty understanding the unique needs of a student who has been identified as having an emotional impairment. People often cannot see beyond the behavior of the student and want the student to be punished or removed from a class or building. In advocating for students, I often find myself explaining and re-explaining the needs or behaviors of a student.

What is the most rewarding part of your career?

Seeing student progress and growth is very rewarding. I rarely get the chance to see monumental changes, like students totally transitioning out of a self-contained program. I do get to see small milestones. Every time I see a student truly smile or laugh is rewarding. When I have the opportunity to see a student show understanding of a concept he or she could not previously grasp, it is rewarding. Being able to share in any triumph my students experience is rewarding. For some students, simply getting to school is a triumph!

What advice do you have for someone in high school or currently at the undergraduate level who might be interested in this career?

Do it! Teaching is a great career. Special education is a unique niche, and if you are drawn to this field it is probably right for you. Take the time to get experience working with an individual student identified as emotionally impaired (or a student with a severe attention deficit). If working with an individual is not an option, then get into some classrooms. It is important to have some experiences in making connections with the types of students you intend to teach before you are the one responsible for the academic aspects of teaching.

(*continued*)

(continued)

What advice do you have for someone currently in a different career/field who might be interested in your career?

Teaching is a great career with a variety of opportunities. Develop a sense of the type of teaching environment you would like to be a part of and the type of students you feel you would be successful in working with.

If you decided to advance your career, what steps would you take and what career(s) might you seek out?

I love what I do. However, I do plan to expand my teaching certifications to include certification in a secondary general education field (math or science) or national certification. If I had to make a career change, I would pursue teaching future teachers at the university level.

47.   ADAPTED PHYSICAL EDUCATION TEACHER

BASIC DESCRIPTION

For students with disabilities, physical education must involve the development of physical fitness, fundamental motor skills, and involvement in games/sports. An adapted physical education teacher ensures that these efforts are carried out by designing achievement-based programs that are developmentally appropriate (preschool through grade 12). Specialized instruction (i.e., one on one, small group, large group, inclusive general physical education class) and high-quality programming in physical education are developed to meet the unique individual needs of the student with disabilities. Monitoring and documenting student progress toward those goals must occur, as this information will need to be shared with other individualized education plan (IEP) team members. The adapted physical education teacher also serves an important role in leadership and advocacy for students with disabilities and their parents within the larger school context. The primary focus of this teaching position is to assist students in maintaining a healthy lifestyle outside the school setting and especially as they transition to the community for postsecondary placements.

CORE COMPETENCIES AND SKILLS NEEDED

The ability to provide age-appropriate and disability-sensitive physical education programs is needed. This includes the need to have a strong understanding of physical education content; assessment and evaluation; disability; and IEP development, implementation, and evaluation. As for other teachers, core competencies in classroom and behavior management, the ability to engage in individual assessment to establish baseline levels of functioning, and the ability to carry out high-quality instructional practices are essential. Familiarity with activity modifications, equipment modifications, assistive devices, specialized equipment, and integration of technology into the curriculum are especially important. Strong interpersonal skills and the ability to relate to a diverse student population are essential. The ability to work effectively as a part of a team and a strong understanding of special education law and practices are needed.

EDUCATIONAL REQUIREMENTS

A bachelor's degree in kinesiology or physical education is typically required. Some universities offer a minor in adapted physical education. Post bachelor's or post master's degree coursework and training in adapted physical education is typical for those working in this career. Often this culminates in the individual becoming a certified adapted physical education teacher. Typically, coursework involves training in inclusive practices, child development (i.e., abnormal, motor, normal, physical), and special education law.

EXPERIENCE NECESSARY

Prior experience in teaching physical education and adapted physical education is necessary. This typically will occur as a part of a major or minor course of study. It may also occur within a certificate or endorsement program that is completed after graduating with a degree.

CERTIFICATION, LICENSURE, AND CONTINUING EDUCATION REQUIREMENTS

States vary in how they credential adaptive physical educators. Some states have a separate teaching license or credential (e.g., Wisconsin, California). It is also possible to become a nationally certified adapted physical educator (CAPE). This credential represents training that meets the highest national standards. Most teachers in this field have prior training, experience, and credentials related to teaching physical education.

SALARY/COMPENSATION

Salaries vary considerably across the country. An average salary for an adapted physical education teacher is between $50,000 and $60,000. Years of experience, characteristics of the school district/community, and one's degree will all influence compensation.

EMPLOYMENT OUTLOOK

Demand for well-qualified adapted physical education teachers is strong given the limited supply of teachers who are well trained to meet the needs of students in special education. Currently, the demand for teachers at the kindergarten, elementary, and middle school levels is higher than the demand for those interested in working at the high school level.

FURTHER INFORMATION FOR EXPLORATION

If you are curious about or interested in the field of adapted physical education, please review the Adapted Physical Education National Standards (www.apens.org). In addition, professional organizations such as the Society of Health and Physical Educators (www.shapeamerica.org) provide useful resources and information to review. Resources and handouts related to lesson plans and activities can be found at www.PEcentral.org.

48. MUSIC/ART THERAPIST

BASIC DESCRIPTION

Music and art therapists use an array of activities to promote mental and physical well-being through self-expression and creativity. Using art or music as a medium for expression can be therapeutic and also reinforces the unique talents and skills of students. This is especially true for students with disabilities or those who are experiencing psychological or adjustment issues. Music performance and studio art activities, when combined with psychological therapy techniques, can promote more positive thinking and a healthier outlook on life. Art therapy techniques often include painting, sketching, crafting, or sculpting. Music therapy techniques may include playing instruments, listening to music, or mimicking (feeling, re-creating) music through movement. Art and music therapists work across a broad range of ages and typically do not limit their work to only school-age populations. Therapy techniques can be offered individually, in small groups, or as a part of larger groups depending on the emotional and physical needs of the client. In addition to working in schools, art and music therapists may work in hospitals, rehabilitation centers, psychiatric care facilities, retirement homes, prisons, or community-based mental health agencies.

CORE COMPETENCIES AND SKILLS NEEDED

Creativity, empathy, and compassion are qualities needed to work within this career. The desire and ability to help others to foster their self-expression and promote well-being are essential. Working effectively as a part of a team and collaborating with other staff to develop, implement, and monitor a comprehensive treatment plan are essential qualities to possess for this profession. Effectively communicating with families or other members of the client's support network is also required.

EDUCATIONAL REQUIREMENTS

A bachelor's degree in music or art therapy will involve courses in music/ art theory, psychological theory, therapy techniques, legal/ethical issues, and life-span development. In some cases, an unrelated bachelor's degree combined with advanced graduate study in art/music therapy can lead to the appropriate credentials for work within this field. There are also doctoral degree programs that can be completed to further one's understanding of the science and practice of art/music therapy.

EXPERIENCE NECESSARY

Prior supervised experience working as a therapist with diverse populations and clinical challenges is necessary. Clinical-hour requirements for therapist credentials may be as high as 1,200 hours, but state criteria should be examined closely for specific requirements.

CERTIFICATION, LICENSURE, AND CONTINUING EDUCATION REQUIREMENTS

Certification is required. Art therapists must be certified by the Art Therapy Credentials Board. Following completion of a master's degree in art therapy, one can then become a registered art therapist (ATR). To become a board-certified art therapist (ATR-BC), one must pass the national examination. Music therapists must be board certified (MT-BC), which requires successfully passing the national examination following degree completion. Continuing education is expected and required to maintain one's credentials.

SALARY/COMPENSATION
Guidance on salaries for art/music therapists can be seen within the field of recreation therapy. Average salaries will typically fall between $45,000 and $50,000. Years of experience, credentialing, and graduate degree completion will certainly influence one's salary.

EMPLOYMENT OUTLOOK
The employment outlook for art/music therapists, along with recreational therapists, appears strong in the near term. As the population of the United States gets older, the need for therapists working with the senior citizen population will likely be substantial.

FURTHER INFORMATION FOR EXPLORATION
The American Music Therapy Association (www.musictherapy.org) and the American Art Therapy Association (www.arttherapy.org) provide additional information for those interested in a career in art/music therapy. International, regional, or state professional associations can also be consulted (e.g., www.ieata.org, www.mar-amta.org).

49. INTERPRETER FOR THE HEARING IMPAIRED

BASIC DESCRIPTION
Interpreters for the hearing impaired (sign language interpreters) translate the spoken language into sign language for those who are deaf or hard of hearing. The primary responsibilities associated with this career are to provide voice-to-sign and sign-to-voice support. An understanding of the content being signed is essential. Accurate translation of spoken language is important to the work of an interpreter. Interpreters can work in a multitude of settings, including in schools, government agencies, hospitals, and facilities for senior citizens. In school settings, both academic and nonacademic activities may be involved. Participation in school meetings (e.g., individualized education plan [IEP] team meetings), monitoring of student progress, and preparation of lesson plans are examples of the responsibilities of an interpreter working in the school

setting. Other examples of settings in which an interpreter for the hearing impaired may work include translating within public events, court proceedings, office meetings, or one-on-one situations.

CORE COMPETENCIES AND SKILLS NEEDED
Exceptional communication skills (English, American Sign Language [ASL]) are needed with this position. The abilities to listen intently, react quickly, and interpret accurately are core competencies expected of those who work in this career. The need to understand and translate highly technical or complex information can be especially challenging. Exceptional time-management skills and well-developed organizational strategies are essential for this position. Establishing baseline levels of students' language skills and subject proficiency through language assessment measures is important.

EDUCATIONAL REQUIREMENTS
Education, training, or a degree in ASL is required. Bachelor's degrees in English, communications, or a related field are often combined with training in ASL.

EXPERIENCE NECESSARY
Experience in a number of different contexts and under a multitude of conditions is important for those working as an interpreter. Well-developed nonverbal communication skills (e.g., gestures, hand movements, facial expressions) can be very beneficial within the translation process. The use of technology to facilitate interpretation has been steadily growing over the past decade.

CERTIFICATION, LICENSURE, AND CONTINUING EDUCATION REQUIREMENTS
Certification is not necessarily required, but having credentials (e.g., certified interpreter for the deaf, oral transliteration certificate) can help to clearly demonstrate one's skills in interpretation.

SALARY/COMPENSATION
The typical salary for this position is around $40,000 to $45,000, according to data reported by the Bureau of Labor Statistics (2014). Variations in pay are associated with the employment setting, the qualifications

and background of the interpreter, and the sophistication of the content being translated.

EMPLOYMENT OUTLOOK

The employment outlook for interpreters for the hearing impaired appears especially strong. The aging population of the United States combined with the limited supply of highly trained personnel has resulted in a significant demand for highly qualified interpreters.

FURTHER INFORMATION FOR EXPLORATION

For additional information about a career as an interpreter, the National Association of the Deaf (www.nad.org), the American Speech-Language-Hearing Association (www.asha.org), the World Association of Sign Language Interpreters (www.wasli.org), and the American Sign Language Teachers Association (www.aslta.org) offer a comprehensive set of resources to explore. For additional information on credentialing, the Registry of Interpreters for the Deaf (www.rid.org) should be consulted.

50. ENGLISH AS A SECOND LANGUAGE TEACHER

BASIC DESCRIPTION

English as a second language (ESL) teachers or English for speakers of other languages (ESOL) teachers create lesson plans and engage in effective instructional methods to teach non-native speakers (e.g., immigrants) to speak, read, and write English. Specific instruction in English pronunciation, conversational skills, and grammar is required within this career in education. The ability to apply English instruction to real-life situations and everyday living is important. Multiple settings hire ESL teachers, including elementary/middle/high schools, community-based adult literacy programs, vocational schools, and postsecondary education settings. Like other teachers, ESL teachers are expected to develop effective lesson plans, direct classroom-based activities, and engage in assessment of expected mastery of the English language in participating students.

CORE COMPETENCIES AND SKILLS NEEDED

The ability to communicate and work well with learners from a diverse array of backgrounds is essential within this position. The ability to effectively communicate, the possession of strong interpersonal skills, and a commitment to serving others are needed. Patience, empathy, and an interest in multicultural education are especially important for teachers who work to bridge the gap between native and non-native languages and cultural practices. The ability to create games and other fun learning activities can be especially important when students are learning a new language.

EDUCATIONAL REQUIREMENTS

A bachelor's or master's degree is typically required. A degree related to adult education or English as a second language is expected for those working within this career. Coursework in literacy, adult development, child development, linguistics, or academic English is typical.

EXPERIENCE NECESSARY

A history of teaching, including managing classrooms, planning lessons, implementing learning activities, and engaging in assessment of student learning, is expected. Experience working or teaching non-English speakers is necessary. Experience studying abroad or international travel can also be very beneficial to those who become ESL teachers.

CERTIFICATION, LICENSURE, AND CONTINUING EDUCATION REQUIREMENTS

Completion of a teaching training program is a prerequisite to becoming an ESL teacher. ESL teacher requirements vary by state. At a minimum, a state teaching license is required to teach in the public schools. Private schools may have alternative requirements for ESL teachers.

SALARY/COMPENSATION

Salaries for ESL teachers typically align with the pay received by secondary education teachers. An average salary between $50,000 and $60,000 is typical but will vary greatly by state and the characteristics defining the community in which one chooses to teach.

EMPLOYMENT OUTLOOK

Increases in the immigrant population within the United States have created a significant demand for ESL teachers, especially in large cities and towns near the Mexican border. The increased importance on literacy and minimal educational requirements (i.e., General

Education Development [GED]) for employment will result in additional demand for ESL teachers within the United States in the years to come.

FURTHER INFORMATION FOR EXPLORATION

Teachers of English to Speakers of Other Languages (TESOL; www.tesol.org) is a professional association with a mission to advance professional expertise in English language teaching. For a comprehensive listing of ESL teacher resources, see Purdue University's Online Writing Lab website (owl.english.purdue.edu/owl/section/5/24). Other web pages offer teacher handouts, grammar worksheets, and printables (e.g., www.UsingEnglish.com, www.ESLgold.com, www .ESLflow.com).

Career-in-Education Profile
ENGLISH AS A SECOND LANGUAGE TEACHER

Interview With Mary Lou Turnbull (BA, Secondary English Education)

Describe your educational background.

I completed my Bachelor of Arts degree in secondary English education. My minors were bilingual education and teaching English to speakers of other languages (TESOL). I later returned to school for graduate study and earned my elementary education endorsement.

Describe your prior experiences and the path you took to get to this career.

My family was always interested in forming relationships with families and individuals from other countries. We welcomed exchange students from Mexico into our lives for entire school years. I even spent a summer living with the family of one of these students. I always knew that I would work with students from other cultures, but I had never even heard of English as a second language (ESL), either as a class or as a career. I didn't learn of a career as an ESL teacher until I took a Spanish class at my undergraduate institution. After I graduated from college, I taught general education English classes at the high school level for 10 years. I didn't start in my role as an ESL teacher until a position opened in the district in the late 1980s.

Describe the work that you do.

I teach two sections of ESL at the high school and two sections of ESL and an ESL homeroom class at the middle school every afternoon. I also run an after-school academic support program for English language learners (ELLs) for grades 7 to 12. In each of my classes I have from 10 to 20 students from approximately 12 different countries with widely varied levels of English proficiency. My charge is to provide differentiated instruction in areas of literature, vocabulary, reading, writing, speaking, and listening skills. Fortunately, the district has provided me with a paraprofessional who is assigned to my program for 15 hours

(continued)

(continued)

per week. I have also partnered with our local public university to place its students in my program. Generally, 20 college seniors are placed in my program each semester. These students may be assigned to work one on one with a beginner-level ELL or in a small group providing academic support. Some summers I teach summer school over a 3-week period in August. I engage my ESL students in reading, writing, and speaking. We also take field trips to apply what they learn. Because I speak Spanish and used to teach it in our district, I also have led study-abroad trips to Spain. During some of the summers that I don't teach, I have voluntarily run a less formal ESL program for the beginners in my program. I have also been invited to participate in conversation "classes" offered at the library and the community center.

What is a typical day like for you in this career?

Each day we always open with a warm-up, reviewing a key concept from the previous day's lesson. During our short-story unit, we might discuss a short story each student read. Throughout the reading and discussion of the story, I provide background information, preteach vocabulary, and enhance comprehension with illustrations that I project on the screen. After we discuss the story, I distribute to students and display on the overhead a template for writing an expository essay on the short story. The way I set up my middle school program is very similar. However, unique to the middle school setting is that I have an eighth-grade homeroom class called REACH, where assistance is provided on homework.

What is the most challenging part of your career?

Like most teachers, I have a few students who lack motivation. Helping these students stay on track and guiding them to find the motivation to work hard is definitely challenging. It used to be *very* hard for me to say good-bye to students who had to return to their countries. I am grateful that it has become much easier to stay in touch given advances in social media. Even some students from my first year of teaching ESL, back in 1989, have tracked me down. I love seeing what interesting adults they have become!

(continued)

(continued)

What is the most rewarding part of your career?

I think the most rewarding part of teaching is when a former student tells me how I affected his or her learning, assimilation, or acculturation. I also find working with my students' families highly rewarding. Most parents view me as the "school mom" for their kids. It is extremely rewarding to know that what I do makes a positive difference in their lives!

What advice do you have for someone in high school or currently at the undergraduate level who might be interested in this career?

Find an opportunity to volunteer in an ESL classroom or in a refugee center that offers homework help after school or in the evenings. Another possibility would be to contact a local college or university to volunteer as an English tutor. Getting direct experience working with students from other countries would help determine whether this is a career path you might like to pursue.

What advice do you have for someone currently in a different career/field who might be interested in your career?

My advice would be the same as I listed regarding advice for high school or undergraduate students. Volunteer with ESL students and refugees. Get a feel for their struggles and challenges as well as the varied talents and rich experiences they bring to their communities.

If you decided to advance your career, what steps would you take and what career(s) might you seek out?

A person in my position might pursue a master's degree or a PhD in TESOL. With a master's degree or PhD one might consider teaching in college of education teacher preparation courses or doing research. Many teachers trained in TESOL take jobs teaching ESL in other countries. Native speakers of English are highly sought after, and teaching opportunities can be found in almost every country in the world.

51. BILINGUAL TEACHER

BASIC DESCRIPTION

Bilingual teachers provide content instruction to students in two languages, the native language (i.e., English) and a secondary language. These teachers help to create links in specified knowledge (e.g., math, science, literature) between the two languages through bilingual instruction. This position differs from that of English as a second language (ESL) teachers, who provide English instruction to students who speak a different native language. ESL teachers also teach students from multiple backgrounds/languages, whereas bilingual teachers teach students who possess the same native language. In the United States, bilingual classrooms most typically involve English-speaking students and Spanish-speaking students. Teachers will typically teach half of the class in English and half in Spanish. Infusion of both languages throughout the class period is essential. Like other teachers, bilingual teachers are expected to develop lesson plans, direct classroom-based activities, and grade class assignments/tests.

CORE COMPETENCIES AND SKILLS NEEDED

The ability to teach core content in two languages is essential for this career in education. Helping students to learn academic skills by using both the students' native language and the English language also requires a level of mastery of both languages. The skills necessary to mentor and assist students in their efforts to bridge multiple and, at times, conflicting cultures are also essential.

EDUCATIONAL REQUIREMENTS

Bilingual teachers are required to hold at least a bachelor's degree in education, bilingual education, multilingual education, or a related field such as Spanish. A dual major in a foreign language and teacher education may also be sought. For those who major in the non-native language (e.g., Spanish) to be taught, it is essential to meet state certification requirements for additional teacher education coursework and practica/internship experiences. Considerable education in two languages and the specific academic content area to be taught is essential.

EXPERIENCE NECESSARY

Student teaching as a part of a teacher certification program is typically necessary. Experience teaching a foreign language and instruction in two or more languages is also helpful to enter into this teaching career. Prior experience with the history and culture of the language's country of origin is often preferred.

CERTIFICATION, LICENSURE, AND CONTINUING EDUCATION REQUIREMENTS

Most states require completion of a teacher education program in order to achieve certification to teach. Some states may also require a specific bilingual teacher credential or certification.

SALARY/COMPENSATION

Salaries for bilingual teachers typically parallel pay for high school teachers, which typically falls between $50,000 and $60,000. Geographic location and years of experience will certainly influence salary levels.

EMPLOYMENT OUTLOOK

Well-qualified foreign language teachers are currently in high demand within middle and high schools. Advanced content knowledge combined with the ability to instruct in two languages provides a unique set of skills for employment within schools. The number of students in the United States who speak other languages, especially Spanish, is growing. Job prospects are considered strong for bilingual teachers as the diversity within schools in the United States increases.

FURTHER INFORMATION FOR EXPLORATION

For additional information about becoming a bilingual teacher, two professional organizations should be consulted: the National Association for Bilingual Education (www.nabe.org) and the Teachers of English to Speakers of Other Languages International Association (www.tesol.org). Many states have their own professional associations for bilingual educators that provide helpful resources and information for those interested in this career in education (e.g., Colorado Association for Bilingual Education; www.cocabe.org).

52.   OVERSEAS ENGLISH TEACHER

BASIC DESCRIPTION

Overseas English teachers work in a variety of settings and with a diverse array of learners. Teaching of school-age children may occur within primary schools or within the host country's higher education system. Teaching adult learners the English language may take place in the community or within an industry-based setting. For those unfamiliar with the English language, the focus of lessons and instruction typically begins with conversational communication skills. As in other teaching careers, responsibilities include preparation of lesson plans/activities, role-playing/modeling, and specification of clear learning outcomes. Measuring learner outcomes is essential and will require the development of assignments, test, quizzes, and other assessment situations. In addition to instruction and assessment, administrative responsibilities (e.g., communicating with school leaders, carrying out an internationally recognized curricular plan) may also be expected. The main responsibility of being an overseas English teacher is to help learners to understand (listen), speak (pronunciation), and read/write.

CORE COMPETENCIES AND SKILLS NEEDED

A command of the English language and the competencies needed to teach it to others are expected. Teaching overseas requires one to embrace and adapt to other cultures and countries. Travel and mobility are expected within this career. Exceptional communication skills, the ability to speak/understand or quickly learn a foreign language, and strong time-management skills bode well for those assuming this position. Being highly organized, structured, and focused are important characteristics of an overseas English teacher. A high degree of patience, a sense of humor, and strong interpersonal skills are necessary to flexibly deal with language or cultural barriers that may arise when working within a foreign country.

EDUCATIONAL REQUIREMENTS

A bachelor's degree is usually required to be an overseas English teacher. However, educational requirements to teach English overseas vary from country to country. Some countries require a background in teaching or even prior certification as a teacher. Prior training or certification in teaching English as a foreign language (TEFL) or teaching English as a second language (TESL) may be required. Some countries may expect that their English teachers are citizens of a native-English-speaking country. Access to a work visa is essential for this position.

EXPERIENCE NECESSARY

Prior experience in teaching English to non–English-speaking populations is typically expected. A strong commitment to serving others through teaching and an academic background related to teaching English to speakers of other languages (TESOL) are necessary for many positions overseas. Other positions may require little prior experience. Private language schools throughout the world will typically expect considerable experience combined with a bachelor's degree and a certificate related to teaching English to others.

CERTIFICATION, LICENSURE, AND CONTINUING EDUCATION REQUIREMENTS

No single degree, certification, or license will authorize someone to teach English overseas. However, certification to teach English as a foreign language or a certificate in English language teaching to adults (CELTA) may be required or preferred.

SALARY/COMPENSATION

Given the diversity of overseas teaching positions available and issues of supply/demand, salaries greatly vary by location. It is important to look specifically at information provided by the country in which you are interested in teaching for guidance with respect to compensation.

EMPLOYMENT OUTLOOK

There is considerable demand across the world for teachers of English. Numerous agencies that focus on placing English teachers overseas can be found via an Internet search. Networking with teachers working overseas or teachers with a history of teaching English as a second language will help to further understand the parts of the world in greatest need of overseas teachers.

FURTHER INFORMATION FOR EXPLORATION

Teachers of English to Speakers of Other Languages (TESOL; www. tesol.org) is a professional association with a mission to advance professional expertise in English language teaching. For opportunities to teach English abroad, see websites such as www.teachaway.com or www.ciee.org/teach.

REFERENCE

Bureau of Labor Statistics, U.S. Department of Labor. (2014). *Occupational outlook handbook, 2014–2015 edition, Special Education Teachers.* Retrieved July 11, 2015, from http://www.bls.gov/ooh/education-training-and-library/special-education-teachers.htm

8 ■ CAREERS WORKING WITHIN SYSTEMS OF CARE FOR STUDENTS WITH DISABILITIES

53.   OCCUPATIONAL/PHYSICAL THERAPIST

BASIC DESCRIPTION

The Individuals with Disabilities Education Act (IDEA) mandates free and appropriate educational services to students who are eligible for special education. An occupational therapist (OT) helps individuals with disabilities to engage in daily life tasks (i.e., occupations). Occupational therapy services provided within the school setting may target physical, cognitive, sensory, or other aspects of performance expected across multiple settings. Engagement in assessment, intervention, and prevention services regarding occupational issues is typical within this career. Helping students with disabilities to better engage in daily living activities (e.g., toileting, feeding, hygiene), complete classroom responsibilities (e.g., organizing materials, transitioning), and function within the classroom setting (staying on task, engaging in appropriate social skills, following directions) is the primary focus of an OT. A physical therapist (PT) helps in the evaluation, treatment, and prevention of disability, injury, or other health conditions. Physical therapy services are set up to improve an individual's ability to participate in school activities and may include the use of heat, cold, water, massage, or therapeutic exercise. Improving school mobility and involvement in classroom activities, transitioning to postsecondary opportunities, and helping children with disabilities to access all environments within the school setting is the primary focus of a PT. Referral from physicians or the recommendation of a multidisciplinary team as a part of an individualized education plan (IEP) is required for the provision of occupational therapy or physical therapy services. In sum, the primary focus of the OT/PT is to allow students with disabilities to benefit from their individualized special education programming.

CORE COMPETENCIES AND SKILLS NEEDED

Data-based problem solving is an essential competency required of those who provide occupational or physical therapy services. Familiarity with assistive technology and a focus on working with students on future goals are essential for OTs/PTs. Strong written and oral communication skills are needed. The ability to work well with school-age children is essential. Helping students with disabilities to make changes to their daily living activities can be challenging, both emotionally and physically. Patience, focus, determination, compassion, and an optimistic outlook on life are important OT/PT characteristics. Physical stamina and strength are important to provide supportive services for some types of disabilities. A strong commitment to excellence and engaging oneself as a lifelong learner within the field of occupational/physical therapy are important characteristics to perform well within this career.

EDUCATIONAL REQUIREMENTS

Undergraduate degrees that would qualify for earning a graduate degree within the field of occupational/physical therapy include kinesiology, biology, sociology, and psychology. A master's or doctoral degree in physical therapy or occupational therapy is ultimately required to work in this career. Cardiopulmonary resuscitation (CPR) certification may be a requirement for work in this career.

EXPERIENCE NECESSARY

Prior experience as a therapy assistant or some other form of service delivery to those with disabilities is typically needed. Practica, internship, and residency experiences across multiple settings (e.g., schools, rehabilitation facilities, nursing homes, or fitness settings) may be required within an occupational/physical therapy graduate degree program.

CERTIFICATION, LICENSURE, AND CONTINUING EDUCATION REQUIREMENTS

State licensure is required to be an OT/PT. A national exam is required, and it is essential to look at state-level requirements necessary to be an OT/PT. Requirements for continuing education and recertification vary by state.

SALARY/COMPENSATION

Salaries for those providing occupational/physical therapy services depend on geographic region and years of experience. Average salaries within the school setting may range from $60,000 to $70,000, according to the Bureau of Labor Statistics (2014a). Pay for this work outside of school settings is typically higher.

EMPLOYMENT OUTLOOK

The employment outlook for OTs/PTs is strong, especially for work outside of the school setting. Specifically, aging baby boomers are nearing retirement and the elderly population will require a greater number of therapists in the years ahead.

FURTHER INFORMATION FOR EXPLORATION

To learn more about the field of occupational therapy, see the website for the American Occupational Therapy Association (www.aota.org). To learn more about the field of physical therapy, see the website of the American Physical Therapy Association (www.apta.org). For certification requirements, see the National Board for Certification in Occupational Therapy (www.nbcot.org) or the Federation of State Boards of Physical Therapy (www.fsbpt.org).

54. RESPONSE-TO-INTERVENTION COORDINATOR

BASIC DESCRIPTION

A response-to-intervention (RtI) coordinator provides leadership to school districts in the implementation of RtI services (e.g., screening, progress monitoring, multilevel prevention system). RtI strategies are focused on ensuring that all children achieve at grade level. Implementation of a three-tiered approach to improve student achievement is the primary focus of this leadership position. At the first tier, which focuses on implementation of effective reading and mathematics instruction provided to *all* students, RtI coordinators organize, implement, and evaluate school-wide reading and math assessments. Students deemed at risk from the results of those assessments are provided more intensive services, usually within small groups via a second tier of support services. Students who fail to respond to these second-tier intervention services are typically provided resource-intensive services at the individual level (third tier) in an effort to improve basic academic skills. RtI coordinators work closely with staff and administrators to ensure high fidelity to this model of service delivery aimed at ensuring success within the classroom. This school-based model of services parallels a model of public health (i.e., primary prevention, secondary prevention, tertiary prevention) that has long been discussed within health care in the United States.

CORE COMPETENCIES AND SKILLS NEEDED

Substantial knowledge and skills are required pertaining to effective instructional strategies. Collaborative consultation skills (e.g., working with other teachers, administrators) as well as direct intervention skills with students presenting academic challenges are needed. Providing services in both small-group and one-on-one settings is necessary. The ability to meet a diverse array of student needs is required. Skills associated with leadership and time management are particularly important to this coordinator position, as altering existing practices within a school setting can be a long and laborious process. Strong oral and written communication skills are required for this administrative position within schools.

EDUCATIONAL REQUIREMENTS

A degree in teacher education or a closely related field is required. An advanced graduate degree pertaining to reading, instruction, math, special education, or early childhood is typically preferred. An endorsement as a reading or math specialist may be required and will depend on the district. Some districts may also require the candidate to have an administrative license.

EXPERIENCE NECESSARY

Prior experience as a classroom teacher, special education teacher, or academic specialist is expected. A history of providing leadership in the implementation of school-based initiatives and evidence-based practices to promote children's success in schools is preferred. It is important to have prior evidence of engaging in cooperative relationships with students, teachers, parents, and administrators for this coordinator position. Prior experience in training other teachers and providing instruction to students with and without disabilities is very important to working within this model of service delivery.

CERTIFICATION, LICENSURE, AND CONTINUING EDUCATION REQUIREMENTS

A teaching certificate for the grade level and one of the subject areas of emphasis is required. Renewal of a teaching certificate will require continuing education via engagement in professional development activities.

SALARY/COMPENSATION
Salaries vary by region and district. Years of experience and the type of degree held may influence the range of pay. Typically, these coordinator positions pay at the higher end of the teaching salary range ($55,000 to $65,000), based on a review of recent position descriptions/job openings.

EMPLOYMENT OUTLOOK
A focus on early intervention and prevention has emerged recently within school settings. This shift in resource allocation means that RtI coordinators are currently in high demand as schools begin to implement this service-delivery approach to meeting the needs of all students within a district.

FURTHER INFORMATION FOR EXPLORATION
The Center on Response to Intervention (www.rti4success.org) provides helpful information for states, districts, and schools that are implementing this service-delivery model. The Association for Supervision and Curriculum Development (www.ascd.org) is an example of one professional group that has given considerable attention to RtI training for teachers and school systems in recent years.

55. SCHOOL PSYCHOLOGIST

BASIC DESCRIPTION
The Individuals with Disabilities Education Act (IDEA) mandates free and appropriate educational services to students who are eligible for special education. The role of the school psychologist within the special education diagnostic decision-making team is essential. School psychologists use multiple assessment techniques to assess students' behavior, learning, and mental health (e.g., observations, rating scales, standardized assessments), and they communicate with others about the results of this data collection and the hypothesized meaning. This role is essential for the development of a special education student's individualized education plan (IEP). School psychologists provide collaborative consultation

services to families, teachers, school staff, administrators, and other professionals outside of the school setting. In addition, they engage in intervention services with both children (e.g., individual or group counseling) and adults (e.g., parent or teacher training). A considerable portion of the time spent in this profession is devoted to reducing barriers to children's learning and promoting successful development in schools. Those holding a doctoral degree in school psychology from an accredited program may also be eligible to become a licensed psychologist. Holding both a national certificate in school psychology and a license allows a school psychologist to provide psychological services to school-age children across home, school, and community settings.

CORE COMPETENCIES AND SKILLS NEEDED

Skills in research, practice, and dissemination are essential. This means that strong oral and written communication skills are needed. Analytical thinking, data-based decision making, and strong interpersonal skills are important within this career. Developing meaningful relationships with both children and adults is a necessary facet of working as a school psychologist. Specific skills are needed in data collection/analysis, assessment techniques, intervention approaches, and consultation skills. Normal and abnormal child development, psychopathology, classroom management, effective instructional skills, and the schooling process are some of the many areas of expertise necessary for work as a school psychologist.

EDUCATIONAL REQUIREMENTS

Students pursuing a graduate degree in school psychology often have majored in psychology, child psychology, child development, or teacher education as an undergraduate. An advanced degree (e.g., educational specialist [EdS], doctor of philosophy [PhD]) is required to be a school psychologist. Graduate training typically takes 3 to 6 years to complete, and school psychologists typically have the most formal educational training of any of the staff within a school building.

EXPERIENCE NECESSARY

Training to become a school psychologist requires many years of school-based experience in working with children and adults who care for children. Practica and internship experiences in diverse communities and populations will be required during graduate education.

CERTIFICATION, LICENSURE, AND CONTINUING EDUCATION REQUIREMENTS

Certification requirements vary by state, so it is important to look closely at state-specific guidelines. Holding the national certificate in school psychology is typically recognized across the United States and allows for a high level of professional mobility. For the criteria associated with that national credential, see the National Association of School Psychologists (NASP) website at www.nasponline.org. Licensure to become a psychologist for those who complete doctoral training in a program accredited by the American Psychological Association (www.apa .org) also varies by state, and the website of the Association of State and Provincial Psychology Boards (www.asppb.net) should be consulted for state-specific details. Continuing education requirements exist to maintain one's credentials and also vary by state.

SALARY/COMPENSATION

School psychologists have a reported mean salary just over $70,000 (according to recent survey data reported by the NASP), and are among the highest paid social service professionals working within schools. Pay will vary by years of experience and geographic location, as indicated by the variation of pay within the discipline ($35,000 to $110,000). Pay for doctoral graduates in school psychology is typically higher. In recent years, the field of school psychology has been ranked as one of the top social service careers in the country.

EMPLOYMENT OUTLOOK

The United States has experienced a shortage in well-trained school psychologists for the past decade or so. This shortage is expected to continue for the near term as both retirement and the emphasis on mental health in schools increases. The demand for school psychologists, although vast overall, varies by region, as need is greatest in rural and urban parts of the country.

FURTHER INFORMATION FOR EXPLORATION

For entry-level training requirements (i.e., EdS degree) to become a school psychologist and a breadth of information about the field, see www.nasponline.org. For doctoral-level training (PhD) in school psychology and a better understanding of how school psychologists fit within the world of professional psychology, see www.apadivisions.org/division-16.

Career-in-Education Profile
SCHOOL PSYCHOLOGIST
Interview With John S. Carlson (BS, Child Psychology; MS/PhD, School Psychology)

Describe your educational background.

I majored in child psychology (BS) as an undergraduate student and completed my graduate school studies (MS, PhD) in school psychology. My education involved training as a scientist-practitioner with specific competency development in the areas of assessment, consultation, intervention, and research pertaining to children's mental health functioning. A specific emphasis of my training was on collaboration and consultation with school personnel, families, and professionals working in community-based mental health. As a part of my studies I completed a 2,000-hour predoctoral internship at a large children's hospital. Following completion of my degree, I completed a 1,500-hour postdoctoral placement at a university-based psychology clinic and a reading/math clinic. I am a nationally certified school psychologist and a licensed psychologist at the state level. I receive continuing educational training via my involvement in two professional organizations, the National Association of School Psychologists and the American Psychological Association (Division 16: School Psychology).

Describe your prior experiences and the path you took to get to this career.

As a part of my training to become a doctoral-level school psychologist, I worked in numerous psychological service-delivery systems, including Head Start, K–12 schools, hospitals, and community-based mental health. The focus of my work has been to ensure equitable educational services to all children, especially those presenting with mental health and learning challenges. My interest in pursuing this career path began in high school when taking a psychology course. A requirement for that course was to complete a practicum experience within the community. My placement was within an early intervention

(continued)

(continued)

services program run by our county special educational entity. As an aide to the classroom teacher, I quickly found myself appreciating the interplay between learning, development, disabilities, and the educational environment. Those interests led to pursuit and completion of an undergraduate degree in child psychology and the professional goal to be a child psychologist. It was during my undergraduate studies that I learned about the field of school psychology. Following completion of advanced graduate studies, I was eligible for state and national certification as a school psychologist and also eligible to become a licensed psychologist. With those credentials, I am able to provide psychological services to school-age children, their families, and their teachers in schools and in the community. Being a licensed psychologist allowed me to engage in private practice, and I own a consultation business pertaining to child and adolescent mental health.

Describe the work that you do.

As a school psychologist, I work closely with parents and teachers of children diagnosed with or at risk for disabilities. Working as a part of an interdisciplinary team, I collaborate with others to develop educational supports and interventions (i.e., individualized education plans) that help children better access education and learning. My primary work is with those experiencing school challenges. However, mental health services for all students (i.e., primary prevention) are also a large part of the work done by a school psychologist.

What is a typical day like for you in this career?

A typical day is one filled with unexpected challenges. From intervening with children's depressive symptoms, to assessing suicidal thoughts, to addressing behavior management issues in the classroom, the typical day involves targeting the challenges related to mental health and learning for individual or small groups of children. Such involvement also requires a great deal of contact and consultation with parents and teachers. Finally, strict adherence to comprehensive

(continued)

(*continued*)

documentation such as notes for school files or formal psychological reports is an essential role of the work completed.

What is the most challenging part of your career?

No two problems or challenges are alike. Children, families, and teachers all tend to differ in their values and priorities. Rallying all parties involved in a child's life around the notion of improved school, peer, and family functioning, despite these personal differences, is a difficult part of the job. Keeping up with the thorough documentation required in this position is also difficult to maintain given the fast-paced nature of the work involved in being a school psychologist.

What is the most rewarding part of your career?

Helping others to realize that growth and development are clearly possible despite the presence of disabilities or challenges is the most rewarding part of this career. Being able to effectively communicate and gain the trust of individuals who have a long history of severe mental health problems is also a rewarding part of being a school psychologist. Assisting and supporting teachers and parents too is an incredible privilege associated with this position.

What advice do you have for someone in high school or currently at the undergraduate level who might be interested in this career?

The need and demand for bright and talented individuals to enter this profession is as great as ever. The number of position openings for school psychologists and the emphasis on mental health in schools have increased substantially since I graduated with my degree in the mid-1990s. We need talented professionals to enter our field, especially those who are interpersonally skilled, those with exceptional written language skills, and those with strong oral communication skills. In addition, a commitment to excellence and professional development typifies those who succeed in this career.

(*continued*)

(continued)

What advice do you have for someone currently in a different career/field who might be interested in your career?

The rewards associated with retraining to become a school psychologist are substantial even though full-time study within a graduate training program in school psychology is typically required.

If you decided to advance your career, what steps would you take and what career(s) might you seek out?

Many in the role of school psychologist contemplate becoming a supervisor of psychological services or they go on to receive additional special education administration/leadership training/education to become a special education director. Additionally, many psychologists who work in schools or communities engage in training and/or supervision of future school psychologists. Adjunct teaching or moving full time into a graduate training program in school psychology is also possible, especially for those trained at the doctoral level.

Both organizations provide links to all of the nationally approved and accredited programs across the country, making the search for a graduate program in school psychology very efficient.

56. SCHOOL SOCIAL WORKER

BASIC DESCRIPTION

School social workers are problem solvers who are focused on addressing challenges in students' lives. They are trained to address social and psychological factors that impede children's learning and functioning within the school setting. Examples of challenges to be addressed include aggressive behavior, bullying, and truancy. School social workers are integrally involved in the provision of special education services through social and emotional assessment (e.g., classroom observations, interpreting rating scales), consultation (e.g., parents, teachers), and intervention (e.g., family and child techniques). Making connections and developing relationships with children's caregivers are essential roles within this position. School social workers might engage in some or all levels of prevention, including primary prevention (e.g., teaching a bullying-prevention curriculum), secondary prevention (e.g., providing group interventions to those who have trouble managing their anger), and tertiary prevention (e.g., providing individual support to a student who is homeless).

CORE COMPETENCIES AND SKILLS NEEDED

The ability to work well under stressful situations and the ability to consistently demonstrate a high degree of empathy are required to work in this mental health profession. Analytical and critical thinking skills are needed given the complexity of issues facing children and families. Strong time-management skills and a high degree of self-awareness/management are necessary given the demanding and varied nature of the roles played during a typical day. Both oral and written communication skills are needed. Legal requirements pertaining to documentation and communication with others about assessment findings result in a strong need for exceptional skills in speaking and writing.

EDUCATIONAL REQUIREMENTS

An undergraduate degree in psychology, sociology, political science, anthropology, and child development are common for those who pursue careers in social work. In most states, an advanced graduate degree requiring 2 years of study (i.e., master of social work, or MSW) is required to work in the schools. Other states may only require a bachelor's degree in social work combined with a certain level of experience. A specialty certificate in school social work might also be necessary in some states.

EXPERIENCE NECESSARY

Given the important role that school social workers play in linking home, school, and community settings, it is essential to have prior experience providing social services in each of these contexts. In schools, the importance of working with teachers, administrators, and other school staff is essential, and prior practica or internship experience in providing school social work services is necessary.

CERTIFICATION, LICENSURE, AND CONTINUING EDUCATION REQUIREMENTS

Certification and licensure requirements to be a school social worker vary by state; therefore the Social Work License Map (www.socialworklicensemap.com) and the website of the Department of Education for the state in which you would like to work should be consulted. Supervised clinical experience following an advanced degree is often necessary for licensure.

SALARY/COMPENSATION

School social workers earn close to $55,000 per year, on average, based on data from the Bureau of Labor Statistics (2014b). Providing social work services in the schools appears to pay considerably higher than working in a community or hospital setting, where average salaries are closer to $40,000. School social worker salaries vary by district, community, and state. Years of experience and degree achieved will also influence the level of one's pay.

EMPLOYMENT OUTLOOK

There is a great demand for social workers across the country, especially in the area of geriatric care. The need for school social workers will grow substantially in the coming years given pending increases in student enrollment. Like many social service careers, federal, state, and local budgets will continue to influence the pay and demand for social work services.

FURTHER INFORMATION FOR EXPLORATION

For additional information about the field of school social work, explore resources from the School Social Work Association of America (www.sswaa .org) and the American Council for School Social Work (www.acssw.org).

57. SPEECH AND LANGUAGE PATHOLOGIST

BASIC DESCRIPTION

Speech and language pathologists assess, diagnosis, and treat communication disorders (e.g., stuttering). The primary focus of speech pathologists within the school setting is to help students be able to access and benefit from their educational programming. Examples of treatment include helping with articulation problems and teaching alternative communication techniques. Helping students to improve their reading, writing, receptive language, and expressive language are also important roles carried out by speech and language pathologists who work in the school setting. Working as a part of a multidisciplinary team is essential for both the special education diagnostic process and progress monitoring.

This means that frequent collaboration and communication with staff and parents are important to carrying out this work.

CORE COMPETENCIES AND SKILLS NEEDED

Listening and communication skills are especially needed in this profession. A high degree of knowledge pertaining to listening, speaking, reading, writing, and other academic performance is required. In addition, strong time-management and organizational skills are essential. Patience and compassion are especially important, as communication disorders can be frustrating and embarrassing to children who struggle with them. Being detail oriented and possessing exceptional written communication skills are very important given the intensive documentation required to both diagnose and treat individuals with speech and language challenges. This high level of record keeping is essential for being accountable and in compliance with special education law. Finally, providing culturally competent services is especially important given the diversity found within our nation's school systems.

EDUCATIONAL REQUIREMENTS

A master's degree in speech and language pathology is necessary to work within this career. Courses pertaining to special education services, schooling processes, communication disorders, and specialized services (e.g., assessment, consultation, intervention) used to address speech and language challenges across multiple settings are typically required when pursuing an advanced degree in this field. Many undergraduate degrees are represented in those within this career.

EXPERIENCE NECESSARY

As a part of graduate training, students will be required to complete an extensive array of practica and internship experiences. This clinical experience typically will cut across multiple service-delivery settings, in addition to schools.

CERTIFICATION, LICENSURE, AND CONTINUING EDUCATION REQUIREMENTS

Certification and licensure are required and vary by state. Licensure requires an advanced degree and a set number of supervised clinical hours. It may require that an individual graduate from an accredited training program. Be sure to consult the Department of Education certification website for the state in which you are considering practicing.

SALARY/COMPENSATION
The average salary for speech and language pathologists is close to $70,000, according to survey data within the field. The range of pay varies considerably by district, state, and geographic region. Years of experience and issues of supply/demand can also have a substantial influence on the salaries ($40,000 to $110,000) of those providing speech and language services in the schools.

EMPLOYMENT OUTLOOK
There has been great demand for well-trained speech and language pathologists for at least the past decade. This need is anticipated to continue through the near future, as increases in both school-age children and professionals nearing retirement will affect the profession.

FURTHER INFORMATION FOR EXPLORATION
Detailed information about this career and helpful resources can be found at the website of the American Speech-Language-Hearing Association (www.asha.org). In addition, most states have a professional organization dedicated to speech, language, and hearing that can be consulted through an Internet search.

58. GIFTED AND TALENTED COORDINATOR

BASIC DESCRIPTION
The primary responsibility of gifted and talented coordinators is to implement a school district's method for referral and identification of children who meet criteria for being gifted. Gifted identification plans lay out specific referral, testing, and, determination procedures. Once children are identified, coordinators work with other school staff to place gifted students in appropriate educational programs. They also must share the assessment results with parents and consult with them about programming. An individualized education program (IEP) for each child identified as gifted is developed in collaboration with school administrators and staff. Finally, when working with school personnel who are

providing gifted services, it is essential for the gifted and talented coordinator to implement progress monitoring and evaluation methodology. Oversight of extensive documentation is necessary, including generation, maintenance, and dissemination of yearly reports for each gifted student.

CORE COMPETENCIES AND SKILLS NEEDED
Expertise in working with gifted populations is needed. This includes a thorough understanding of effective instructional practices and evidence-based curriculum. The ability to collaborate and consult with both parents and teachers is essential for this position. Strong oral and written communication skills are required. In addition, excellent organizational and time-management skills are expected. The ability to adapt to frequent changes amid competing priorities within a school setting is essential for this position.

EDUCATIONAL REQUIREMENTS
A bachelor's degree in an education-related field is required, but preference will likely be given to those who have an advanced degree related to curriculum, exceptional students, or instructional design. In addition, prior experience as a gifted and talented teacher and clear evidence for leadership will be sought for this coordinator position.

EXPERIENCE NECESSARY
A background in teacher education, a history of teaching in the grade levels being served, and experience with educating groups of students from diverse backgrounds is important for those who will assume the coordinator position. Prior experience and education related to gifted populations and instruction are necessary.

CERTIFICATION, LICENSURE, AND CONTINUING EDUCATION REQUIREMENTS
A teaching certificate appropriate for the grade level being taught and special training in the area of gifted and talented services are required. Continuing education is expected, and consultation with other coordinators is essential for the purpose of continuous improvement of services.

SALARY/COMPENSATION
Salary for this coordinator position varies depending on the district and geographic region. Years of experience will also play a role, as the teacher

pay scale will typically apply to this position. The average salary for this position is between $40,000 and $50,000.

EMPLOYMENT OUTLOOK

The demand for gifted and talented coordinators will increase in the future due to expected enrollment increases. A recent focus on differentiated instruction within the classroom may mean a greater focus on consultation services within this position in the years ahead.

FURTHER INFORMATION FOR EXPLORATION

For additional information about becoming a specialist in the area of gifted education or a gifted and talented coordinator, visit the website of the National Association of Gifted Children, which offers helpful resources and guidance (www.nagc.org). In addition, be sure to seek out colleagues (e.g., coordinators, specialists) in the area of gifted education in nearby school districts to share knowledge, experience, and expertise.

59. EDUCATIONAL DIAGNOSTICIAN

BASIC DESCRIPTION

Educational diagnosticians in some states are referred to as teacher consultants, learning consultants, or learning disabilities teachers. The primary focus of this career is to promote children's successful learning within the school setting. This role involves engagement in assessment, consultation, and intervention services regarding student learning. Assessment services involve completion of psychoeducational batteries (e.g., initial, re-evaluations) to help better understand a child's learning problems. Interpretation and use of that data would occur within the context of a multidisciplinary team involving social workers, counselors, school psychologists, speech/language pathologists, teachers, administrators, special educators, and occupational/physical therapists. Collaborative decision making regarding educational programming would then be monitored for implementation and effectiveness by the educational diagnostician. Close communication and consultation with parents and school staff via case management are other important responsibilities of those in this position.

CORE COMPETENCIES AND SKILLS NEEDED

Core competencies related to diagnostic assessment, test interpretation, and experience with a diverse array of assessment tools are needed. Graduate coursework will likely involve learning theories, test interpretation, applied behavior analysis, instructional techniques, and standard test administration. Analytical skills and attention to detail are essential. Strong organizational and time-management skills are necessary given the multitude of assessments and consultations that one may be managing at a given time. Excellent communication skills are needed, and the ability to develop rapport with students is important for this role. Strengths in close working relationships and the ability to work as a team are also characteristics sought in those selected to be educational diagnosticians.

EDUCATIONAL REQUIREMENTS

A master's degree pertaining to learning disabilities, psychometry, or educational assessment is required. Educational requirements vary widely between states, so it is essential to look closely at the Department of Education website of the state in which you would like to work for additional guidance. Typically, 2 to 3 years of teaching experience is required to become an educational diagnostician.

EXPERIENCE NECESSARY

Practica and internship experiences associated with assessment, consultation, test interpretation, and data-based decision making will be an important part of advanced graduate education. A background in teaching is also necessary in a number of states. Prior work as a part of a special education team can also be helpful.

CERTIFICATION, LICENSURE, AND CONTINUING EDUCATION REQUIREMENTS

Certification and licensure of educational diagnosticians varies by state. It is essential that those in this profession are engaged in continuing education given the ever-changing nature of assessment instruments and technologies.

SALARY/COMPENSATION

Salary varies based on years of experience, location of the school district, and geographic location. Some school districts use administration pay scales, whereas others use teacher pay scales. Average salaries for educational diagnostician positions appearing on employment service websites are in the $40,000 to $60,000 range.

EMPLOYMENT OUTLOOK
The role of the educational diagnostician is likely to increase as the importance of accountability for special education services continues to increase.

FURTHER INFORMATION FOR EXPLORATION
Professional organizations related to learning disabilities, school psychology, or special education should be sought for additional information. Some states have professional associations dedicated to educational diagnosticians (e.g., www.txeda.org). In addition, looking closely at university graduate programs aimed at training educational diagnosticians will also provide those interested in this career with a better understanding of the educational requirements and experiences needed to work in this special education–related field.

REFERENCES
Bureau of Labor Statistics, U.S. Department of Labor. (2014a). *Occupational outlook handbook, 2014-2015 edition, Occupational Therapists.* Retrieved July 8, 2015, from http://www.bls.gov/ooh/healthcare/occupational-therapists.htm

Bureau of Labor Statistics, U.S. Department of Labor. (2014b). *Occupational outlook handbook, 2014-2015 edition, Social Workers.* Retrieved July 11, 2015, from http://www.bls.gov/ooh/community-and-social-service/social-workers.htm

IV ■ CAREERS IN SCHOOLS: SERVING GROUPS AND SYSTEMS

9 ■ CAREERS WORKING IN EDUCATIONAL ADMINISTRATION AND LEADERSHIP

60. PRESCHOOL DIRECTOR

BASIC DESCRIPTION

Preschool directors oversee the care and education of young children from birth to 5 years of age in preschool centers. They hire and train new personnel. They can work in either public or private facilities. Directors work closely with staff and teachers to coordinate daily activities. They supervise and evaluate early childhood teaching practices and support professional development within their centers. They work closely with parents and provide leadership in developing good practices in home–school communication. Developing budgets, setting tuition/fees, adhering to state regulations/guidelines, and overseeing operations may all be assumed under this administrative position. Directors may work in family-centered, community-centered, or nationally franchised facilities. Directors of Head Start programs are also responsible for ensuring that the program, policies, staff, and facilities meet both state and federal standards for comprehensive care and education of children who come from families that are financially challenged.

CORE COMPETENCIES AND SKILLS NEEDED

Effective leadership and management skills are needed for this position. The ability to develop professional relationships with both staff and parents is important. Strong oral and written communication skills are essential. One needs to be able to engage in efficient and effective problem solving given the challenges that arise when caring for young children. The ability to manage stressful situations is needed. Directors also should be effective teachers and care providers in those times when their staff members are ill or not able to make it to work.

EDUCATIONAL REQUIREMENTS

Preschool directors typically have a bachelor's or associate's degree in early childhood education. A master's degree may also be required in some states or by some programs. Some private programs within high-need areas might only require a high school diploma combined with extensive experience in working in preschool settings. Examples of the type of coursework that is necessary to embark on a career as a preschool director include child development, effective early childhood instructional and care practices, teacher preparation, center/facility management, and evaluation/assessment.

EXPERIENCE NECESSARY

Training and prior experience as an early childhood education teacher are necessary. Many years of experience in providing care to young children and working closely with other staff is important for this leadership position.

CERTIFICATION, LICENSURE, AND CONTINUING EDUCATION REQUIREMENTS

Preschool directors often hold the Child Development Association (CDA) national certificate or the National Administration Credential (NAC). Licensing and certification requirements vary by state.

SALARY/COMPENSATION

The median salary, according to the Bureau of Labor Statistics (2014), is just under $45,000.

EMPLOYMENT OUTLOOK

The need for preschool directors is strong given the increases in the preschool-age population and a trend in greater use of preschool/day-care settings.

FURTHER INFORMATION FOR EXPLORATION

For guidance and information pertaining to networking, training, program quality, and education related to the field of early childhood administration, please see the website of the Association for Early Learning Leaders (www.earlylearningleaders.org). The mission of this professional association is to ensure high-quality child-care administrators and programs.

61. MENTAL HEALTH COORDINATOR

BASIC DESCRIPTION

Mental health coordinators oversee care coordination services for those in need of mental health or special education services. They may or may not provide direct services to children and adults (i.e., clients). In many situations, mental health coordinators primarily supervise and provide oversight of the mental health staff. This position may be in schools, in communities, or within hospital settings. One example is found within Head Start programs. Head Start programs are federally mandated to provide mental health consultation services to enrolled children and their families/teachers. The coordinator overseeing that work hires, trains, and monitors the delivery of mental health consultation services within the Head Start programs and classrooms. This service delivery must adhere to national standards. Leadership in developing, implementing, and evaluating effective agency policies and evidence-based practices is required. Working as a mental health coordinator within a school context will require oversight of individualized education plans (IEPs) for students with disabilities and management of mental health staff members' engagement and effectiveness in working as a part of an interdisciplinary special education team.

CORE COMPETENCIES AND SKILLS NEEDED

Effective oral and written communication skills are essential. The ability to lead others and work effectively with other administrators within the service-delivery system is needed. In this position, it is important to be able to manage one's time effectively and to possess strong organizational skills. Core competencies related to mental health diagnoses and treatment are necessary. Strong interpersonal skills are especially important when working with parents and other team members. An understanding of the challenges faced by low-income families or those in transition is necessary. Collaborative consultation skills, coordination of service providers, development of meetings/trainings, and a focus on interdisciplinary care fit well with this leadership position.

EDUCATIONAL REQUIREMENTS

A master's degree in counseling, social work, or psychology is typically required. However, a bachelor's degree or an associate's degree in early childhood development, public health, public administration, or education, along with many years of experience, may be sufficient.

EXPERIENCE NECESSARY

Prior experience working with students with special needs and their families/care providers is necessary. A history of providing mental health services to children and families is especially important for moving into the leadership role associated with the coordinator position. Prior work with families experiencing discord or challenges can also be helpful to fully understand the importance of a child's context when trying to make improvements in his or her mental health functioning. A history of providing leadership to agencies, training in management, or developing mental health policies or procedures is important for those who seek this administrative position.

CERTIFICATION, LICENSURE, AND CONTINUING EDUCATION REQUIREMENTS

Certification or licensure within the field of study is required. This could include a licensed marriage and family therapist, a certified school psychologist, a licensed clinical psychologist, or a licensed clinical social worker.

SALARY/COMPENSATION

Salaries vary by geographic location. Years of experience, educational background, and possession of licensure/certification will all influence pay levels. Typical salaries for mental health coordinators usually range between $50,000 and $60,000.

EMPLOYMENT OUTLOOK

Social service managers will be in high demand in the years to come. Local, state, and federal budgets will certainly impact the level of growth within this career. Yet, the need for mental health services and a societal focus on early intervention will continue to influence this growth.

FURTHER INFORMATION FOR EXPLORATION

For additional information on the services provided within this administrative position for young populations, see www.ecmhc.org. For additional information about mental health services in adult populations, see www.nami.org. The National Association of State Mental Health Program Directors (www.nasmhpd.org) provides a number of valuable resources and links for those holding mental health service administrative positions.

Career-in-Education Profile
MENTAL HEALTH COORDINATOR

Interview With Marta Kermiet (BA, Elementary Education;
MA, Social Work; LMSW, ACSW)

Describe your educational background.

I completed a bachelor's degree in elementary education with a minor
in psychology. My career choice was ultimately shaped by volunteer
experiences in urban schools and a community center. One lasting
memory is of a teacher quietly reading aloud while children screamed
and jumped from desk to desk. Another was of driving two children
home after tutoring. When delivering them to the door, I saw into
the dark living room where adults slept as children tried to play (with
10 people occupying the two-bedroom house). I realized that I had a
strong desire to focus my career on the barriers to success in school.
I later took courses in human services management and grant writing.
After functioning as a Child Protection Team coordinator/pediatric
social worker, I obtained a master's degree in social work.

Describe your prior experiences and the path you took
to get to this career.

A common background seen in supervising early childhood consultants is one of child advocacy. In my case, it was seeing that kids
from our neighborhood were treated differently when bused to a more
affluent school district. My early experiences were in the area of child
abuse and neglect, and I was lucky to work directly with two pioneers
in the area of the newly defined "battered child syndrome." A job as
a child-care worker with abused/neglected infants and toddlers in a
residential institution was an eye opener. I challenged/changed the
practice of keeping children in cribs so much of the time. A stint at
the Crisis Nursery and parent hotline of the National Center for Prevention of Child Abuse and Neglect allowed me to sit in on a model
Child Protection Team's case conferences. After years in tertiary care
settings, I took a rather prevention-oriented job as a part-time early
childhood mental health (ECMH) consultant.

(continued)

(*continued*)

Describe the work that you do.

As the mental health coordinator for Head Start/Great Start, I plan and supervise the work of the ECMH consultants. I also offer supervision of direct assessment/therapeutic intervention sometimes necessary to link children to further services. The mental health coordinator (MHC) articulates and facilitates the agency plan to meet the Head Start "Performance" requirements regarding promotion of mental health in students, staff, and families. The MCH designs a system of data collection, analysis, and use about child and program needs/outcomes. A primary focus is on the hiring, orientation, supervision, and ongoing support of the ECMH coordinators. The MHC translates data and recommendations from her or his observations to the various internal leadership teams—administrators, site supervisors, Health Advisory group, and the Promoting Nurturing Environments advisory committee.

What is a typical day like for you in this career?

One perk of this job may be that there is no routine day. As barriers to a child's well-being and school success are found, much of the work is in building communication "teams" of adults to respond effectively. Gaps in services needed require meeting with community or local university partners to coordinate existing or build new service options for families. Creating training for staff in such topics as burnout prevention and programming to remediate impacts of trauma are part of the job.

What is the most challenging part of your career?

A challenge in this role is the increasing frequency of stressful/crisis-oriented experiences for families, children, and staff, which has led to more staff burnout. The exposure to second-hand trauma coupled with the attachment and empathy staff feel for children and families truly challenges them (and the consultants/supervisors) to find the value in what we are able to offer. The insufficient resources in social services, public schools, and mental health services often

(*continued*)

(*continued*)

leave us "holding the bag" after assessing a need when referrals are not accepted.

What is the most rewarding part of your career?

It is gratifying when you are able to pull together the puzzle pieces (information, resources) to help staff/parents see the bigger picture and guide a group to effective outcomes. When team members are able to process in a way that allows them to speak a similar language, validate one another's perspectives, and tap into their common goals, they successfully change outcomes for children who have, at age 3, already too many obstacles to overcome. To see a child blossom in spite of serious symptoms or trauma experienced continues to keep the mental health team returning each year.

What advice do you have for someone in high school or currently at the undergraduate level who might be interested in this career?

As is probably evident, this job requires a good bit of motivation, flexibility, and stamina. Judging by the consultants I have known, this often is as much a "calling" as a career choice. One should be aware that the pay range for Head Start is the same as that for most poverty programs—dependent on the federal budgets or fluctuating funds for prevention.

What advice do you have for someone currently in a different career/field who might be interested in your career?

Find mentors along the way who have become adept at speaking the many languages of early childhood education, special education, and mental health. Volunteering or working in a toddler/preschool setting will be most valuable as you learn from the teachers who have found the "tricks" to therapeutically and empathetically respond to the needs of these little people. Consider whether you will be satisfied in a role that is often one step removed from direct intervention.

(*continued*)

(continued)

If you decided to advance your career, what steps would you take and what career(s) might you seek out?

After 25 years in early childhood mental health consultation, I am looking for ways to disseminate Head Start data that better define the need for and the impact of early services. I hope to advocate locally and possibly at the state level in promoting the use of early childhood mental health consultants. I will look for ways to contribute to university-level curricula in social work, psychology, and special education.

62. HEAD START HEALTH MANAGER

BASIC DESCRIPTION

Head Start health managers provide administrative oversight and leadership to a group of Head Start staff and partners who plan, implement, and evaluate the health systems and services in Head Start and Early Head Start programs. These systems and services include a focus on children's health, mental health, dental health, safety, and nutrition. Individuals in this management position work to create systems, policies, protocols, monitoring, and technical assistance that ensure compliance with Head Start performance standards. Individuals in this leadership position work closely with the administrative team under the guidance and support of the Head Start director. It is one of a few positions in Head Start that is year round, as opposed to following the school year.

CORE COMPETENCIES AND SKILLS NEEDED

A thorough understanding and a prior history in effectively implementing the Head Start Performance Standards are needed. Specific content knowledge pertaining to health and nutrition is necessary. A thorough understanding of local, state, and federal health and nutrition regulations is important. Effective written and oral communication skills are very important for this position. The ability to work with professionals and families within a system of care that is continuously experiencing strains on resources requires a unique set of skills. Remaining calm when faced with stressful situations, using data to solve problems, and networking with other health managers are essential qualities for this position. Facilitating and leading staff success in obtaining positive health results for Head Start enrollees and their families are the primary functions of this position.

EDUCATIONAL REQUIREMENTS

Typically, a master's degree in health, public health, or administration is needed. Education related to early childhood education, child health, nursing, mental health, maternal health, nutrition, and health administration is required.

EXPERIENCE NECESSARY

Prior experience in health and nutrition administration is necessary. Effective teaming and a history of hiring staff or consultants who are well qualified (e.g., dietician, nutritionist, social worker, psychologist) to meet the needs of the Head Start health system are essential. Familiarity with and expertise in using technology to track health outcomes are important.

CERTIFICATION, LICENSURE, AND CONTINUING EDUCATION REQUIREMENTS

It is expected that individuals in this management position will be trained to meet national training standards in their field of study. The need to engage in continuous professional development regarding state/federal regulations and Head Start Performance Standards means that the health manager needs to be committed to continuous improvement.

SALARY/COMPENSATION

Salaries for administrative positions in Head Start typically range from $55,000 to $65,000. However, geographic region, years of experience, and degree/credentials (e.g., nurse, dietician) will certainly influence the range of salaries.

EMPLOYMENT OUTLOOK

the need for effective leadership personnel within a number of agencies providing health and mental health services will remain high in the years to come. many of those who currently hold administrative positions will be retiring in the near future. typically, those holding positions within the agency and those possessing additional management training are best positioned to be selected for these important management positions in head start.

FURTHER INFORMATION FOR EXPLORATION

The website of the National Head Start Association (www.nhsa.org) provides a number of resources and links to learn more about Head Start services and to explore employment opportunities within Head Start agencies. In addition, the website of the Health Resources and Services Administration (www.hrsa.gov) and the Association of Maternal and Child Health Programs (www.amchp.org/Pages/default.aspx) may be of particular interest to those seeking leadership positions in Head Start or other early childhood education settings.

63. DAY-CARE OWNER

BASIC DESCRIPTION

Day-care owners are responsible for the care, educational development, and well-being of young children. This care may occur within homes, community-based settings, or a commercial facility. This self-employed position requires close oversight of the daily operations of the day-care setting, including budgeting, marketing, and human resource management. As a small-business owner, hiring and training well-qualified day-care providers is an important part of this position. Making sure that all required certifications and licenses are obtained and maintained is essential. Meeting national or state accreditation standards (e.g., state preschool program standards) may also be an important responsibility of day-care owners. Maintaining close and effective communication with parents and staff members can help to promote a positive learning environment for the care of young children.

CORE COMPETENCIES AND SKILLS NEEDED

A high degree of competence across a diverse array of areas is necessary for this leadership position. One must have a keen mind for running a business (e.g., accounting, payroll, financial record keeping), in addition to a firm understanding of how to care for early childhood populations. This will require excellent time-management and organizational skills, along with prior knowledge, training, education, and experience in running a day-care center. Patience, problem-solving skills, and listening skills are important when working with families. In addition, a clear vision or mission for the business is needed, and a decisive approach to decision making is important within this leadership position.

EDUCATIONAL REQUIREMENTS
An associate's or bachelor's degree in early childhood education, child development, or preschool administration is typically required. Owners are also likely to have prior education in management or business operations. Graduate education (master's degree) might also be helpful given the multiple roles and responsibilities associated with this early childhood administrative position. Prior coursework may involve child psychology, classroom management techniques, nutrition, parenting, home–school communication, and first aid/safety.

EXPERIENCE NECESSARY
Prior experience providing day-care services or within the field of early childhood education is necessary. Working under the mentorship and guidance of a day-care owner or director can be especially helpful for those interested in pursuing this career.

CERTIFICATION, LICENSURE, AND CONTINUING EDUCATION REQUIREMENTS
Many states require day-care centers to meet clearly defined early childhood education standards. These include standards in the areas of health and safety. Professional development and continuing education are especially important given the changing knowledge base associated with the care of young children. A day-care owner might be interested in obtaining the Child Development Associate (CDA) credential or the Certified Childcare Professional (CCP) designation. A criminal background check, immunizations, cardiopulmonary resuscitation (CPR) training, and first aid certification are typically required of all those who work in a day-care center.

SALARY/COMPENSATION
Salaries will vary considerable based on the size of the day care, as owners will pay their salaries based on the profits from the business. In addition, geographic region and demand for child-care services may also influence pay for day-care owners. Typically, salaries have been reported to be about $40,000 to $45,000.

EMPLOYMENT OUTLOOK

Working families increasingly must turn to day-care providers. High-quality child care can have a positive influence on children's social and educational development. The demand for high-quality care is expected to lead to continued strong growth in the need for day-care owners.

FURTHER INFORMATION FOR EXPLORATION

For additional information about a career as a day-care owner, see the Association for Early Learning Leaders (www.earlylearningleaders.org), the National Association for Family Child Care (www.nafcc.org), or the National Child Care Association (www.nccanet.org). In addition, the National Association for the Education of Young Children (www.naeyc .org) provides a number of exceptional links to resources that may be helpful to day-care owners.

64. SCHOOL PRINCIPAL

BASIC DESCRIPTION

Principals provide leadership by example to the staff, students, and the parent community. They provide a vision for high expectations and improvement of the educational program. Most important, they establish a safe environment that is conducive to student learning, creativity, and academic performance. Principals oversee the development and evaluation of the curriculum. The principal reports to the superintendent or the assistant superintendent for leadership and learning.

CORE COMPETENCIES AND SKILLS NEEDED

Principals need to demonstrate effective speaking and writing skills in communicating with staff, students, and the school community. The position requires the ability to listen and evaluate input, and requires the integration of information in the decision-making process, which in many instances must occur with minimal time for reflection. A personal philosophy of relationship building is crucial in that how a decision is communicated often is as important as the actual message. Other competencies include knowledge of and demonstrated leadership in educational standards, the ability to effectively communicate with the school community, and administration of all school activities. Principals must also be skilled at developing and administering the annual school-building budget. Coordinating and overseeing the employment, supervision, and evaluation of school personnel requires skills in human resource management.

EDUCATIONAL REQUIREMENTS
The position requires an advanced degree or evidence of working toward an advanced degree in educational administration.

EXPERIENCE NECESSARY
A principal must have a minimum of 3 years of teaching experience, demonstrated involvement and leadership in extra- or cocurricular activities, and demonstrated involvement in community activities. Prior experience working as a part of a team and involvement in support roles in school administration are helpful for those seeking this position.

CERTIFICATION, LICENSURE, AND CONTINUING EDUCATION REQUIREMENTS
Principals should be prepared to provide a portfolio reflecting appropriate certification, evidence of licensure for the position, and a plan showing either what has been done in continuing education or what continuing education the individual is planning on completing within the next 5 years.

SALARY/COMPENSATION
Compensation will vary from district to district, and most boards of education are willing to provide an attractive compensation plan to attract someone who they feel will provide the desired educational leadership. Boards of education will look to meet or exceed the comparable salaries of like-sized districts. There may be some flexibility in what a district will provide regarding fringe benefits. Most principal contracts are 12-month contracts, and salaries are typically in the $75,000 to $85,000 range but vary by geographic location and years of experience. Salary and fringe-benefit information is updated annually for all districts, and seeking this information out on the State Department of Public Instruction website is recommended.

EMPLOYMENT OUTLOOK
The employment outlook is very positive, as there is continued turnover caused by retirement and promotions. In many cases individuals aspiring

to the position of principal will have to move and relocate. In some of the larger districts, individuals desiring to pursue a position as principal may have the opportunity for an in-district promotion.

FURTHER INFORMATION FOR EXPLORATION

Prospective candidates should become familiar with activities sponsored by professional organizations such as the National Association of Secondary School Principals (www.principals.org). In addition, state association websites should be consulted, such as the website of the Association of Wisconsin School Administrators (www.awsa.org), which offers information relating to workshops, regional and state conferences, continuing education information, and other information that may be helpful in preparing oneself to be a principal.

65.   AFTER-SCHOOL COORDINATOR

BASIC DESCRIPTION

An after-school coordinator oversees the academic programs and enrichment activities provided after the regular school day is over. This position may also include programming prior to the start of the school day. The position may be in either a school- or community-based setting. This coordinator position involves managing staff, facilitating student enrollment, and ensuring the overall well-being of students being served. It is essential to work closely with the school administration and community agency partners within this leadership role. Responsibility for developing a program budget and managing the finances of the program may be expected. In some locations, grant writing may be a part of this position. Record keeping is a substantial responsibility within this position. Activity documentation, personnel files, and evidence of meeting mandated program requirements are examples of this record keeping. Managing staff training and parent meetings highlights the adult-focused nature of the after-school coordinator position.

CORE COMPETENCIES AND SKILLS NEEDED

Strong interpersonal skills are needed. The ability to work with a diverse array of individuals and groups is essential. Establishing and maintaining professional relationships with staff and parents are important. Strong organizational skills and effective time management are two qualities that are important to bring to an after-school coordinator position. Evidence of well-developed administrative and supervisory skills should be in place.

EDUCATIONAL REQUIREMENTS
A background in youth development, education, or community development is required. A bachelor's or master's degree is preferred. Prior coursework in effective classroom management, child development, adolescent mental health, recreation therapy, personnel development, or youth development is expected.

EXPERIENCE NECESSARY
Previous success in working in an after-school program and providing leadership in implementing activities with youth is necessary. Working as a part of a team and the ability to relate to youth are important. Prior work engaged in administration (i.e., supervisory role) of school activities or community-based programs would be helpful for this position.

CERTIFICATION, LICENSURE, AND CONTINUING EDUCATION REQUIREMENTS
As with most school employees, a background check (fingerprinting), a tuberculosis (TB) test, and cardiopulmonary resuscitation (CPR)/first aid training are required. The ability to engage in continuous program improvement, develop innovate programming, and refine staff management practices is required.

SALARY/COMPENSATION
In many cases, especially in smaller cities, this position is paid on an hourly basis and benefits may not be included. The pay range may span from $15 to $20 per hour. Geographic location and years of experience may influence pay. In some larger communities, this may be a full-time salaried position and the pay range may begin in the low $20,000 range and extend up to $60,000, according to position postings found on the web.

EMPLOYMENT OUTLOOK
The need for after school-care has grown substantially given the time constraints of working families. The demand for high-quality, after-school directors is anticipated to increase in the years to come.

FURTHER INFORMATION FOR EXPLORATION

For further exploration of a career as an after-school coordinator, see the website of the National AfterSchool Association (www.naaweb.org). For ideas about different activities to feature in after-school care, see www .kidactivities.net.

66. SUPERINTENDENT OF SCHOOLS

BASIC DESCRIPTION

The superintendent of schools strives to achieve school district goals by providing educational leadership and supervision to the professional staff and the support staff and by acting as a role model for staff and students. Superintendents oversee all aspects of the district's mission, objectives, and initiatives. Together with school board members, the superintendent is in charge of all aspects of the educational system within that community. Ultimately, the superintendent is accountable for the short- and long-term financial health of a district.

CORE COMPETENCIES AND SKILLS NEEDED

The core competencies and skills essential for success as a school superintendent include a personal philosophy of servant leadership, the ability to communicate effectively in writing and speaking, an understanding of the importance of relationship building, and a demonstrated ability in establishing an environment conducive to collaboration, creativity, motivation, and lifelong learning. It is also critical for a superintendent of schools to quickly understand the culture of the school district and to have a sense of some of the critical educational issues that the specific community has experienced. This can be done by visiting the community, by exploring the stability of the board of education leadership and membership, and by reviewing published minutes of past board meetings.

EDUCATIONAL REQUIREMENTS

Educational requirements include having previously met the qualifications of a teacher educator. A license to teach at either the elementary or secondary level is commonly expected. In addition, a state-issued administrator's license is required. Typically, it is expected that an applicant will be able to provide evidence of working toward or having completed a doctoral degree (PhD, EdD) in educational administration, educational leadership, or an equivalent course of study.

EXPERIENCE NECESSARY

Necessary experience includes 3 or more years of teaching; building-level and/or district-wide program leadership; and involvement or experience in any areas of school program leadership, such as finance, personnel, curriculum, transportation, food service, supervision of extracurricular activities, organization/development of referendum projects; as well as evidence of a superintendent license issued by the respective State Department of Education. Additional experience is needed in negotiating contracts, understanding and having experience with school crisis plans, and having the ability and/or experience in dealing with the public relations aspect of the position (e.g., television, radio, or newspaper requests).

CERTIFICATION, LICENSURE, AND CONTINUING EDUCATION REQUIREMENTS

The following are generally required for any superintendent of schools position: (a) a minimum of 3 years of public school teaching experience; (b) a master's degree plus at least 30 additional hours of graduate credit (not less than 30 semester hours of graduate credit shall have been in administration, supervision, and related fields); (c) graduate credits and courses in school administration, supervision, and school business administration and in at least three of the following areas: curriculum, problems or trends in education, measurements, psychology, guidance, and school finance and school law; and (d) evidence of continuing education.

SALARY/COMPENSATION

Compensation is influenced by the size of the district and the educational experience one brings to the position. Typically, superintendents are the highest paid educator in the district. Salary ranges vary considerably. Median salary for this career in education is just under $150,000. It is important to examine the school district's size and numbers when thinking about salary. Generally, a prospective candidate can expect to receive a salary equal to or more than that of the individual who is being replaced. In addition to a salary, school districts also offer other amenities and benefits (e.g., car expenses, support for additional education, life insurance, tax-deferred annuities, additional vacation, moving expenses).

217

Compensation information for each district is published annually on the respective State Department of Education's website.

EMPLOYMENT OUTLOOK

The outlook for a career as a superintendent of schools is excellent. One has to realize that the position is a chief executive officer (CEO) position that is directly responsible and responsive to the board of directors, which is the respective Board of Education. Many superintendents are able to reconcile their personal educational objectives and leadership styles to fit the expectations of the culture of the community and the respective Boards of Education and enjoy long-term employment. However, the average length of employment for a school superintendent in Wisconsin's 425 school districts is approximately 3 years. Thus, there is a high turnover in this field, much of it related to the inability of superintendents to adapt to the culture of their respective districts.

FURTHER INFORMATION FOR EXPLORATION

For additional information about a career as a school superintendent, see the websites of the School Superintendents Association (www.aasa.org) and the National School Boards Association. State-level resources are also important to explore (e.g., Wisconsin Association of School District Administrators, www.wasda.org).

Career-in-Education Profile
SUPERINTENDENT OF SCHOOLS

Interview With Richard L. Carlson (BS, Economics; BS, Broad Field Social Studies; MA, Counseling)

Describe your educational background.

I majored in economics, with a minor in geography/sociology. To earn my teacher certificate/license, I returned to school to complete the state credentialing requirements, which was augmented with coursework related to certification in driver education and school administration.

Describe your prior experiences and the path you took to get to this career.

The path started from my interests and involvement in activities during my early adolescent, high school, and college experiences. These included experiences such as working with children teaching Sunday school, serving as a playground director, and being a coach/advisor of several different youth activities. When I graduated from college, I took a sales position. Although the compensation was good, after about a year, I was second-guessing my career decision. I decided I wanted to pursue a career in education, which meant that I needed to return to school and obtain my teaching certification. After 3 years of teaching I took advantage of an opportunity to use some of my undergraduate work in the area of business. I was offered and accepted a position as an assistant business manager for the school district where I was working. Although I enjoyed that experience, it convinced me that I needed to pursue my interests in counseling and school administration. Fortunately, I was able to complete the necessary coursework while still employed in that position. That advanced degree afforded me the opportunity to pursue my interests in school administration.

Describe the work that you do.

My primary responsibility is to the Board of Education to ensure that I carry out the established board policies and procedures. Areas include:

(continued)

(*continued*)

- Ensuring that all students are provided maximum opportunities commensurate with their abilities
- Developing and executing the annual school district budget
- Ensuring that the adopted K–12 curriculum is implemented and evaluated
- Hiring all staff, including aides, bus drivers, custodians, teachers, building principals, and administrative assistants
- Being responsible for all school district communications and public relations initiatives
- Serving as legal counsel with professional assistance for the Board of Education
- Managing all school programs and ancillary services

What is a typical day like for you in this career?

A myriad of unanticipated issues arise in the role of superintendent. They can include personnel conflicts; concerned parents; student discipline issues; bomb scares; injuries or deaths; fire alarms; power, water, or other service issues; or weather-related issues. It is important to have regular contact with the school board president to establish a consistent, open communication channel. My daily schedule involves visits to buildings, participation in classroom activities, meetings involving volunteer work with community agencies and service clubs, and attendance at school-related activities during and after the school day. Visibility to your constituents is critical to success as a school district leader.

What is the most challenging part of your career?

Specific challenges may include the need to develop a network of resources. In addition, the high-stakes nature of personnel selection can be difficult. Creating an environment of trust, respect, and confidence is essential.

What is the most rewarding part of your career?

There are numerous rewards that I have realized from my role as a superintendent. Some of the most profound from my perspective

(*continued*)

(continued)

include comments from students who return to the community who state that they had been well prepared for post–high school education and the world of work. A high degree of mutual respect and a compatible working relationship with represented employee groups also is rewarding. Helping to support capable associates in moving their careers forward is a wonderful aspect of the position.

What advice do you have for someone in high school or currently at the undergraduate level who might be interested in this career?

I would suggest a self-assessment in terms of some of the critical components needed for the position. The position is about relationships and serving others. It also requires the following:

- Strong people skills and the ability to communicate verbally and in writing
- A passion for working with not only students but with all types of individuals
- A well-rounded education and a commitment to obtain as many different experiences as possible
- Experience being in the role of a classroom teacher
- Recognition and understanding that the position is very political in nature
- Conflict resolution skills
- Strong organizational skills
- An understanding that you answer to and are responsible to the Board of Education
- A realization that you are involved in a lifetime of continuing education

If you make a commitment to the career as a professional educator, compensation will take care of itself, as personal satisfaction and enjoyment in what you are doing will ultimately overshadow everything else.

(continued)

(continued)

What advice do you have for someone currently in a different career/field who might be interested in your career?

Make plans to change as soon as you can. One piece of advice is that once you make a decision to change careers, do not lament on what might have been. Stay positive and keep your focus on the future.

If you decided to advance your career, what steps would you take and what career(s) might you seek out?

I had the experience of trying something else, realized that my interests were in the educational profession, and was fortunate enough to be able to redirect my career. In retrospect I would not change a thing. Finally, let me provide a few thoughts for those interested in advancing their career in education, or in any field, for that matter. Remember to be true to yourself and follow your passionate interests. Also, be sure to take advantage of opportunities, even though they may require a move, a salary reduction, or other initial negative aspects. Be sure to continue your education and take advantage of every experience that you can, as somewhere in the future it will be advantageous to you. Finally, don't burn any bridges, as you do not know what the future may hold, and be sure to move on from disappointments and focus on the positives.

67. DIRECTOR OF SPECIAL SERVICES

BASIC DESCRIPTION

The director of special services (assistant superintendent) is responsible for personnel, programs, and services for students to ensure the program's compliance with district, state, and federal guidelines. This would include but is not limited to at-risk and alternative school options, students with limited English proficiency, speech and language support, students with disabilities, custodial and residency issues, open enrollment information, homebound instruction, expulsion procedures, and grant initiatives to support any or all of those activities.

CORE COMPETENCIES AND SKILLS NEEDED

The position requires knowledge and some experience in any or all of the special services disciplines, organizational skills, and the ability to plan and facilitate all aspects of the program areas. Situations faced will require effective interpersonal communication skills, the integration of information in assessing specific needs, and the ability to make decisions and recommendations based on input and data related to a specific situation.

EDUCATIONAL REQUIREMENTS

An advanced degree in educational administration with an emphasis on one or more of the specific special services areas is required.

EXPERIENCE NECESSARY

Experience should include a minimum of 3 years of teaching experience in a K–12 special services area. Other experiences, work related or volunteer, in any of the areas under the special services umbrella would augment a candidate's résumé.

CERTIFICATION, LICENSURE, AND CONTINUING EDUCATION REQUIREMENTS

Appropriate certification/licensure as a director of special education services or evidence of the ability to obtain the appropriate licensure is required. The license renewal would be contingent upon continuing education.

SALARY/COMPENSATION

Compensation varies considerably from district to district. Salaries, including fringe benefits and salaries for other duties that may be assigned to this position, range from $60,000 to $135,000, with some outliers on either end of the spectrum.

EMPLOYMENT OUTLOOK

The outlook for professionals seeking to enter the field is outstanding. State and federal requirements dictate that school districts provide specific services for special needs students. Many districts have an enrollment sufficient to support a director of special services, whereas smaller districts may select options to contract specific services for some or all of their services with a state-supported cooperative education service agency or other certified health providers at the local or regional level.

FURTHER INFORMATION FOR EXPLORATION

Information related to special education legal and federal mandates is available on the respective State Departments of Public Instruction special education website. This would include information on state statutes, as well as information on federal statutes such as the Individuals with Disabilities Education Act (IDEA) of 2004 and the No Child Left Behind Act. For Wisconsin, the website is the Wisconsin Council of Administrators of Special Services (www.wcass.org), which includes information relative to the mission of the organization, state conferences, regional professional development opportunities, resources, legislative agendas, and affiliate information.

68. DIRECTOR OF CURRICULUM/INSTRUCTIONAL SERVICES

BASIC DESCRIPTION

The director of curriculum/instructional services (assistant superintendent) is responsible for providing leadership to administration and faculty related to the development and implementation of curriculum, instruction, and assessment. Some of the program areas that typically fall within the responsibilities of an individual in this position include the gifted and talented program, the library media program, and the district's summer school program. An important role to play in this position is to promote the building principal as an instructional leader. The director also assists the K–12 department chairs in providing and coordinating curriculum leadership and instruction. Finally, the director must effectively communicate with the public regarding pre-K–12 assessment, accountability, educational reform and restructuring, school improvement, and related educational initiatives.

CORE COMPETENCIES AND SKILLS NEEDED

Numerous competencies and skills will contribute to being an effective instructional leader. Understanding the importance of relationships, being receptive to input, and being able to reach consensus on issues are essential competencies needed within this position. Specific expertise in research-based "best practices" in one or more of the core content areas (reading, language arts, mathematics, science, and social studies) is important. Demonstrated expertise in curriculum design, development, and implementation is necessary. Specific knowledge of contemporary policies, evidence-based assessment practices, data analysis, data-based decision making, and school improvement is required in this leadership position. Finally, demonstrated expertise in the strategies, processes, implementation, and facilitation of educator professional development must be provided.

EDUCATIONAL REQUIREMENTS
The requirements are licensure as a classroom teacher and a master's degree in educational administration.

EXPERIENCE NECESSARY
The director of curriculum/instructional services should have a minimum of 3 years of successful teaching experience, preferably in one of the core content areas. In addition, some administrative experience or program leadership experience is preferred.

CERTIFICATION, LICENSURE, AND CONTINUING EDUCATION REQUIREMENTS
The position requirements consist of a master's degree in educational administration with certification as a director of instruction and curriculum, or evidence of progress to obtain such certification. The license renewal is contingent upon meeting continuing education requirements.

SALARY/COMPENSATION
Salary varies from district to district based on the responsibilities assigned to the position. For example, total compensation for most of the 424 districts in Wisconsin ranges from $65,000 to $145,000, with some outliers on either end based on the size of the district and other areas of responsibility assigned to the position.

EMPLOYMENT OUTLOOK
The employment outlook is excellent in this field, as school districts are continually striving to focus on student achievement by updating, revising, and evaluating curricula, and responding to state and federal curricular recommendations.

FURTHER INFORMATION FOR EXPLORATION

Most states have a statewide organization that focuses on the broad area of curriculum. For example, in Wisconsin it is the Association of School Curriculum Directors (www.wascd.org). The website of the equivalent national organization, the Association of Supervision and Curriculum Development (www.ascd.org), also should be explored. These websites will provide a broad overview of issues, initiatives, membership information, state/national conference information, regional professional development opportunities, and other information that is helpful in assisting individuals interested in this specific career.

69. COLLEGE/UNIVERSITY DEAN

BASIC DESCRIPTION

College/university deans provide leadership to specific academic units or collections of departments (e.g., college of education, college of medicine). Deans are responsible for the academic, personnel, financial, and administrative affairs of the college. They approve all faculty hiring, evaluate faculty performance and promotion decisions, and work with faculty to create academic policies. A college dean is one of many higher education administrators (e.g., dean of students, provost, president) who help to lead and manage the university. College deans work closely with central administration and work to represent the views of their college faculty. Additionally, fund-raising and networking with alumni are major responsibilities of college deans, especially at private universities and, more recently, in public universities, where state funding has dwindled considerably.

CORE COMPETENCIES AND SKILLS NEEDED

The ability to lead others is essential. Confidence, an effective leadership style, determination, and a high degree of motivation are needed to be successful in this management position. The ability to work effectively as a member of the university administration team is important. Having strong interpersonal skills is central to this position given the multitude of relationships (e.g., with other administrators, faculty, donors, students) associated with the roles and responsibilities of a college dean. A strong grasp of contemporary issues in higher education and an accurate perception of the strengths and weaknesses of college faculty and procedures are needed.

EDUCATIONAL REQUIREMENTS
A doctoral degree in higher education is typically required. However, many college deans have doctoral degrees in other areas along with years of experience serving in administrative roles within the university setting. Coursework or training in higher education administration/ leadership, student affairs, school finance, educational policy, and politics in education is expected.

EXPERIENCE NECESSARY
Prior success within a university faculty position is expected. In addition, a track record of leadership and success in administrative positions (i.e., program director, department chair, associate dean) is necessary.

CERTIFICATION, LICENSURE, AND CONTINUING EDUCATION REQUIREMENTS
College deans typically are certified or licensed at the highest level nationally within their respective fields. Continuing education pertaining to higher education administration is essential for this position.

SALARY/COMPENSATION
Salaries vary by institution and geographic region. Most college deans make at least $100,000, with some requiring salaries as high as $250,000.

EMPLOYMENT OUTLOOK
The outlook for university administrators is strong due to pending retirements, mobility resulting from a high demand for effective leaders in university settings, and the fact that not all hired deans are effective within the position.

FURTHER INFORMATION FOR EXPLORATION
For additional information about contemporary issues within higher education, see *The Chronicle of Higher Education* publication or website (www.chronicle.com). There are also a number of professional associations aimed at supporting those in higher education administrative positions, including the Association of Deans & Directors of University Colleges and Undergraduate Studies (www.adandd.org) and the American Association of University Administrators (www. aaua.org).

70. WRITING CENTER DIRECTOR

BASIC DESCRIPTION

Writing centers are set up to assist undergraduate and graduate students to be more effective writers. The primary goal of writing centers is to help students to express their ideas clearly through written products. Linking writing, literacy, and teaching practices is another common goal of writing centers on university campuses. A writing center director within a university setting oversees all operations of the center. This includes hiring and training undergraduate or graduate writing tutors/consultants, supervising staff members, creating policies and procedures, and documenting the effectiveness of the writing center efforts. Teaching writing courses to first-year undergraduate students may also be involved. Outreach to faculty and advertising to student groups are important aspects of this position. In addition, the director oversees the development and implementation of writing workshops to be held in the center or across campus. This position may be associated with the university library or housed within student support services/academic affairs.

CORE COMPETENCIES AND SKILLS NEEDED

Core competencies in literacy and composition are important. Evidence of effective writing and, more important, being able to teach writing are essential. Training in evaluation and assessment is important. Strong organizational skills, the ability to prioritize tasks, and good time management will be needed within this fast-paced career on a college campus. A director should have strong interpersonal skills and the demonstrated ability to work as a part of a team. Respect for the diversity of writing expertise that is typical within undergraduate student populations and a great deal of patience will be important. A passion for supporting and facilitating students' success in writing can be very helpful within this role. Understanding how to link technology to improvements in writing also can be helpful. This may include prior training in a learning management system, a tutor scheduling system, or computer applications focused on improving writing.

EDUCATIONAL REQUIREMENTS

A master's degree (fine arts in writing) or doctoral degree in education, English, literacy, composition, or a related field is required. Coursework may include adult development, best practices in tutoring, writing instruction, and discipline-specific courses that link closely to common majors within the university (e.g., psychology, education).

EXPERIENCE NECESSARY

Prior experience working in a writing center or teaching composition courses is necessary. Evidence of increasing responsibilities or engagement in a supervisory role within a tutoring program, writing center, or some other aspect of student support services will be helpful preparation for this management position.

CERTIFICATION, LICENSURE, AND CONTINUING EDUCATION REQUIREMENTS

A commitment to professional development and continuous improvement is important for writing center directors. Involvement in professional organizations and networking with other directors on campus or at other campuses can be especially helpful for staying abreast of the latest knowledge and practices.

SALARY/COMPENSATION

Salary ranges vary widely depending on the nature of the position and the location. A review of position openings indicates a range from $30,000 to $70,000. In some cases, it appears that graduate students may be hired to serve as writing center directors. In those situations, the position may be part time and the pay considerably lower.

EMPLOYMENT OUTLOOK

Undergraduate writing skills have been noted as being especially problematic within some universities. Combined with an increase in the number of students entering formal postsecondary education programs, a substantial demand exists for the services provided by college campus writing centers.

FURTHER INFORMATION FOR EXPLORATION

For further information needed to explore a potential career as a writing center director, see the website of the International Writing Centers Association (www.writingcenters.org). In addition, most universities have a specific web page for the writing center (e.g., writing.msu.edu) where helpful resources and information can be found.

71. DIRECTOR OF ADMISSIONS

BASIC DESCRIPTION

The primary role of the director of admissions is to recruit students through management of the admissions process, staff, policies, and practices. Working closely with university administrators, alumni, and donors is likely to be an important part of this position. Providing oversight of all aspects of the admissions process, including selecting scholarship recipients, is necessary. Supervision and training of a multidimensional admissions team (associate director, assistant directors, admissions counselors, recruiters) will be required. Working with a variety of university committees across campus is expected. Typically, the director of admissions will work under the guidance of the vice president for academic affairs.

CORE COMPETENCIES AND SKILLS NEEDED

Strong interpersonal and managerial skills are necessary. The ability to interact with colleagues, students, and parents is important for this position. Organizational and problem-solving skills are especially important for this position given the need for extensive record keeping and the need to evaluate the activities of members of the admissions team. Skills in developing and managing the admissions office budget are expected. Strong written and oral communication skills are needed.

EDUCATIONAL REQUIREMENTS

A master's or doctoral degree in higher education administration, student affairs, communications, business, marketing, or a related field is typically required. However, a bachelor's degree combined with knowledge, competence, and experience in admissions or enrollment management may be sufficient.

EXPERIENCE NECESSARY

Prior experience in a management position is important, preferably within the registrar's office or within student affairs. A history of working within the leadership team of an academic dean would also be highly sought for those who will be likely to succeed in this management position. A background of extensive training or professional development with undergraduate or graduate student groups may also position one to work well within this admissions position. Prior experience as an assistant or associate director of admissions would be most ideal prior to assuming the director position.

CERTIFICATION, LICENSURE, AND CONTINUING EDUCATION REQUIREMENTS

Certification and licensure requirements consistent with the background or training of the admissions director are expected. Membership in a professional association or a state-level organization devoted to contemporary issues in college admissions would typically be required. A focus on continuous improvement and engagement in professional development is expected. This will involve attending national conventions and conferences to maintain knowledge of best practices in recruiting and admissions.

SALARY/COMPENSATION

Salaries for admissions directors vary considerably based on type and size of institution. Typically, those in this leadership position within universities will make between $85,000 and $100,000.

EMPLOYMENT OUTLOOK

The employment outlook for university administrators is projected to grow in the coming years. Projected retirements and expected increases in college enrollment will lead to growth within this career in education.

FURTHER INFORMATION FOR EXPLORATION

For additional information about a career in university admissions, see the websites of the National Association for College Admission Counseling (www.nacacnet.org) and the American Association of Collegiate Registrars and Admissions Offices (www.aacrao.org).

72. UNIVERSITY ATHLETIC DIRECTOR

BASIC DESCRIPTION

University athletic directors oversee and administer all aspects of the collegiate athletic program. This includes hiring, managing, and evaluating (i.e., team goals, player/team achievements, player academic performance) the coaching staff and other members of the athletic department staff.

Oversight of facility use and management, along with coordination of team transportation and travel, is required. Overseeing the management of the athletic department budget is an especially important responsibility of this career. The size and scope of that budget will largely influence the variety of responsibilities that can be seen in this position when comparing universities. For example, assistant or associate athletic directors might take on many administrative roles and responsibilities at larger universities. Fund-raising activities and serving as the face of the athletic program to the institution and the media are especially important parts of this position. In larger universities, athletic directors often work closely or in collaboration with the university president to address the mission and goals associated with student athletes. They also will serve as a representative of the university to the national association governing their athletic program/conference.

CORE COMPETENCIES AND SKILLS NEEDED
Extensive knowledge in management, college athletics, and human resources is needed. Strong oral communication skills are essential when working with the public and the media. A thorough understanding of the rules and regulations surrounding athlete recruitment, retention, and graduation is essential.

EDUCATIONAL REQUIREMENTS
A master's degree in physical education, educational administration, sports management, or a related field is typically required. At a smaller university, a bachelor's degree combined with many years of experience in working within an athletic department may be sufficient.

EXPERIENCE NECESSARY
Most athletic directors have prior experience as a coach and/or student athlete. A history of managing athletic budgets and athletic program procedures/policies is ideal.

CERTIFICATION, LICENSURE, AND CONTINUING EDUCATION REQUIREMENTS
Consistent with a background as a coach, some athletic directors may maintain their coaching credentials. Professional development through involvement in a professional organization or via networking with colleagues at peer institutions is important.

SALARY/COMPENSATION

University athletic directors typically make close to $100,000. However, salary will certainly depend on the size and nature of the university. Additional compensation might also be provided (e.g., car allowance, conference travel allowance, professional membership fees).

EMPLOYMENT OUTLOOK

The employment outlook for those working within collegiate athletics and specifically those interested in athletics management is strong. This demand is the result of an increase in the growth of athletic teams, largely the result of an influx of money into college athletics from television rights and gate receipts (e.g., basketball, football).

FURTHER INFORMATION FOR EXPLORATION

For additional information about a career as a university athletic director, see the National Association of Collegiate Directors of Athletics (www.nacda.com), the National Association of Collegiate Women Athletics Administrators (www.nacwaa.org), the National Interscholastic Athletic Administrators Association (www.niaaa.org), or the 1A Athletic Directors Association (www.d-1a.com). Specific conference websites might also be helpful when considering the scope of work involved in being a university athletic director (e.g., www.naia.org, www.ncaa.org, www.bigten.org).

Career-in-Education Profile
UNIVERSITY ATHLETIC DIRECTOR
Interview With Don Maslinski (BA, French; MS, Education Leadership and Supervision)

Describe your educational background.

I graduated from a college preparatory high school in a large urban city. At a small private college, I received certification as a secondary teacher in French and language arts. After about 20 years of teaching, I returned to graduate school at one of our state's public universities to pursue my master's degree in administration so that I could become certified to be a high school principal.

Describe your prior experiences and the path you took to get to this career.

I spent 27 years as a high school teacher on a full-time and part-time basis. During that time I was the head baseball coach and an assistant football coach at the varsity level. My part-time teaching experience ran concurrently to my work as an athletic director/activities director and lasted for 15 years until I was appointed principal for the high school for 7 years. At the end of my principal position, I began my career as a college director of athletics at the same college where I completed my undergraduate studies. I worked in that role for 6 years when I stepped down to become the director of fund-raising for athletics, a position I continue in to this day.

Describe the work that you did.

First and foremost, I had to make sure our athletic program followed our institutional philosophy and mission statement while operating within the parameters of the National Collegiate Athletic Association (NCAA). I was responsible for building our department budget and making sure that all of our programs operated under budget. I was responsible for supervising and evaluating 70 to 80 coaches, some

(continued)

(*continued*)

part time; two athletic trainers; a sports information director; a business manager; secretarial staff; and many student part-time workers. I was responsible for recruitment and hiring of the best possible staff. I built playing schedules for 20 teams. I arranged for all facets of team travel, to include busing, lodging, and meals. I hired officials for all contests. I scheduled workers for all events. I was responsible for public relations, promoting attendance at all events, and maintaining solid relationships with members of the working media. I acted as the athletic department liaison with our faculty. I served on the Dean's Council, an advisory group to the academic dean of the college. I was responsible for the Student Advisory Council (SAC) composition and activities.

I had primary responsibility for the college's adherence to the provisions of Title IX, the legislation that ensures that women have equal opportunities and support in intercollegiate athletics. I was responsible for determining the eligibility of all of our athletes. I had to provide appropriate facilities in which our athletes could train and compete. In short, a college director of athletics needs to be the "face" of the program.

What was a typical day like for you in this career?

There is no such thing as a typical day in the life of an athletic director, and that is what makes the position so intriguing and challenging. For the most part, an athletic director spends a good deal of time as a problem solver. Because there are so many varied constituencies associated with this role, it seems that meetings become an almost constant element of any work day. On any day you might find yourself working with faculty, students/athletes, coaches, trainers, business department staff, media, parents, game officials, vendors, campus facilities personnel, student life professionals, counselors, law enforcement, college administrators, residence life staff, the office of admissions, food service personnel, transportation providers, the NCCA, city officials, college neighbors, and any one of a myriad of standing college committees.

(*continued*)

(continued)

What was the most challenging part of your career?

Due to the complexity of the position, finding the time to complete all of your tasks can be very challenging. Time-management skills are of the utmost importance. It is imperative to acquire the skill of prioritization. The immense workload can become stressful, and it is so very important to be constantly aware of your persona. An athletic director needs to develop positive relationships with all those with whom he or she comes in contact. There is a definite need to be personable and not allow the pressures of the position to create any negativity.

What was the most rewarding part of your career?

There is no doubt that the most rewarding part of being an athletic director is watching young men and women reach their full potential in the classroom, in their athletic participation, and then in social development. It is exciting to see young people excel in their education and their athletic endeavors while developing as positive and effective members of their communities.

What advice do you have for someone in high school or currently at the undergraduate level who might be interested in this career?

Teach, coach, and find good mentors. Acquire as many experiences as possible in the area of athletic administration. Earn degrees that will help position you for this career. Degrees in business, education, sports management, psychology, physical education, leadership, supervision, marketing, and planning would all be an asset to becoming an athletic director.

What advice do you have for someone currently in a different career/field who might be interested in your career?

If you are in a totally different career at the moment and would like to become a college athletic director, the first step would be to earn a degree in a related field and then gain experience in this "arena."

(continued)

(*continued*)

If you decided to advance your career, what steps would you take and what career(s) might you seek out?

If I wanted to advance my career, most likely by trying to get a position at an institution with a higher profile, I would begin to do the appropriate networking, and at the same time, identify what skills I might need to acquire to successfully land the job. I would most likely do an inventory and assessment of my current skills to identify my strengths and then pursue positions in which my skill set could prove valuable.

73. OFFICE OF STUDENT DISABILITIES— STUDENT SUPPORT PROVIDER

BASIC DESCRIPTION

Student support providers (coordinators/counselors) are responsible for implementing support services and linking students with disabilities to college resources. The disabilities targeted within this position typically include attention deficit hyperactivity disorder, mental health issues, learning disabilities, chronic health conditions, and other developmental/medical challenges. These support providers may work individually with a student to provide academic coaching. They may also consult with faculty or university personnel across the campus about instructional modifications or curricular accommodations (i.e., course, exam, housing, transportation) necessary to meet a student's individual needs. Training faculty and administration in how to be inclusive of persons with disabilities within the university setting is another important aspect of this position. Working closely with community-based service providers or agencies may be another facet of this position. The primary focus of this position is to ensure academic success and student retention. The dean of student services/affairs typically provides oversight of the office of student disability.

CORE COMPETENCIES AND SKILLS NEEDED

A respect for individual differences and the diversity of learners that exist on campus is essential. Skills in assessment, consultation, and academic intervention are needed. Good people skills are important, including being a good listener, showing empathy, and displaying positive regard for a student's well-being. Meeting deadlines, handling stress, juggling multiple clients, paying close attention to details, and working well as a member of a team are essential for this position. Strong oral and written communication skills are important. Thorough documentation/record keeping is essential.

EDUCATIONAL REQUIREMENTS

A master's degree in student services, counselor education, student affairs, special education, or school psychology is typically required in this specialized career in working with students with disabilities. A strong background in coursework pertaining to special education, learning disabilities, adult mental health, and postsecondary instruction/accommodations is necessary.

EXPERIENCE NECESSARY

Many years of experience in working with young adults with disabilities is needed. A history of documenting disabilities within the university setting along with prior work in consulting with faculty about accommodations and instructional practices is necessary.

CERTIFICATION, LICENSURE, AND CONTINUING EDUCATION REQUIREMENTS

Ideally, the student services provider will meet national and state certification within his or her field of study (e.g., special educator with endorsement in learning disabilities, nationally certified school psychologist).

SALARY/COMPENSATION

Salary typically varies by university. Full-time support providers might earn between $30,000 and $40,000. The salary range may be higher based on years of experience or one's background and training. In addition, serving as the director of these services would also result in a considerably higher salary. Part-time hourly ($15–$25 per hour) positions might also appear within some universities, whereas others might hire graduate assistants from programs in school psychology or special education to serve in this role.

EMPLOYMENT OUTLOOK

The population of students attending college is anticipated to increase substantially in the coming decade. In addition, inclusion practices have become commonplace within many university systems. This has opened the door for students with disabilities to seek postsecondary educational opportunities.

FURTHER INFORMATION FOR EXPLORATION

To further explore the field of disability services within higher education, see the Association on Higher Education and Disability (www.ahead .org). Websites aimed at advocacy and improved services for specific disability populations might also be consulted (e.g., www.ldaamerica.org, www.chadd.org, www.pacer.org).

74. STUDY-ABROAD COORDINATOR

BASIC DESCRIPTION

Study-abroad coordinators advise students about educational opportunities (course credit) in foreign countries (i.e., study abroad). This includes developing informational materials and flyers. Helping to oversee the application process, including selection of students to study abroad, is an important part of this career. The coordinator may be assigned specific study-abroad opportunities (e.g., country, continent, language spoken) and works closely with other study-abroad office staff and faculty leaders to ensure the educational program and experience are carried out as intended. This includes helping selected students to prepare for and learn from their study-abroad opportunity. Most study-abroad coordinators work in university settings (i.e., office of international studies/affairs), but government programs or private companies offer other employment setting options.

CORE COMPETENCIES AND SKILLS NEEDED

The ability to manage complex programs and coordinate multiple facets of an educational experience for undergraduate or graduate students is needed. Strong oral and written communication skills are important. Attention to detail and being highly organized are qualities that will bring success to this career. Strong interpersonal skills and cultural competence are especially needed within this position.

EDUCATIONAL REQUIREMENTS

A master's degree in international education or a related field of study is preferred. A minimum of a bachelor's degree in student affairs, international business, international studies, or some other similar program of study is required. Prior language training (e.g., French, Spanish, German, Chinese) also can be very beneficial for those entering into this career. Knowledge pertaining to international travel regulations, immigration rules, and overseas travel credentials are particularly helpful within this position.

EXPERIENCE NECESSARY

Experience working or living abroad is important. Prior involvement in a study-abroad program, while an undergraduate student, would be very helpful to those who are interested in this coordinator position. The ability to speak multiple languages, having cultural diversity training, or being a dual resident of the United States and another country would all position one favorably for this career.

CERTIFICATION, LICENSURE, AND CONTINUING EDUCATION REQUIREMENTS

Engagement in continuing education is essential for this coordinator position through regional or national study-abroad conferences. In addition, it may be important to be in close communication with overseas partners regarding continuous improvement or even to explore future study opportunities through international travel.

SALARY/COMPENSATION

Salaries for a study-abroad coordinator vary considerably based on the size and location of the university or other type of setting. Moreover, some programs may be relatively new or emerging, which would also influence levels of pay. Typical salaries range between $40,000 and $50,000 based a review of recent postings found on the Internet.

EMPLOYMENT OUTLOOK

An increase in college enrollment and an expansion of learning opportunities in other countries will continue to push the demand for study-abroad personnel.

FURTHER INFORMATION FOR EXPLORATION

The Forum on Education Abroad (www.forumea.org) provides a number of helpful resources and links related to the field of overseas education. Most important, you should consult the website of the office of study abroad at the university where you would like to be employed (e.g., www.studyabroad.isp.msu.edu) or the study-abroad office at the university from which you graduated.

75. CAREER COUNSELOR

BASIC DESCRIPTION

Career counseling involves working with others to assist them in career exploration, problem solve about a change in career, or discuss other employment issues. A career counselor may work in a variety of settings, including colleges, universities, community colleges, government agencies, and career centers. Within a university setting, a career counselor primarily functions in the role of assisting students with career exploration. Helping students to explore and identify their talents and skills is an important first step in the career counseling relationship. The next step is linking those interests and aptitudes to a set of careers or employment options. Finally, an action plan to pursue additional information in the short term can be developed and monitored. Additional services may include interview preparation, document review (curriculum vitae, résumé, personal statement), and assistance with professional networking.

CORE COMPETENCIES AND SKILLS NEEDED

Career counselors need to be good listeners and be able to help their clients be data-based problem solvers through use of aptitude and interest assessment tools. Career decision making can be especially stressful, and it is important to empathize and support those seeking career counseling services. Strong interpersonal skills are especially important, as good relationships with students are prerequisites to effective counseling. Strong oral and written communication skills are essential. In addition, adept record keeping and maintaining confidentiality are necessary when working within a counseling relationship. Expertise in using technology to assist the career counseling process is needed.

EDUCATIONAL REQUIREMENTS

A master's degree in school counseling, rehabilitation counseling, counseling psychology, guidance counseling, social work, career development, student affairs, or a related field is required. Coursework related to counseling techniques and theory and adult development should be completed.

EXPERIENCE NECESSARY

Prior experience in working in a career center, an academic support office, or as a counselor is necessary. A history of working with diverse populations is especially important within a university setting. In a career counselor position, it is important to demonstrate sensitivity and understanding of differences in culture, disability, ethnic background, and income. Evidence of experience in using career assessments and career counseling techniques is necessary.

CERTIFICATION, LICENSURE, AND CONTINUING EDUCATION REQUIREMENTS

Possession of the required discipline-specific credential (e.g., counselor) or license (licensed psychologist) is required. It is expected that professional development will occur frequently through national/state conference attendance, participation in training, and active involvement in professional associations.

SALARY/COMPENSATION

Average salaries for career counselors typically fall between $45,000 and $60,000. The size and type of the university setting or the government agency along with years of experience may influence the level of pay.

EMPLOYMENT OUTLOOK

An increase in enrollment in university/college settings has resulted in a significant need for career counselors who are well trained to work with undergraduate and graduate students. Pending retirements within the university system will further affect the positive outlook for future employment in this area.

FURTHER INFORMATION FOR EXPLORATION

Two professional associations should be explored for further information about becoming a career counselor: the National Career Development Association (www.ncda.org) and the National Employment Counseling Association (www.employmentcounseling.org). In addition, the career center within your community (e.g., www.camw.org) or local university/community college (e.g., www.careernetwork.msu.edu) can also be consulted.

REFERENCE

Bureau of Labor Statistics, U.S. Department of Labor. (2014). *Occupational outlook handbook, 2014-2015 edition, Preschool and Childcare Center Directors.* Retrieved July 13, 2015, from http://www.bls.gov/ooh/management/preschool-and-childcare-center-directors.htm

V ■ CAREERS IN EDUCATION: NONTRADITIONAL POSITIONS

10 ■ EDUCATION-RELATED CAREERS IN COMMUNITY, INDUSTRY, AND GOVERNMENT SETTINGS

76. RELIGIOUS EDUCATION TEACHER

BASIC DESCRIPTION

Religious education teachers provide instruction in a particular religion (e.g., catechism teacher—Catholicism) or about religions in general (e.g., history, beliefs, rituals, customs). This work may be situated within a number of developmental levels, including preschool, school-age, or adult populations. The ability to adapt teachings to the skill level of the audience is essential. This position is usually within church, community, or parochial school settings.

CORE COMPETENCIES AND SKILLS NEEDED

As is true of most educators, the most important skill needed to be a religious education teacher is the ability to carry out a curriculum effectively so that learning objectives are met. This means it is essential to be competent in knowledge of the religion, to bring an enthusiastic approach to learning through an engaging presentation style, to be open to questions, and to be a good listener. The ability to share passionately the culture, teachings, and faith of the church is needed.

EDUCATIONAL REQUIREMENTS

The educational requirements for this career depend on the context in which the work is completed. For example, a religious education teacher who instructs within a Sunday school program at his or her church would not need any specialized education. Instead, the individual would need to be motivated and willing to volunteer his or her time. Religious education teachers who work within parochial schools are likely required to have a degree in teacher education.

EXPERIENCE NECESSARY

Prior involvement in teaching others is necessary. This may occur through student teaching within a degree program or it may instead mean that one is well experienced in making presentations. A history of teaching any subject area along with a background in measuring learning outcomes is ideal for this position.

CERTIFICATION, LICENSURE, AND CONTINUING EDUCATION REQUIREMENTS

Some religions offer a certificate in religious education. Working within a parochial school setting will likely require a teaching license from the state in which the school is located. See state-level teacher credential requirements for additional details. Background checks are likely to be required regardless of the setting in which the religious education instruction is being provided.

SALARY/COMPENSATION

Given that this career in education can vary substantially from a volunteer position (i.e., no pay) to a full-time position as a teacher within a religious education program, salaries vary widely. A typical salary for those working in this position within a parochial elementary school would be between $40,000 and $45,000. For additional guidance on salaries, see the Internet for job postings with those details or network with those who are in these positions.

EMPLOYMENT OUTLOOK

The employment outlook for this career in schools would be similar to that for the field of elementary education, which appears to be steady in the years ahead. Work as a volunteer in this position within your local church is typically readily available, and you should consult your church's administrative team for additional information.

FURTHER INFORMATION FOR EXPLORATION

For further information about a career as a religious education teacher, see the websites of the Association for Professors, Practitioners, and Researchers in Religious Education (www.religiouseducation.net) and the American Academy of Religion (www.aarweb.org). For additional information about becoming a religious education teacher within a specific faith, search online. For example, for such positions within the Catholic Church, see www.thereligionteacher.com.

77. SUMMER CAMP COUNSELOR

BASIC DESCRIPTION

Summer camp counselors perform multiple duties during their time working with campers during the summer months. This may be in the form of a day or overnight camp. The work assignment may last from days to months. This work will include ensuring campers' safety, health, and enthusiasm for their experience. Carrying out the camp's daily schedule, including engaging campers in indoor and outdoor activities, is required. Counselors will also develop and implement special activities, plan group excursions, provide emotional support to campers, and enforce camp rules. As primary caregivers for the campers, summer camp counselors plan, teach, coordinate, and implement activities that are focused on developing daily living skills and personal growth.

CORE COMPETENCIES AND SKILLS NEEDED

The ability to communicate effectively with both campers and staff is needed. Maturity, patience, excellent decision-making skills, and good conflict resolution skills are important. Empathy, emotional support, and the ability to provide clear expectations in a calm and confident manner are essential for those working in this position. Carrying forward the full scope of responsibilities with skill and talent requires one to keep the needs of both the camp director and the campers in mind. Failing to meet those dual needs can be particularly problematic.

EDUCATIONAL REQUIREMENTS

Many camp counselors have not yet completed an undergraduate degree, as they are often of high school or college age and often work at the camp during the summer break. During the academic year, camp counselors may be working on a related degree, such as child psychology, social work, counselor education, leisure studies, recreational therapy, or parks/recreation. On-the-job training combined with an orientation covering camp policies and procedures is usually required. Cardiopulmonary resuscitation (CPR) training and/or lifeguard certifications may be necessary depending on the camp position assumed.

EXPERIENCE NECESSARY

Prior experience with school-age populations in a caregiving capacity is the most common requirement. Having expertise and experience in the activities counselors will teach—such as art, athletics, archery, canoeing, drama, or music—is highly desirable. Those with strong leadership skills may go on to be mentor counselors for camp counselors.

CERTIFICATION, LICENSURE, AND CONTINUING EDUCATION REQUIREMENTS

No prior certifications or licenses are required. Continuing education related to camp safety, health, and recreational activities is a common requirement. Training in first aid or life-saving measures may result in the necessary certifications desired for some of the summer camp counselor positions.

SALARY/COMPENSATION

Room and board combined with a stipend (e.g., $300 to $400 a week) is typical for those working as summer camp counselors. The specific nature of the position or the talents required for the position may influence the salary provided.

EMPLOYMENT OUTLOOK

The employment outlook for camp counselors or, more broadly, recreation workers is expected to grow in the years ahead. In addition, the high rate of turnover within this profession for college-age individuals leads to a yearly demand.

FURTHER INFORMATION FOR EXPLORATION

For additional information about the diverse array of positions available in summer camps and to further explore becoming a summer camp counselor, see the American Camp Association Website (www.acacamps.org).

78.   CAMP DIRECTOR

BASIC DESCRIPTION

Camp directors are responsible for the smooth daily operation of the camp. This will include development and management of the camp to meet the mission of the organization. Providing a camp curriculum that matches the needs and interests of the campers is especially important in this role. Being the camp director will involve all staff recruitment, hiring, training, retention, and termination responsibilities. Budgeting and marketing are also typically the responsibility of the camp director. This career in education is typically a year-round position, but it may also be seasonal depending on the camp.

CORE COMPETENCIES AND SKILLS NEEDED

Exceptional writing and verbal communication skills are needed. The ability to work effectively as a leader of a team is especially important for this management position. A firm grasp of both child and adult development is essential. Exceptional time-management skills and highly developed organizational skill are essential in this position.

EDUCATIONAL REQUIREMENTS

A minimum of a college degree and prior administrative experience within a camp or a youth development program is required. A graduate degree in a related field (e.g., counselor education, sports management, recreation therapy, parks/recreation, child development, child psychology, teacher education) may be expected for this leadership position. Coursework in human development, counseling, youth development, or leadership development is expected.

EXPERIENCE NECESSARY

Prior experience working as a camp counselor, prior engagement in youth development curriculum, or a background working in parks/recreation is expected. Most typically, a camp director will have gradually worked his or her way up the leadership command within the camp (e.g., youth development program), or a similarly run camp, for which he or she is being considered for the position of director.

CERTIFICATION, LICENSURE, AND CONTINUING EDUCATION REQUIREMENTS

Certification from the National Recreation and Parks Association or a similar professional organization may be required. First aid and CPR training are typically expected within this management position.

SALARY/COMPENSATION

Salaries for camp directors vary considerably by location and type of camp. Typically, pay will fall between $25,000 and $45,000 for year-round positions. A close review of open camp director positions via an Internet search is recommended to help get a more accurate sense of pay within a camp program comparable to the one to which you are considering applying. Summer term appointments will likely be paid via a stipend, room/board, and other benefits.

EMPLOYMENT OUTLOOK

As a result of increases in the child population, the need for camp staff and recreational services personnel will increase in the years to come. The need for an undergraduate or graduate degree combined with relatively low salaries means that turnover and attrition result in the continuous demand for camp directors.

FURTHER INFORMATION FOR EXPLORATION

For additional information about becoming a camp director, see the American Camp Association website (www.acacamps.org). For learning about a career more generally in the field of parks and recreation, see the website of the National Recreation and Parks Association (www.npra.org).

Career-in-Education Profile
CAMP DIRECTOR

Interview With Kathy Jurichko (BA, Sociology; MA, Religious Education; MA Candidate, Counseling and Psychological Services)

Describe your educational background.

I majored in sociology and minored in child psychology. I completed an advanced degree in religious education at a theological seminary. Currently, I am pursuing my advanced degree in counseling and psychological services. My educational background and preparation to be a camp director started well before I finished high school and took many years of on-the-job training and years of gradual increases in my responsibilities.

Describe your prior experiences and the path you took to get to this career.

I began at this summer camp program as a child participant. Later, in my teens, I volunteered on a short-term basis. In college, I was asked to work all summer as a cabin counselor. I stayed with this camp program for many years—2 years as a cabin counselor (children ages 8–14), 1 year as a trip leader (camping and canoeing), 1 year as the assistant director, and a total of 12 years as the camp director. My college degree in sociology and child psychology contributed well to the knowledge I needed for this career.

Describe the work that you do.

My responsibilities included:

1. Hiring, training, and supervising staff and volunteers (training included topics such as child development and behavior management, general safety expectations and emergency procedures, waterfront safety, and camping techniques)
2. Planning program curriculum for swimming lessons and outdoor living skills (e.g., tenting, low-impact camping)

(continued)

(*continued*)

3. Maintaining the camp's American Camp Association accreditation status
4. Overseeing all aspects of daily camp life, such as foodservice, property maintenance, transportation, and camper and staff well-being
5. Assisting camp staff with camper behavior issues
6. Maintaining camp budget

What is a typical day like for you in this career?

September–May: Planning, recruiting campers and staff, training volunteers, fund-raising, regular meetings with camp board of directors, facility project planning, updating staff and camper information manuals and staff training materials.

June–August: A typical day on site would include the following:
8:30 a.m.: Breakfast
9:00 a.m.: Flag-raising ceremony
9:15 a.m.–12:15 p.m.: Assist staff, attend to camper health or behavior needs, make parent phone calls as necessary, transport groups to overnight camping site and/or canoe landing, plan menus, place food order, create to-do list for janitorial/maintenance staff
12:30 p.m.: Lunch
1:00–4:00 p.m.: Assist staff, accounting/pay bills, payroll, prep for staff meetings, inspect property for maintenance needs, assist in kitchen with inventory, check up on any behavior issues
4:00–5:00 p.m.: Quiet break
5:30–6:30 p.m.: Dinner with campers and staff and post dinner camp rituals
6:30–8:30 p.m.: Prepare evening activities with program directors and plan for the next day
8:30 p.m.: Help supervise and/or participate in evening camp activity
9:30 p.m.: Help distribute evening snack and visit with campers
10:00 p.m.: Assist with supervision of campers as they prep for bedtime, assist with health care needs (including home sickness)
10:30 p.m.–12:00 a.m.: Be available to talk over camp-related or staff issues

(*continued*)

(continued)

12:00 a.m.–1:00 a.m.: Personal time to reflect on the day and prepare for the next day

What is the most challenging part of your career?

Dealing with staff members who don't want to follow the rules or work according to the established plan/procedures/routine is challenging. Staff members who don't get along with others or do not "pull their weight" can be very challenging. I never had trouble deciding when to let staff go, but did find it very difficult to try to work to improve staff morale and work performance once camp activities were in full swing.

What is the most rewarding part of your career?

I worked with some people in the camp program starting when they were just children then encouraging them to become volunteers as teenagers and then fostering them along to fill adult staff roles. Seeing long-term positive relationships develop between people was an awesome part of being a director. Also, every once in a while, in the middle of the winter, I would get a phone call at my office from a former staff member to thank me for the way I handled a tough situation with them. Those phone calls were very rewarding.

What advice do you have for someone in high school or currently at the undergraduate level who might be interested in this career?

Work at a residential summer camp and expect to work very hard. Be open to working at different camps to get exposure to different program formats and leadership styles. Volunteer for the camp during the off season (fund-raising, recruiting campers, maintenance on camp property). Choose a college major that contributes to the summer camp setting that you are interested in (e.g., youth development, environmental studies, psychology, education, science, second language, music). Get certified in summer camp–related skills such as first aid/cardiopulmonary resuscitation, lifeguarding, or archery, or as a canoe instructor. Explore the information provided through the

(continued)

(continued)

American Camp Association website at www.acacamps.org. Travel abroad if you get the opportunity. The potential of expanding your worldview and your cultural skills is so valuable for working at a camp.

What advice do you have for someone currently in a different career/field who might be interested in your career?

Volunteer with a camp program that you are interested in. Volunteer with the same population of campers (e.g., physically challenged, behavior issues, special medical population, veteran families, music- or language-focused programs, adults with disabilities, the general youth population) in the off season. Network with other camp professionals.

If you decided to advance your career, what steps would you take and what career(s) might you seek out?

I will soon become a mental health counselor (licensed professional counselor, or LPC) in the college campus setting. As a camp director, most of my time was spent coaching and encouraging my camp staff, primarily college-age students. I really enjoy working with the college-age population. I value education and seek to support struggling students who seek success through a college education.

79. PRISON EDUCATOR

BASIC DESCRIPTION

Prison educators provide education to inmates to help them gain knowledge, skills, and qualifications to assist them when they are released. They oversee all vocational, technical, and academic classes and programs within the correctional facility. Basic skill development and preparation for the General Educational Development (GED) certificate are examples. Preparation for gainful employment of those incarcerated is an effective approach to prevent reoffending. Prison educators prepare lesson plans, carry forward effective instructional approaches, measure learner outcomes, and evaluate the overall effectiveness of the courses taught. Instruction may be provided individually, in small groups, or in larger groups. A prison educator may have a history of working as a prison officer who has gone through retraining to become a teacher. This teaching career may fall under the broader term of *vocational* or *adult education.*

CORE COMPETENCIES AND SKILLS NEEDED

Working with individuals from disadvantaged populations who are experiencing significant learning challenges is expected within this career. The ability to implement a curriculum effectively that meets the unique needs of the prison setting and the prisoner is an important aspect of this teaching career. Having a background in providing computer-assisted instruction may be particularly important for this teaching position. Ultimately, the need to adapt the instructional process to meet the individual learning needs of the prisoner is paramount.

EDUCATIONAL REQUIREMENTS

A bachelor's degree in postsecondary teaching, adult education, high school equivalency preparation, or a related field is typically required. Appropriate credentials and certifications are necessary, and state requirements should be consulted for specifics.

EXPERIENCE NECESSARY

Prior teaching experience, specifically within disadvantage populations, is necessary. A history of effective adult education classroom instruction (e.g., adult literacy, high school equivalency courses) is important. Familiarity and/or comfort with working in a correctional facility is ideal.

CERTIFICATION, LICENSURE, AND CONTINUING EDUCATION REQUIREMENTS

Typically, a secondary teaching certificate or credentials related to adult literacy are required. Consult the state in which you will become a prison educator for additional information about expected certification and licensure. Continuing education in the area of adult education or teaching incarcerated populations would be expected.

SALARY/COMPENSATION

According to the Bureau of Labor Statistics (2014a), a prison educator may be paid similarly to adult literacy and high school equivalency diploma teachers, who have a median annual wage just under $50,000. Pay will vary considerably by geographic location, type of prison setting, and the responsibilities of the position. Many prison educator positions are part time and may pay an hourly wage.

EMPLOYMENT OUTLOOK

The employment outlook for prison educators will continue to grow in the years ahead. The need for part-time teachers will be especially strong, as state prison budgets are likely to remain tight.

FURTHER INFORMATION FOR EXPLORATION

For additional information about a career as a prison educator, see the Correctional Education Association website (www.ceanational.org) or look for a state-level association such as the Correctional Education Association of Wisconsin (www.ceawisconsin.org). To look for job postings for a prison educator, see the Bureau of Prisons website (www.bop.gov) or the prison system website of a particular state.

80.   ADULT EDUCATOR

BASIC DESCRIPTION

An adult educator may teach a number of subjects to adult learners (18 years or older) in a variety of settings, including high schools, university extension programs, community colleges, or community agency settings. Identification of student learning needs and establishing lesson plans to meet those needs are required aspects of this career. Instruction may include adult basic education (e.g., reading, writing, math), adult secondary education, or English literacy. Adult basic education is geared toward skills that are not yet developed at a middle school level or higher. Adult secondary education is focused on teaching adults wishing to obtain a certificate or to meet specific credentialing requirements. English literacy provides instruction to adults with limited English proficiency. Assessment of learning outcomes and modification of instructional processes to meet the needs of the adult learners are especially important within this position.

CORE COMPETENCIES AND SKILLS NEEDED

An adult educator should have excellent instructional skills and be a good communicator. Having expertise in the field or subject being taught is necessary. Patience and empathy regarding the difficulties faced by adult learners are essential to one's success within this teaching career. A respect for individual differences is especially important.

EDUCATIONAL REQUIREMENTS

A bachelor's degree in teaching, adult education, literacy, or an equivalent area of study is necessary. A master's-level degree or coursework might also be required. Some states offer a special credential or certificate in adult education.

EXPERIENCE NECESSARY

Prior teaching experience is expected. Work with adult learners via community education or professional development programs would be desired. Prior secondary education experience or teaching children of younger ages may also be appropriate.

CERTIFICATION, LICENSURE, AND CONTINUING EDUCATION REQUIREMENTS

A teaching certificate is typically required. It is recommended that you seek guidance from the Department of Education of the state in which you are considering applying to be an adult educator, as requirements may vary. Continuing education and professional development pertaining to adult education are required.

SALARY/COMPENSATION

Years of experience, location, and level of education all affect the level of salary one receives. Data from across the country indicate that the average salary for an adult educator is between $45,000 and $50,000. It is important to note that many positions may be part time and pay considerably less.

EMPLOYMENT OUTLOOK

Continued immigration to the United States and an increased demand for adult education programs make the employment outlook positive for adult educators in the years ahead. The increasing need for workers to demonstrate at least a high school–level education further increases the importance of this teaching career.

FURTHER INFORMATION FOR EXPLORATION

For additional information about a career as an adult educator, see the website of the American Association for Adult and Continuing Education (www.aaace.org) and the Coalition of Lifelong Learning Organizations (www.thecollo.org).

81. HEALTH EDUCATOR

BASIC DESCRIPTION

Health educators work to promote and improve people's health by teaching them about behaviors that promote wellness. They work with individuals to encourage healthy behaviors and may also work within communities to promote population-based behavioral health changes. Health and wellness assessments serve as the basis for the educational objectives carried forward by health educators. Some examples include how to prevent illness, how to manage existing health conditions, how to eat a healthful diet, and how to maintain an active lifestyle. Specific health curriculum or programs may be implemented. Data collection and evaluation of services are essential aspects of this career that is aimed at continual improvement of health education approaches. Health educators may work in schools, health care facilities, nonprofit organizations, or public health agencies.

CORE COMPETENCIES AND SKILLS NEEDED

A strong understanding of health, wellness, illness, and disease is needed for this teaching position. Exceptional instructional skills and the ability to teach both small and large groups are important. Strong verbal and written communication skills are needed. Excellent analytical and problem-solving skills are important to be able to think creatively about how health education programs can affect individuals and communities. The ability to form relationships with individuals and to maintain confidentiality is especially important in this health education career.

EDUCATIONAL REQUIREMENTS

A bachelor's degree in health education or health promotion is required. Coursework in theories, methods, and best practices in health education is required and may be sought by those who already hold a bachelor's degree in teacher education. Some positions may require a master's or advanced graduate degree in areas such as community health, school health, or public health.

EXPERIENCE NECESSARY

Postsecondary coursework typically will include an internship experience carrying forward a health curriculum or program under the supervision of a health educator. Specialized training in a specific population or associated with a specific area of health promotion may be required.

CERTIFICATION, LICENSURE, AND CONTINUING EDUCATION REQUIREMENTS

Specific preparation in health education that meets national training standards may result in the credential of Certified Health Education Specialist (CHES), offered by the National Commission for Health Education Credentialing (www.nchec.org). This credential requires specific coursework, experiences, and successful completion of the national exam. Continuing education in health education is required to maintain the CHES credential.

SALARY/COMPENSATION

Salary will depend on years of experience, prior background and training, educational credentials, and location. The median wage for health educators according to the Bureau of Labor Statistics (2014d) is just under $50,000.

EMPLOYMENT OUTLOOK

A focus on public health and health outcomes within society has created a significant demand for health educators. Teaching people to take care of themselves and live healthy lifestyles is viewed as an effective approach to reducing health care costs.

FURTHER INFORMATION FOR EXPLORATION

For additional information about a career as a health educator, see the following professional organizations: the Society of Health and Physical Educators (www.shapeamerica.org); the Society for Public Health Education (www.sophe.org); the Alliance for Health, Physical Education, Recreation, and Dance (www.aahperd.org); and the National Commission for Health Education Credentialing, Inc. (www.nchec.org). The Centers for Disease Control and Prevention (www.cdc.gov) also provides numerous resources on health and wellness that may be of interest to those pursuing a health educator career.

82. EDUCATIONAL CONSULTANT/PROFESSIONAL COACH

BASIC DESCRIPTION

An educational consultant works closely with parents/students/clients to help with educational planning through establishment of goals and methods to meet those goals. This planning may focus on preparation for postsecondary education, success within current academic studies, or the creation of educational programming to best accommodate a student's disability or learning challenges. Educational consulting is guided by the individual academic needs identified. A professional coach (e.g., business, life, health, fitness, relationship, spirituality) serves a similar purpose but may instead be focused on assisting in occupational planning, maximizing success outside of the educational setting, meeting specific individual life goals, or assisting in adapting to major life changes (e.g., divorce, new job). The process of helping others with self-discovery through discussion, self-monitoring, and homework activities is the primary focus of work within this career. A focus on an individual's goals, motivations, and actions through regular one-on-one meetings is a major part of the work of an educational consultant/professional coach.

CORE COMPETENCIES AND SKILLS NEEDED

Exceptional interpersonal skills are required for this position. The ability to listen intently, to be empathetic, to assist in establishing attainable goals, to provide motivation and encouragement, and to assist an individual's efforts to monitor his or her own progress toward the individual's goals is needed. A particular focus on serving others and a positive outlook on problem solving are essential within this career in education. The need to be flexible and adaptive to change is especially important.

EDUCATIONAL REQUIREMENTS

A bachelor's degree in teaching, counseling, psychology, or education is typical for those within this profession. However, no specific educational or licensure requirements exist within this unregulated career in education. An advanced degree in curriculum and instruction, student personnel development, career development, counseling psychology, or a closely related career may be particularly helpful for those who run their own consulting/coaching business.

EXPERIENCE NECESSARY

Prior teaching experience and a deep understanding about the area in which consulting/coaching is taking place are particularly important. Extensive life experience or experience in overcoming the challenge being focused on within the consultant/coaching position is expected. With extensive content knowledge, an educational consultant/ professional coach is able to collaboratively problem solve and guide the consultee toward effective outcomes.

CERTIFICATION, LICENSURE, AND CONTINUING EDUCATION REQUIREMENTS

Educational consultants and professional coaches are relatively new occupations. Specific licensure requirements do not exist. Qualifications necessary to engage in this career in education may vary by state, and attention to those varying expectations for individuals working in these positions is essential. Consulting and coaching training programs are available for those interested in this career. Most of these programs lead to some type of specific certification.

SALARY/COMPENSATION

Many educational consultants/professional coaches work part time and may make as much as $100 an hour. Pay will greatly vary based on location, years of experience, and success within the business. For those who work full time, the pay may be similar to the pay for those working within the counseling profession. Median salary would likely fall between $45,000 and $50,000.

EMPLOYMENT OUTLOOK

The employment outlook for educational consultants/professional coaches appears to be strong, as individuals will continue to look for ways to engage in self-improvement and get ahead when it comes to occupational success.

FURTHER INFORMATION FOR EXPLORATION

For additional information about a career as an educational consultant, see the websites of the Higher Education Consultants Association (www .hecaonline.org), the National Career Development Association (www .ncda.org), and the Independent Educational Consultants Association (www.iecaonline.com). For more information about a career as a professional coach, see the International Coach Federation website (www .coachfederation.org).

Career-in-Education Profile
EDUCATIONAL CONSULTANT/PROFESSIONAL COACH
Interview With Regina Carey (BA, Special Education;
MEd, Special Education)

Describe your educational background.

I majored in special education. After graduation, I went immediately into teaching at the middle and high school levels for 3.5 years, the career span of many special education teachers. I left teaching to pursue a grant opportunity and get an advanced degree in special education—learning disabilities. I am continually engaged in professional development, conferences, and consulting with other professionals in the fields of education, health care, and psychology.

Describe your prior experiences and the path you took to get to this career.

From an early age, I knew I would be an educator. In high school I worked at a facility for severely mentally handicapped children and adults. My roles as caregiver and daily-life-skills facilitator directed me even further into a passion for special populations. While obtaining my master's degree, I worked as a teacher trainer and programs' coordinator. It was during this time that I began making formal presentations about "invisible disabilities" (e.g., learning disabilities [LDs], attentional disabilities) to a variety of campus and community groups. I then worked as a learning specialist within a university athletic department. I began connecting with a number of agencies across the state. After being trained by one of the pioneers in attention deficit disorder (ADD) coaching, I took on clients of my own. I then became a consultant with a university's Center for Persons with Disabilities. I continue to serve as a professional coach, I also serve as a volunteer with the Learning Disabilities Association, and I do public speaking in the field of special education.

Describe the work that you do.

As an educational consultant, I work with agencies, institutions, and corporations to develop an awareness of ADD/LD issues that interfere

(continued)

(continued)

with productivity. I work with supervisors and administrators to train and educate their staff about invisible disabilities. As a consultant and professional coach, I work with a client to do the following:

- Highlight strengths that support job efficiency.
- Examine issues interfering with productivity.
- Develop action plans to attack each obstacle.
- Conduct on-site visits.
- Maintain constant contact with the client during the service period.
- Produce a written report of my services.

Unlike therapy, which targets emotional well-being, or tutoring, which provides academic support, coaching is about action! As a coach, I strive to help clients learn new behaviors and skills. I remind them of what is important to them. I help them break down tasks into manageable pieces, translate their ideas into actions, and act as a pillar of support and encouragement.

What is a typical day like for you in this career?

My work is extremely flexible. My many roles ebb and flow throughout the day among coach, consultant, and advocate. There really is no typical day, which I love! Phone or Skype appointments with clients last from 30 to 60 minutes, and I provide each client with a follow-up report so he or she can begin to take action. Face-to-face meetings involve hands-on tasks, such as organizing, filing, throwing out unnecessary clutter, or improving efficiency in a work or living space. I write a weekly blog on a website for persons with ADD, and I speak at conferences nationwide to help empower people with invisible disabilities.

What is the most challenging part of your career?

The most challenging part of my career is the many transitions that occur throughout the day. Billing for my services can get blurred due to all aspects of the job overlapping each day. When I spend a day traveling to see clients, I have to factor in my family responsibilities with travel time and client time. It can get overwhelming, as with any career. Working out of my home also adds to the challenge.

(continued)

(continued)

What is the most rewarding part of your career?

The most rewarding part of my career is watching clients learn about themselves and their brains! My goal is for clients to live strong without me eventually. Once we've worked together for a period of months or years, it's rewarding to have them release me as their coach and go off on their own. The strategies and techniques have been practiced to the point of evolving into great habits.

What advice do you have for someone in high school or currently at the undergraduate level who might be interested in this career?

The best way to experience success is to further your education. Some may stop with a bachelor's degree and get additional certification in areas of interest. Others may pursue a master's degree and/or a PhD to further career options. The key is to find out what you can do within the community where you live to make the most impact.

What advice do you have for someone currently in a different career/field who might be interested in your career?

Create a mission statement identifying what it is that you can pull from your current career experience into your work as a consultant or coach. Find someone who is doing what you want to do and make an appointment to talk with that person. Get face to face, job shadow, ask great questions, and then make it happen for yourself.

If you decided to advance your career, what steps would you take and what career(s) might you seek out?

I have never publicized my services, until now. Putting a border around my life's work is no easy task. Currently, I am designing a website, a logo, and explanations around all of my areas of expertise. Ultimately, I want to be speaking at an international level. My career has unfolded thanks to continual life change, which some may see as an obstacle. I see it as an opportunity to embrace what's next!

83. TEST PUBLISHER

BASIC DESCRIPTION

A test publisher works with authors to publish tests and assessment tools for career, personal, or organizational development. These tests are typically associated with screening, selection, certification, or licensing purposes and are to be used in educational and other clinical contexts. Test publishers work closely with test authors to validate the instrument and ready it for publication. They are responsible for editing, printing, and selling the instrument and distributing it to buyers. They also work closely with marketing and accounting personnel to increase sales and expand the reach of the instrument to additional markets. A focus on increasing profits and reducing losses is the primary indicator of success as a test publisher. Most of these positions are found within industry, business, or government settings.

CORE COMPETENCIES AND SKILLS NEEDED

Strong interpersonal, time-management, and organizational skills are required. The ability to work as a member of a production team under the challenge of timelines and deadlines is especially important within this career. Familiarity with and expertise in using computers and knowledge of multiple publishing and word-processing software programs are essential. Excellent verbal and written communication skills are needed. Leadership skills are especially important given the project management aspects of this work.

EDUCATIONAL REQUIREMENTS

A bachelor's degree in business, training/development, technology, or a field closely related to the focus of the test publishing company is expected. Coursework in instructional design, educational software, and word processing link well to the skills expected for working as a test publisher.

EXPERIENCE NECESSARY

Prior experience in the field of education, professional development, book publishing, or educational technology is necessary. A long history of working with computers and computer applications is expected. Project management experience within a publishing company is preferred.

CERTIFICATION, LICENSURE, AND CONTINUING EDUCATION REQUIREMENTS

No certification or licensure is necessary for a career as a test publisher. Educational background and prior experience are most important. A commitment to on-the-job training and continuing education is expected.

SALARY/COMPENSATION

Salaries for test publishers vary greatly by the size of the company, the individual's work experience, and the geographic location. Comparable publishing careers (e.g., book, magazine, newspaper) have salaries that range from $50,000 to $150,000, with starting salaries typically on the low end of the range.

EMPLOYMENT OUTLOOK

The focus on accountability and outcomes within education has created considerable demand for assessment tools and test instruments. Combined with the use of technology and computer applications, the career of test publisher is expected to grow as test practices expand to other parts of the world.

FURTHER INFORMATION FOR EXPLORATION

For additional information about a career as a test publisher, see the websites of the Association of Test Publishers (www.testpublishers.org) and the Association of American Publishers (www.publishers.org). For additional information about assessment practices and tools, a close review should be conducted within the specific discipline of interest. For example, in the field of psychology, see Assessment Psychology Online (www.assessmentpsychology.com) and PsychCentral (www.psychcentral.com).

84. CORPORATE TRAINER

BASIC DESCRIPTION

Corporate trainers organize, lead, and implement programs to improve the knowledge and skills of a corporation's workforce. Their primary responsibility is to engage employees in staff development and training. This will involve the use of a needs assessment within the context of the corporation's mission and stated objectives. Specific goals and objectives for training will be developed. Materials, resources, and training materials will be purchased. A specific program or curriculum will provided. Assessment of the effectiveness of trainings is monitored. Continually improving the knowledge and skills of a workforce is believed to be a wise business decision. Corporate trainers may supervise a staff of training and development specialists, depending on the size of the corporation. Being responsible for the corporation's training budget may also be a part of this career.

CORE COMPETENCIES AND SKILLS NEEDED

Strong organizational and management skills are needed in this position. Effective oral and written communication skills are especially important in this leadership position. The ability to work effectively as a member or leader of a team is essential. Effectiveness as an instructor of both small and large groups must be demonstrated. In addition, the ability to facilitate high-quality professional development programs and effective staff training is needed. A background in educational or instructional technology may be particularly important for corporate trainers. Critical thinking skills are especially necessary to make decisions about "what, why, how, and when" training offered to a corporation's employees.

EDUCATIONAL REQUIREMENTS

A bachelor's degree in human resources, business management, business administration, communications, adult education, or a related field is required. Management positions overseeing instructional staff may require the completion of an advanced degree. Prior coursework and skills in training and development are especially important for work as a corporate trainer. Depending on the size of the company and its reliance on technology, a background in instructional design or educational technology may be needed. Public speaking training is expected.

EXPERIENCE NECESSARY

Prior experience of involvement in staff training, public speaking, and group instruction is necessary. A background in human resource management, instructional design, staff training, personnel development, or educational technology may be particularly helpful when working as a corporate trainer.

CERTIFICATION, LICENSURE, AND CONTINUING EDUCATION REQUIREMENTS

No specific credential or licensure is required, as this profession is not regulated by a state's Department of Education. Instead, specialized training or certifications pertinent to staff training or instructional design may be helpful for those pursuing this career. Certifications can be particularly helpful in distinguishing one's expertise and training from those of other applicants. Continuing education is required to keep up to date with innovations in training methods and learning technology.

SALARY/COMPENSATION

Salaries vary based on the size of the company, the geographic location, and the individual's years of experience. Typical salaries may fall between $50,000 and $60,000. However, management positions will yield considerably higher salaries, with some reports indicating upwards of $130,000.

EMPLOYMENT OUTLOOK

The influence of social media and other business technologies has resulted in a considerable need for employee training, and the outlook for corporate trainers is anticipated to be strong in the coming years.

FURTHER INFORMATION FOR EXPLORATION

For additional information about a career as a corporate trainer, see the websites of the following professional organizations: the Association for Talent Development (www.td.org), the International Society for Performance Improvement (www.ispi.org), and the Society for Human Resource Management (www.shrm.org).

85. TEST PREPARATION CENTER DIRECTOR

BASIC DESCRIPTION

Test preparation centers aim to provide individuals with the information necessary to help with high school, graduate, and professional school admission tests that are necessary for educational or occupational attainment. Centers provide instruction on what to expect on a test and how to prepare for the examination, and usually will provide extensive practice opportunities in taking simulated examinations. Usually, access to computer programs or web-based tutorials/materials is also provided to those who pay for the services provided by the test prep center. The test preparation center director manages all aspects of the business. He or she will be responsible for the center's staff, budget, and materials. This includes all aspects of hiring and training center staff. Securing and arranging office space, marketing and advertising, and managing the daily activities of the center are required within this administrative position.

CORE COMPETENCIES AND SKILLS NEEDED

Strong management and organizational skills are needed in this leadership position. Excellent communication and interpersonal skills are especially important in directing the center's activities. Extensive knowledge of, familiarity with, and expertise in assessment and testing services are needed within this career in education. A focus on customer service and close attention to meeting revenue goals are essential to running a successful test preparation business. An entrepreneurial spirit is especially important for this director position.

EDUCATIONAL REQUIREMENTS

A bachelor's or master's degree in education or a closely related field combined with a degree in business administration or management would typically be required to assume the position of test preparation center director. Extensive training or coursework in human resource management, sales, marketing, or accounting might also be expected.

EXPERIENCE NECESSARY

Experience in providing tutoring or instruction in high-stakes assessments and tests is expected. Prior experience in managing retail staff or a history of managing test preparation services is typically sought for this position. A background in successfully developing a business or proof of growing a business would be particularly important to assume this position. Familiarity with national testing companies and the diversity of examinations offered is also expected.

CERTIFICATION, LICENSURE, AND CONTINUING EDUCATION REQUIREMENTS

No specific licensure or credentials are required for this position. However, certification or a background in training with national testing companies may help one to prepare for this position.

SALARY/COMPENSATION

According to a search of the web, the median salary for a test preparation center director at a test preparation company such as Kaplan would be about $100,000. Salaries would be considerably lower for those running their own business and will also vary based on geographic location.

EMPLOYMENT OUTLOOK

The use of test preparation centers has grown tremendously over the past decade due to the increased focus on the importance of securing admissions into high-quality college and graduate programs. The continued focus on educational attainment and the continued influx of international students into the United States is expected to create a positive employment outlook for this administrative position in the years ahead.

FURTHER INFORMATION FOR EXPLORATION

For additional information about the world of high-stakes testing and assessment, see the website of one of the largest test preparation centers, Kaplan Test Prep (www.kaptest.com). The website of the Education Industry Association (www.educationindustry.org) might also be particularly helpful for those interested in starting their own test preparation business.

86.   BOOK EDITOR

BASIC DESCRIPTION

Book editors work with authors to acquire books for the employing company. They read book proposals (prospectus) and work with a team to make a determination of whether the book should be published. Once a book contract is established, a book editor will work closely with authors to secure the manuscript and ready it for publication. This will include reading the text and recommending improvements. They will work closely with authors to ensure the writing conforms to the publication policies of the company. This will include making sure all permissions and copyright agreements are in place prior to publication. Book editors may work in a diverse array of publishing companies, from those aimed at niche markets to those publishing for mass markets. Book editors often supervise a small group of copy editors and publication assistants who work out the final details associated with proofing the book and readying it for final printing.

CORE COMPETENCIES AND SKILLS NEEDED

Book editors need to be very detail oriented and have strong written communication skills. Working with numerous writing projects at one time also requires strong time-management skills. Book editors need to have a good understanding of the book market and products that will be received positively. Strong interpersonal skills and the ability to form relationships and foster the work of authors are especially important for this position. Working under strict time deadlines may create stressful conditions, which must be handled calmly and professionally. Having a love for learning and a passion for writing are qualities especially well aligned with this career in education.

EDUCATIONAL REQUIREMENTS

A bachelor's or master's degree in English, journalism, communications, or a related field is typically required to be a book editor. Prior course-work or training in marketing, computer word processing, and web-based publishing is also helpful.

EXPERIENCE NECESSARY

A background as a copy editor or editorial assistant is necessary. Experience with the publishing process within a variety of media, such as newspapers, magazines, and web pages, is essential. An internship or other work experience as a part of an undergraduate degree program is often needed.

CERTIFICATION, LICENSURE, AND CONTINUING EDUCATION REQUIREMENTS

No specific certification or licensure requirements exist for this career in education. It is expected that a book editor will engage in professional development and continuing education to keep up with the latest innovations in publishing and marketing.

SALARY/COMPENSATION

Salary will largely be determined by the size of the company and the number of projects for which the book editor is responsible. According to the Bureau of Labor Statistics (2014c) website, the median salary for editors will typically fall between $50,000 and $60,000. Years of experience and attainment of a graduate degree may also influence salary levels.

EMPLOYMENT OUTLOOK

Disseminating information and knowledge has taken on a global perspective and expanded to parts of the world seldom reached. Although traditional book publishing has dwindled considerably as computer technology and web-based publications have grown, positions related to online book publishing look very promising. Computer skills and knowledge of web-based publishing applications will be especially important for work in this career in the future.

FURTHER INFORMATION FOR EXPLORATION

For additional information about a career as a book editor, the following websites may be of assistance: the American Copy Editors Society (www.copydesk.org), the Association of American Publishers (www.publishers.org), and the Editorial Freelancers Association (www.the-efa.org).

87. HISTORIAN

BASIC DESCRIPTION

Historians conduct research and analyze historical information to shape public knowledge of past events. They turn to archives, books, images, and other artifacts to validate and verify historical information. Sometimes there is a need to go to the source (e.g., building, area) directly or to engage others in interviews to collect additional information. Findings from their data-collection methods are often presented in reports and exhibits, or shared online. They may also publish books based on their extensive research and documentation. Their work may influence policy or regulations. Historians are often employed by government agencies, universities/colleges, businesses, nonprofit organizations, and historical associations. Some historians may also secure, preserve, catalogue, and maintain artifacts. Most historians specialize in a particular subject, time period, or part of the country. The primary work of a historian is to influence understanding in others and to document one's research.

CORE COMPETENCIES AND SKILLS NEEDED

Historians must have strong analytical skills. They need to able to examine a vast amount of information and make data-based conclusions about what they find. Strong research skills are needed along with exceptional written communication skills. Public speaking and presentation skills are also important for those who work as historians, given the important influence of their work on shaping others' thoughts and ideas about the topic. Strong interpersonal skills are also needed due to the importance of using interviewing techniques and working with others to gather and report information.

EDUCATIONAL REQUIREMENTS

A bachelor's or master's degree in history or a closely related field is often required. Other fields of study may include museum studies, library science, historical preservation, and archival management.

EXPERIENCE NECESSARY

Practica and internship experiences are often a part of a course of study necessary to become a historian. Prior experience with a diverse array of artifacts, including written documents, images, and museum pieces, is necessary. A background in professional writing or public speaking may also be expected.

CERTIFICATION, LICENSURE, AND CONTINUING EDUCATION REQUIREMENTS

No specific licensure or credentials are required to be a historian. However, certification as an archivist, preservationist, or in some other relevant aspect of this work can be particularly helpful. A desire to further your knowledge through continuing education and professional development is expected.

SALARY/COMPENSATION

One's salary will certainly be influenced by the agency of employment. The median salary for historians, according to the Bureau of Labor Statistics (2014e), is between $50,000 and $60,000. Years of experience, an advanced degree, and location may also influence wages. Some positions may be part time, likely yielding an hourly wage.

EMPLOYMENT OUTLOOK

The employment outlook for historians is considered to be slower than that for most other occupations. Very few jobs coupled with an abundant supply of well-qualified candidates will make finding a position challenging. Extensive experience, a high level of expertise, or unique qualifications may improve the likelihood of finding a position as a historian in the future.

FURTHER INFORMATION FOR EXPLORATION

For further information to explore a career as a historian, see the Organization of American Historians (www.oah.org), the American Association for State and Local History (www.aaslh.org), and the American Historical Association (www.historians.org).

Career-in-Education Profile
HISTORIAN

Interview With Chad Carlson (BA, Spanish;
MA, Historic Preservation)

Describe your educational background.

I have a BA in Spanish (1999), an MA in historic preservation (2005), and graduate certificates in city planning and advanced Spanish translation.

Describe your prior experiences and the path you took to get to this career.

I dropped out of college for 6 years and worked as a dishwasher, then bus boy, then bartender, at a tavern. During this time I went back to college to finish my undergraduate degree. I taught high school Spanish for 1 year, but I became disillusioned with the behavior of the kids and the collusion among educators in ensuring that the children received state scholarships through grade inflation. Next, I worked at the registrar's office of a university. After 2 years in the registrar's office, I had to ask myself what it is I like to do when I am not at work, and that is reading history texts and watching documentaries. I entered graduate school for historic preservation at a university. In addition, I applied, and was accepted, to a graduate school for journalism. I attended the open house of the school but was disappointed with the director of the program, and the program generally, so I decided not to attend. I was hired as a historian and transportation planner for a highway department in 2005.

Describe the work that you do.

Federal law mandates that any project that accepts federal funds must assess the effects of that project on cultural resources. I survey any resource over 50 years old, assess its eligibility for the National Register of Historic Places, and then assess the effects of the proposed project on that resource. In addition, I film documentaries. Whenever we have an adverse effect on a resource, when there is no

(continued)

275

(continued)

prudent or feasible alternative to avoid the effect on the resource, we have to mitigate the effect by giving something back. Filming documentaries on local history is a way to do this. For example, a documentary film I made on the relocation of a 19th-century African American cemetery, because of a highway project, has won numerous awards and drawn national attention to the fact that there are unmarked African American cemeteries throughout the South. I also use video, via YouTube, to share cultural resources we encounter with American Indian tribes in Oklahoma. (American Indians are always invited to be consulting parties on our projects.)

What is a typical day like for you in this career?

A lot of our field work is now done by consultants. So I do a lot of reviewing of reports by others.

What is the most challenging part of your career?

By far, the biggest problem is communication. Historians are challenged with math, and engineers are challenged with English, so it is often difficult for us to understand each other.

What is the most rewarding part of your career?

I really enjoy being able to represent people in local communities in the face of large state highway projects. Often they feel that they don't have a voice. I take pride in giving them that voice. Government agencies can be secretive and arrogant when it comes to dealing with the public; I try to be as transparent and open as possible with the public about what is happening. After all, as taxpayers, they own the project. People appreciate being respected, and all they really want is to be a part of the process. By being open with them you establish trust, which in the end helps expedite project delivery. "The greenest building is the one already built"—I feel that I am an environmentalist as well. We have become a disposable society, so to be looking out for resources that were built with high-quality materials and craftsmanship is noble work. Oftentimes, buildings are torn down because

(continued)

(continued)

they are considered out of fashion. We often don't appreciate these buildings until after demolition, decades later, when we say, "how did we let that happen?" I can see the significance of these buildings far before they are widely appreciated by the public.

What advice do you have for someone in high school or currently at the undergraduate level who might be interested in this career?

Be sure you are passionate about history and able to work hard.

What advice do you have for someone currently in a different career/field who might be interested in your career?

You must have passion for history.

If you decided to advance your career, what steps would you take and what career might you seek out?

I wouldn't consider another career. I like what I do, and it is important work. I wouldn't want to advance within my career field, because I don't want the stress that comes with a management position.

88. ARCHIVIST

BASIC DESCRIPTION

Archivists accumulate, organize, and maintain historical records and documents. They preserve these documents for easy access and use by others in the future. In addition to performing research on these historical documents, archivists share their findings and collections with others through outreach programs, workshops, seminars, museum displays, and conference presentations. With the increasing use of technology, archivists are more frequently turning to digital formats of artifact cataloguing to ensure the preservation, safety, and security of these materials. Use of electronic storage methods also can improve access by the general public. Some archivists also serve to authenticate and appraise the documents or materials; such efforts would involve close collaboration and consultation with colleagues. Archivists may also be responsible for developing policies and guidelines regarding public access to the archived materials. Most archivists specialize in a specific area and have specialized subject-matter knowledge.

CORE COMPETENCIES AND SKILLS NEEDED

Strong organizational skills are especially important in helping to catalogue and maintain a logical storage system for future retrieval. Research and analytical skills are useful to uncover historical facts associated with the material. Strong written and oral communication skills are essential given the interface of the archivist's work with others. Computer skills and familiarity with electronic database storage programs are increasingly more important as materials are increasingly digitized.

EDUCATIONAL REQUIREMENTS

A bachelor's or master's degree in history, library science, archival science, records management, or a closely related field is required. Working as an archivist within a museum, university, or college setting likely will require a doctoral degree in a related field. Discipline-related knowledge may also be necessary depending on the material to be archived. Coursework or training in computers, software, and electronic databases is also necessary.

EXPERIENCE NECESSARY

Internship experience or field work is commonly associated with degree-program training in history, historical preservation, library science, or related fields of study. In addition, prior work experience or volunteering within an organization focused on history or archiving would be desirable.

CERTIFICATION, LICENSURE, AND CONTINUING EDUCATION REQUIREMENTS

Archivists with appropriate educational training and experience are eligible for certification as an archivist by the Academy of Certified Archivists (www.certifiedarchivists.org). Requirements for renewal of this certificate include completion of continuing education credits.

SALARY/COMPENSATION

According to the Bureau of Labor Statistics (2014b), the median salary for archivists is between $40,000 and $50,000. Compensation within governmental positions appears to be significantly greater. Geographic location, years of experience, and attainment of an advanced degree may also influence one's salary.

EMPLOYMENT OUTLOOK

Public and private organizations are increasingly requiring digitization of records and materials. Use of electronic record management systems for archiving purposes appears to be an area for considerable employment growth in the years ahead. Those with specialized knowledge associated with the materials to be kept will be most highly sought after for these positions.

FURTHER INFORMATION FOR EXPLORATION

For additional information or to further explore a career as an archivist, see the Society of the American Archivists (www.archivists .org), the National Association of Government Archives and Records Administration (www.nagara.org), the Council of State Archivists (www .statearchivists.org) and the National Archives (www.archives.gov).

89.   SCIENCE MUSEUM EDUCATOR

BASIC DESCRIPTION

Science museum educators focus on teaching others about the museum's collections and exhibits through talks, activities, seminars, and workshops. Linking educational programming to national or state science curriculum allows for close connections to schools, colleges, and science instructors. Science museum educators often partner with school educators to arrange field trips to the museum, or they partner with schools to bring a part of the collection to the district. They also collaborate with teachers through partner programs to provide science-related materials or resources to enhance student learning experiences. Planning, creating, developing, and implementing educational programs is the primary role of the science museum educator. In addition to offering and managing educational activities within the science discipline, they may work closely with other museum staff to market and promote scientific learning opportunities. Networking with professionals in other science museums or science-related agencies is also expected within this career in education.

CORE COMPETENCIES AND SKILLS NEEDED

An excellent grasp of science curriculum is essential for this position. The ability to create educational activities and experiences that link closely to the goals and objectives of science educators and science enthusiasts is necessary for this position. A passion for teaching science and helping others to explore the field of science is essential for those who become science museum educators. Strong presentation and organizational skills are important. A focus on effective instructional science education practices is especially important.

EDUCATIONAL REQUIREMENTS

A science-related bachelor's or master's degree is required. In some positions, a doctoral degree may be desired. Prior training in conducting science experiments or simulations would be expected. Some who assume this position may have a background in teacher education or science education. An increasing emphasis on the use of educational technology and electronic instructional methods is influencing the need for advanced skills in computers and web-based applications.

EXPERIENCE NECESSARY

Many years of experience within the sciences or as a science educator is the most ideal characteristic for those who wish to become science museum educators. Prior instructional effectiveness and experience with science curricula are necessary.

CERTIFICATION, LICENSURE, AND CONTINUING EDUCATION REQUIREMENTS

Although a teacher certificate may be desired within this position, no specific certification or licensure is required to be an educator within a museum. Networking and learning from other science museum educators would be expected of those who assume this career. This may include attending national conferences or becoming involved in a staff exchange program with other museums.

SALARY/COMPENSATION

Science museum educators may be hired on a part- or full-time basis depending on the size of the facility or collection. Full-time salaries for museum educators are typically between $40,000 and $50,000, according to the Bureau of Labor Statistics (2014b). An advanced degree and years of experience will certainly influence salary levels.

EMPLOYMENT OUTLOOK

The employment outlook for educators working in museums will likely remain steady in the coming years. Those with specialized science knowledge and the ability to use effective educational technology methods to disseminate information will likely find the greatest success in securing future openings.

FURTHER INFORMATION FOR EXPLORATION

For additional information about a career as a museum educator, see the websites associated with the following organizations: Museum-Ed (www .museum-ed.org) and Smithsonian (www.si.edu).

90. ART MUSEUM EDUCATION DIRECTOR

BASIC DESCRIPTION

Art museum education directors are in charge of creating educational activities and opportunities related to an art museum's collections or special exhibits. Facilitating an appreciation of artistic expression and art mediums in a diverse array of learners is the primary focus of this work. Typically, this work will involve oversight of youth programs, family educational opportunities, museum tours, interpretive materials, and community outreach initiatives. Art museum education directors often direct a small group of staff who work directly with school and general public audiences. Directors oversee partnerships with school districts to arrange field trips to the museum or partner with art teachers to bring educational experiences to their classrooms through visits or via educational technology. Overseeing all aspects of planning, creating, developing, and implementing art educational programs is the primary role of the art museum education director. Networking with professionals in other art museums is also expected within this education career.

CORE COMPETENCIES AND SKILLS NEEDED

Exceptional administrative and leadership skills are needed for this director position. Extensive knowledge and experience within art education is needed. The ability to effectively partner with community and school-based partners is especially important. The ability to work collaboratively with other museum administrators regarding collections and exhibits, outreach, and marketing is also an essential competency needed for this position.

EDUCATIONAL REQUIREMENTS
A master's or doctoral degree is typically required to assume the art museum education director position. Educational training in administration or management would also be important for those assuming this leadership position in art education.

EXPERIENCE NECESSARY
Prior experience as an artist, an art teacher, or more generally as an educator would be necessary for this position. A number of years of supervising and managing programs and staff would also be ideal.

CERTIFICATION, LICENSURE, AND CONTINUING EDUCATION REQUIREMENTS
No specific licensure or credential is required for this position. However, possession of specialized training or certification pertaining to art education can help an individual to stand apart from other applicants.

SALARY/COMPENSATION
Art museum education directors are typically employed full time, although the number of staff they oversee will likely be influenced by the type of setting in which they are employed. Full-time salaries for public museum educators are typically between $50,000 and $60,000, according to the Bureau of Labor Statistics (2014b). An advanced degree, location, years of experience, and size/prestige of the art museum will influence salary levels.

EMPLOYMENT OUTLOOK
The employment outlook for art museum education directors will likely remain steady in the coming years. Those with specialized knowledge and experience in effectively using educational technology methods to disseminate information will likely find the greatest success in securing future openings.

FURTHER INFORMATION FOR EXPLORATION
For additional information about a career in art education, see the National Art Education Association (www.arteducators.org). To explore a leadership career within an art museum, see the Association of Art Museum Directors (www.aamd.org). Many states also have professional

organizations devoted to art education, such as the New York Foundation for the Arts (www.nyfa.org).

91. NATIONAL PARKS GUIDE/INTERPRETER

BASIC DESCRIPTION
National parks guides/interpreters (e.g., naturalists, rangers) work directly with the public to tour points of interest, provide educational information, and answer questions. They interpret the natural and historical relevance of the park for visitors. They work to make park visits educational, memorable, and meaningful through their knowledge of the park's history and their overall familiarity with the park's surroundings and inhabitants. Interpreters typically will live on site and work closely with other park staff to ensure the safety, security, and well-being of guests. In addition to providing guided hikes and tours, national parks guides/interpreters also work on other educational activities associated with the park, such as creation of online resources, workshops, or public outreach efforts. Interpreters will often specialize in a particular subject matter and may teach outdoor survival skills.

CORE COMPETENCIES AND SKILLS NEEDED
An outgoing personality and a love of nature are two qualities especially well aligned with the characteristics needed for this career in education. The ability to communicate effectively is especially important for the give and take associated with hands-on learning activities. Working well as a member of the park staff is important. Being physically fit and adaptable to a wide variety of climate conditions is especially essential for what is typically considered an outdoor occupation. Patience is also important given the diversity of people visiting national parks.

EDUCATIONAL REQUIREMENTS
A bachelor's degree in biology, botany, zoology, environmental studies, history, communication, education, parks and recreation management, or a closely related field is typically required. Prior training as an outdoor guide, tour director, or group instructor would be expected. Specialized knowledge related to state and national parks would be ideal.

EXPERIENCE NECESSARY

Prior internship experience as a part of an undergraduate or graduate degree program is expected. Experience in leading groups and providing outdoor education to others would be necessary for this position. Prior experience and expertise in camping or other outdoor activities would be well suited for this career. Part-time or seasonal work is one way to enter into this career.

CERTIFICATION, LICENSURE, AND CONTINUING EDUCATION REQUIREMENTS

No specific certification or license is needed to be a park interpreter. However, credentials and training from the National Association for Interpretation (www.interpnet.com) may be expected. On-the-job training is required, and continuing education is expected.

SALARY/COMPENSATION

National parks guides/interpreters may be full- or part-time employees. Seasonal work for those who are full-time college students is also available. For those who are employed full time, a typical salary may be between $30,000 and $40,000, although a nice benefit is that often room and board are also provided. Geographic location and type of park will also influence salary levels.

EMPLOYMENT OUTLOOK

The employment outlook for national parks personnel is largely dependent on federal budgets. As government positions are by contract, a limited number of positions may be available. Those with specialized knowledge, training, or background will likely compete more successfully for these positions.

FURTHER INFORMATION FOR EXPLORATION

For additional information about certification and training as an interpreter, see the National Association for Interpretation (www.interpnet.com). To learn more about the national park system, see the National Park Service (www.nps.gov). A professional organization called the Association of National Park Rangers (www.anpr.org) may also provide helpful information for those interested in this career.

92. HUMAN RESOURCE MANAGER

BASIC DESCRIPTION

Human resource managers are in charge of all of the administrative functions of an organization, including recruiting employees, hiring, compensation/benefits, training/development, and performance management systems. They also provide leadership pertaining to organizational policies, such as providing training to personnel in equal opportunity employment practices, sexual harassment within the workplace, medical/family leave, and other issues that may affect an employee's success. Through strategic planning, they work closely with other leaders of the business to ensure that personnel meet the company's needs. A challenging aspect of this position is dealing with difficult staffing issues such as termination, workplace disputes, and disciplinary procedures. In some larger companies, a human resource director may oversee the work of multiple managers. In smaller companies, the human resource manager will perform all aspects of this position.

CORE COMPETENCIES AND SKILLS NEEDED

Exceptional interpersonal skills, including well-developed communication skills, are essential for this position. Critical thinking and analytic skills will be especially important when engaging in making data-based decisions within the company. Excellent time-management and organizational skills are expected within this position. The ability to lead others and to be competent in workforce training is also needed in this administrative position.

EDUCATIONAL REQUIREMENTS

A bachelor's or master's degree in human resources, business administration, or a closely related field is typical of those managers who work in larger companies. In smaller companies, a bachelor's degree in a variety of fields (e.g., education, psychology, labor relations) combined with extensive training or coursework in human resources would be expected.

EXPERIENCE NECESSARY

Prior experience working in human resources would be expected. Familiarity with labor laws, compensation practices, employee benefits, and staff recruitment/training is necessary. A background in public speaking or extensive work in carrying out adult education or professional development programs would be ideal.

CERTIFICATION, LICENSURE, AND CONTINUING EDUCATION REQUIREMENTS

No specific licensure or credentials are required to be a human resource manager; however, a number of organizations, such as the HR Certification Institute (www.hrci.org) and the Society for Human Resource Management (www.shrm.org), do offer certification programs to those interested. Such certification processes and other continuing education opportunities are especially important for those who have degrees in areas not directly related to the field of business administration.

SALARY/COMPENSATION

According to the Bureau of Labor Statistics (2014f), human resource managers earn a median salary just under $100,000, with pay varying substantially depending on the size of the company and number of employees.

EMPLOYMENT OUTLOOK

As the economy expands and business growth occurs, the need for employees well trained in human resource management will likewise grow. The employment outlook looks quite positive for the years ahead.

FURTHER INFORMATION FOR EXPLORATION

To further explore a career as a human resource manager, the websites of the following professional organizations should be consulted: the National Human Resources Association (www.humanresources.org), the Society for Human Resource Management (www.shrm.org), and the International Public Management Association for Human Resources (www.ipma-hr.org).

Career-in-Education Profile
HUMAN RESOURCE MANAGER
Interview With Shelly Carlson (BS, Elementary Education)

Describe your educational background.

I attended a 4-year university program and majored in elementary education. I student taught within both first- and fifth-grade classrooms. My degree and training to become a teacher was instrumental in providing me the opportunity to assume a number of different careers (special education assistant, private tutor, administrator of educational services, human resources personnel) as my personal circumstances and professional interests have shifted across my lifetime.

Describe your prior experiences and the path you took to get to this career.

I honestly didn't know what to study in college. As a child, I always played school. As a teenager, I enjoyed babysitting and working with kids, so I thought a degree in education would be a good fit. I thought it would allow me the chance to make a positive difference in children's lives. My career began as substitute teacher as I struggled to find and secure a full-time position in the area in which I resided. I also note that I was not the best interviewee, as I struggled to adapt to the interview process and the need to think well on my feet within this performance situation. After a few years of substitute teaching, I obtained a full-time elementary classroom teaching position. I taught multiple grades, including third grade, split fourth/fifth grade, and fifth grade, in a public school system during a 4-year span. I preferred teaching the older students and appreciated the independence and maturity they brought to the learning environment. Following a family move to a different state, I was a special education instructional assistant at a middle school for 1 year. I then went on to teaching at Sylvan Learning Centers and eventually became an associate director of education and then a floating director of education. The desire to work within a creative environment and also the lure of fringe benefits led to my switch to an administrative assistant with

(continued)

(*continued*)

my current employer. I have since worked my way into my current position of human resources (HR) manager. While in my HR position, I left that career to pursue my passions pertaining to real estate. However, the downturn in the economy and the opportunity to rejoin my prior employer (benefits, stability, flexibility to work part time) resulted in my decision to leave the realty world behind me and return to my HR position.

Describe the work that you do.

My work as an HR manager entails being responsible for all aspects of HR, payroll/compensation, and office management, with the goal to ensure overall success of the company by maintaining an organized and efficient work environment.

What is a typical day like for you in this career?

There really is no typical day in my position! One moment I can be tending to a jammed copier, then answering phones, working on invoices, and responding to job applicants, and then reviewing business insurance and processing payroll. My responsibilities are greatly varied and span both ends of the HR and office management spectrum. Every day is different for me in this job.

What is the most challenging part of your career?

The most challenging part of my career is keeping up with employment law. This was especially difficult when my company was operating in two different states. Employment law was vastly different across these two locations and resulted in the need to have different conversations about benefits with people at each location.

What is the most rewarding part of your career?

The most rewarding part of my career is helping and educating employees (e.g., new employee orientation, the company's HR policies

(*continued*)

(continued)

and insurance plans). I also enjoy knowing that I am contributing to the overall success of the company by helping to develop/retain productive and satisfied employees and by helping to provide an enjoyable work environment.

What advice do you have for someone in high school or currently at the undergraduate level who might be interested in this career?

My advice is to take courses focusing on business administration, psychology, accounting, and marketing. Also remember to diversify your talents, skills, and competencies. I would recommend that those interested in this career should pursue a bachelor's degree in human resources management. Excellent listening skills, attention to detail, well-developed communication skills, and organizational skills are a must as well.

What advice do you have for someone currently in a different career/field who might be interested in your career?

My advice is to join a professional association, such as becoming a member of the Society for Human Resource Management (SHRM), and network with HR professionals in your area. Look for an entry-level HR position or possibly an internship to gain work experience. Work toward HR certification and take coursework related to the HR area of interest.

If you decided to advance your career, what steps would you take and what career(s) might you seek out?

I would first work toward becoming certified as a professional in human resources (PHR) or a senior professional in human resources (SPHR) through the SHRM. I would also consider pursuing a master's degree in HR. If I were to advance my career, I would do so through attainment of an advanced graduate degree in HR, and my next step up the career ladder within this field would be to hold the position of HR director.

REFERENCES

Bureau of Labor Statistics, U.S. Department of Labor. (2014a). *Occupational outlook handbook, 2014–2015 edition, Adult Literacy and High School Equivalency Diploma Teachers.* Retrieved July 14, 2015, from http://www.bls.gov/ooh/education-training-and-library/adult-literacy-and-ged-teachers.htm

Bureau of Labor Statistics, U.S. Department of Labor. (2014b). *Occupational outlook handbook, 2014–2015 edition, Archivists, Curators, and Museum Workers.* Retrieved July 14, 2015, from http://www.bls.gov/ooh/education-training-and-library/curators-museum-technicians-and-conservators.htm

Bureau of Labor Statistics, U.S. Department of Labor. (2014c). *Occupational outlook handbook, 2014–2015 edition, Editors.* Retrieved July 13, 2015, from http://www.bls.gov/ooh/media-and-communication/editors.htm

Bureau of Labor Statistics, U.S. Department of Labor. (2014d). *Occupational outlook handbook, 2014–2015 edition, Health Educators and Community Health Workers.* Retrieved July 12, 2015, from http://www.bls.gov/ooh/community-and-social-service/health-educators.htm

Bureau of Labor Statistics, U.S. Department of Labor. (2014e). *Occupational outlook handbook, 2014–2015 edition, Historians.* Retrieved July 12, 2015, from http://www.bls.gov/ooh/life-physical-and-social-science/historians.htm

Bureau of Labor Statistics, U.S. Department of Labor. (2014f). *Occupational outlook handbook, 2014–2015 edition, Human Resources Managers.* Retrieved June 27, 2015, from http://www.bls.gov/ooh/management/human-resources-managers.htm

11 ■ CAREERS PERTAINING TO WEB-BASED LEARNING AND EDUCATIONAL TECHNOLOGY

93. ONLINE LEARNING (HIGH SCHOOL TEACHER)

BASIC DESCRIPTION

Online learning high school teachers provide instruction in curriculum via an online forum. They may teach for either a public (free tuition) or private online education system. Online teachers communicate with their students through e-mail, message boards, and learning management systems. Multiple methods of instruction, including the use of media (e.g., podcasts, video-based lectures) and other technological innovations (e.g., social media, blogs, group messaging), are commonly employed. Course assignments, quizzes, tests, and questions/answers/discussion occur through the use of the Internet. In some instances, a hybrid format may be used that includes some face-to-face meetings. Most times, however, the entire course and its content are taught fully online and all aspects of evaluating student competencies in that content are done remotely. This format provides an alternative for high school students who may benefit from the convenience and flexibility of online courses in completing their graduating requirements. This may include a diverse array of students, such as those with special needs, those living in districts where curricular options may be limited, or those unable to attend the typical school day due to work or other commitments. Online teachers can work from home or in school settings. Course instruction may involve multiple sections or distinct courses within/across disciplines.

CORE COMPETENCIES AND SKILLS NEEDED

Content knowledge is essential for the courses taught. A comprehensive understanding of how to utilize online resources within instruction is needed. Use of effective techniques to promote active engagement within an online course is very important within this position. Being available for student inquiries and questions will require work outside of the traditional school day. Frequent check-ins to the online course management system and timely responses to student concerns or challenges are expected. Exceptional written communication skills are especially important for this career in education.

EDUCATIONAL REQUIREMENTS

Online teachers must have completed a teacher education program and be certified to teach in the state in which they work. A focus on secondary education and the high school curriculum should be demonstrated. Prior coursework and knowledge in the content area taught are necessary. In addition, demonstration of effective instructional practices for that content is required.

EXPERIENCE NECESSARY

Prior experience in teaching course content in traditional formats is typically necessary. It is important to demonstrate the ability to merge that expertise with technology and best practices in online learning/teaching. Working closely with a technology support team or a company specializing in offering online high school curriculum is required.

CERTIFICATION, LICENSURE, AND CONTINUING EDUCATION REQUIREMENTS

A teaching certificate is necessary. Endorsements or certificates related to online teaching might also be required. See state-specific credentialing requirements for additional information.

SALARY/COMPENSATION

Salary may be similar to that of a traditional-format teacher (average range of $52,500 to $58,500). Alternatively, a stipend approach might be set up in which each online course results in a set payment (e.g., $2000) to the instructor. Some teachers will supplement their regular teaching positions by teaching online courses.

EMPLOYMENT OUTLOOK

The use of online courses to teach high school students has increased substantially over the past decade. This trend is anticipated to continue in the years to come. A lack of well-trained online teachers further complicates the challenges in meeting the demand for this career in education.

FURTHER INFORMATION FOR EXPLORATION

The International Association for K–12 Online Learning (www.inacol .org) and the National Education Association (www.nea.org) provide additional information and a number of resources that can be helpful in further exploring the possibility of a career in teaching online courses to the high school-age population. To get a sense of the proliferation of online schools across the country and review local options in your community for taking online K–12 courses, see www.k12.com.

94. SCHOOL TECHNOLOGY SPECIALIST

BASIC DESCRIPTION

School technology specialists (also known as instructional technology specialists, learning development specialists, and school technology coordinators) are responsible for overseeing the district's website, learning management/grade system, and other assigned aspects of the use of technology within the district. Their primary responsibility is to help teachers and staff to use technology effectively to enhance student learning outcomes. They do this by conducting staff training and professional development activities. The school technology specialist will serve as a consultant to those school personnel with questions or concerns about the use of technology to enhance student learning. In addition, they may serve as the point of contact for technology vendors who provide services to the district. Often, those who are well qualified for this career will also be well trained to work with publishing companies or nonprofit groups that design and develop instructional materials.

CORE COMPETENCIES AND SKILLS NEEDED

An extensive knowledge of instructional technology materials and techniques is necessary. Effective oral communication skills and strong interpersonal skills are especially important given the frequent interface expected with school staff. Although school technology specialists are not likely to have a teaching certificate, a passion for effective teaching and a curiosity about how technology might improve student outcomes are very important for this position.

EDUCATIONAL REQUIREMENTS

A bachelor's degree in teacher education, information technology, educational technology, or a related field is required. Certified teachers who move into these positions will often have completed a master's degree in educational technology or a related field of study. Courses in effective instructional practices, curricular assessment, student learning, data analysis, website development, computer science, and teacher consultation would all be helpful for this line of work.

EXPERIENCE NECESSARY
Extensive experience in using technology to enhance learning and student outcomes is desired. The ability to consult effectively and work closely with others is important. Evidence of engagement in collaborative problem solving is also necessary given the diversity of issues and challenges that will arise when using technology in the classroom.

CERTIFICATION, LICENSURE, AND CONTINUING EDUCATION REQUIREMENTS
Certification as an educational technology specialist may be required, especially in those schools that use specialists to help provide direct instruction to students. Ultimately, work experience, background knowledge, and prior training will be most important in a candidate for this unique position in schools.

SALARY/COMPENSATION
Typical salaries for this position range between $40,000 and $50,000. Years of experience, geographic location, and possession of a graduate degree or advanced certificate will all influence salary levels.

EMPLOYMENT OUTLOOK
The use of technology to enhance student learning holds considerable promise within the field of education. Accountability for educational effectiveness can be efficiently investigated and analyzed using technology. Given recent advancements in technology and the anticipated changes that will occur in technology, coupled with the effects of those changes, this career in education is expected to grow substantially in the years to come.

FURTHER INFORMATION FOR EXPLORATION
For additional information about this career, see the Association for Educational Communications and Technology (www.aect.org) and the

International Society for Technology in Education (www.iste.org). State-level organizations focused on the use of technology in education should also be explored (e.g., www.tcea.org). Alternatively, focusing on the nature and scope of a graduate degree in educational technology (e.g., www.edutech.msu.edu) can also be very helpful in deciding whether this career might be one worth pursuing.

95. CHIEF TECHNOLOGY AND INFORMATION OFFICER

BASIC DESCRIPTION

The school district's chief technology and information officer provides leadership in how the district uses technology to educate its students and how it runs all of its systems. The officer will work to establish a specific set of goals related to the use of technology in the district and then will be responsible for working with a team to implement the necessary technology and systems to meet those goals. This position will involve overseeing the implementation of instructional technology, using online assessments, managing district behavior and achievement data, ensuring cybersecurity within the district, and all other aspects involving the use of technology (e.g., attendance, grading system, classroom management systems). This school leader will work closely with the district's administrative team. This collaborative relationship will be especially relevant in regard to working with the director of curriculum and instruction within the district.

CORE COMPETENCIES AND SKILLS NEEDED

Managerial and leadership skills are needed within this position, as much of this work will be completed by other staff members who are a part of the technology team. Excellent verbal and written communication skills are especially important given the need to work with others both within and outside the school environment. Strong organizational skills and the ability to work well under deadlines are necessary. Juggling multiple responsibilities and roles within the complexities of working within the unique characteristics of the school district requires both flexibility and adaptability. Analytical and systems thinking skills are especially essential given the need for data collection within the district and the dissemination of that information to constituents (e.g., parents, state-level Department of Education, policymakers).

EDUCATIONAL REQUIREMENTS

A bachelor's or master's degree in computer science, information science, education, business administration, or a related field is required. Extensive education, knowledge, and background related to the use of information technology (e.g., hardware, software, wireless networks, infrastructure, user support) are important for this career in education.

EXPERIENCE NECESSARY

Prior experience in successfully employing technology within education is imperative for this career. An extensive background demonstrating effective organizational change or continuous improvement within a school district or business is necessary for this leadership position. Prior work experience that provides evidence of effectively working with technology companies and businesses outside of the school system is especially important.

CERTIFICATION, LICENSURE, AND CONTINUING EDUCATION REQUIREMENTS

An advanced certificate in educational technology or technology coordination will likely be required. Demonstrating the highest credential available for the field of study completed will be important for this administrative position. In some districts, completion of a doctoral program or coursework in educational technology may be desired.

SALARY/COMPENSATION

Consistent with other school district administrators, salaries for chief technology and information officers will be some of the highest across the district. Although location, years of experience, and background/training will certainly influence salary levels, average salaries for this position within educational systems will likely fall between $90,000 and $110,000. Pay for chief technology officers who work outside of the school setting (e.g., businesses, government) may be considerably higher.

EMPLOYMENT OUTLOOK

Computer and information management systems are growing and changing continuously. Leaders who are able to guide school districts to cost-effectively and efficiently use technology for the purpose of accountability are currently in high demand. This demand is anticipated to continue to increase in both the near and long term.

Career-in-Education Profile
CHIEF TECHNOLOGY AND INFORMATION OFFICER

Interview With Diane Doersch (BS, Elementary Education; MEd, Educational Technology)

Describe your educational background.

I earned my bachelor of science degree in elementary education (grades 1–8). After 9 years of teaching I earned my master's degree in educational technology. I then moved to a middle school computer applications teaching position. Eventually I made the jump from teacher to administrator when I became the leader of technology for the entire school district. After 1 year in this role, I earned my technology coordinator certification, which prompted a promotion to the director of technology position for the district. Finally, I moved to a different district to assume the position of chief technology and information officer.

Describe your prior experiences and the path you took to get to this career.

Prior life experiences that helped me get to where I am now include the following:

■ Farm kid—I learned the value of hard work, tenacity, and teamwork.
■ Young mom—I learned effective time-management skills, how to multitask, and how to separate home life from my professional life.
■ Cocktail server/bartender—I learned vital "people" skills as well as customer service skills.

Educational experiences:

■ Adjunct faculty—This experience helped me build a professional learning network, an arsenal of resources, and a research pedagogy that improved my organizational/presentation skills.

(continued)

(continued)

- Organizer of professional learning events—This experience helped me to create differentiation in instructional methods. Personalized learning has helped me reach larger audiences.
- Teacher leader—My 21 years in teaching helped me learn about systems and development, management, and sustainability.

Describe the work that you do.

I supervise and am responsible for the operations of 42 members of my teams. Network managers, technical solutions architects and project managers, and programmers are examples of a few of these teams. I work closely in the coordination of technology services (e.g., data/information, technology instruction) with other departments (e.g., special education, pupil services) within the district. It is also my job to make sure our end users (students) have equitable access to technological learning resources that fit their individual needs.

What is a typical day like for you in this career?

My days are usually filled with meeting people face to face:

- **Departmental status meetings:** I hold weekly status meetings with all divisions. We keep an agenda of topics for updates and on it we note collaborative decisions made and tasks to be completed.
- **Internal concept and procedural meetings:** A lot of my time is also spent on researching processes and products for advancement according to the strategic direction of our district—for instance, determining which portable devices will be best as our educators teach within a mobile environment.
- **External concept and procedural meetings:** As our school district works to optimize resources, it often requires working in partnership with like organizations. Those partnerships require governance agreements, financial commitment, and joint leadership.
- **Vendor meetings:** I meet with vendors to make sure we are receiving the products/services for which we are contracted. I also

(continued)

(continued)

spend a substantial amount of time doing product research and developing requests for proposals.

■ **Ambassador and informational meetings:** At times, I serve as the "face" of technology with business leaders, city/county government, and educational institutions at the state and national levels.

What is the most challenging part of your career?

The most challenging part of my career is finding balance between strategic priorities. One must be very careful to keep all priorities on the radar and know when to move on each topic. It requires strategic planning and coordination so that all items "fit" together as a complete, multilayered package that addresses the needs of the district.

What is the most rewarding part of your career?

The innovative nature of my position is the most intriguing and motivating for me. When I am able to build a system and structure that has a valid proof of concept I feel most rewarded. Making sure our students, no matter what their background and socioeconomic status may be, have equal opportunities to learn is the WHAT to all things I do. My belief system and values support my passion to be a servant to others, which answers the WHY. I have been blessed to have a life full of rich experiences that have taught me life lessons and create the HOW I do what I do.

What advice do you have for someone in high school or currently at the undergraduate level who might be interested in this career?

A person in my administrative position must never forget what takes place in the classroom, as our teachers and students are our end users. Learn all you can about the systems that support education. Build a personal learning network via social media to keep up with the latest research-based trends. Attend educational and personal networking events that incorporate large-system thinking with the nuts

(continued)

(continued)

and bolts of how things are operationalized in the classroom. Strive for continuous improvement. Last, when there is a match between your values and your work mission, your passions will be fed and your life will be fulfilled.

What advice do you have for someone currently in a different career/field who might be interested in your career?

Learn all you can. Take what you know from your current field and work to apply it to this career. Job shadow and remember to talk to your end users.

If you decided to advance your career, what steps would you take and what career(s) might you seek out?

Advancement for me would mean working on a larger scale or a very specialized scale such as a technology consultant. Other passions that I could incorporate into another career include leadership coaching, building opportunities for marginalized individuals, filmmaking, and policy reform. I truly do view my future as having no limits—the possibilities are endless and I can write my own future.

FURTHER INFORMATION FOR EXPLORATION

To learn more about what is involved in this profession, see the State Educational Technology Directors Association (www.setda.org) for helpful resources and information.

96. WEB DESIGNER

BASIC DESCRIPTION

Web designers (developers) create, refine, and maintain websites. They develop a website to match the needs of the client (i.e., website purpose), and they create the interface in which a user interacts. The look, feel, and utility of a website are important to its users. Responsibilities associated with this position include content management/updating, programming, website layout, and meeting of technical requirements. Registering the website with search engines to improve ease of access to the site is essential. Analyzing site traffic and running analytics on the data collected can help to further improve functionality. Web designers can work in a variety of different settings, such as businesses, consulting firms, schools, or government agencies. Many are self-employed, and many are also required to work closely with others related to web design. Specialized web developers may include web programmers (create), web designers (implement), and webmasters (evaluate, refine, maintain).

CORE COMPETENCIES AND SKILLS NEEDED

A thorough understanding of website design (e.g., graphic design, software programming skills, Internet presence, programming language familiarity) is essential. The ability to effectively use images, icons, banners, video, and audio is necessary. Attention to and understanding of website functionality are especially important. The ability to listen to a client's needs, identify specific goals for the website, and build a set of pages that meets or exceeds those needs is the primary set of skills needed for this position. Artistic talent, creativity, and imagination are important qualities for web designers to possess. They must also be able to focus intensively on project completion and be very detail oriented. The ability to work under stressful conditions to meet deadlines and skill in communicating effectively with a broad array of clients are especially important for this customer-driven career.

EDUCATIONAL REQUIREMENTS

A bachelor's degree in web design, computer science, programming, multimedia, communications, or a related field is needed. In some cases, an associate's degree in web design or a related field might suffice. No matter the educational background, prior experience in developing websites, working as a part of a team, and meeting deadlines is important.

EXPERIENCE NECESSARY

For those without a bachelor's degree, prior experience with computer programming, graphic design, and website management is necessary.

CERTIFICATION, LICENSURE, AND CONTINUING EDUCATION REQUIREMENTS

Given the fast-paced innovations apparent in the field of technology, the need for continuing education is clearly essential. One must be committed to learning new technologies. Specific certification in or mastery of programming languages or multimedia publishing tools may be required.

SALARY/COMPENSATION
Salaries for web designers vary considerably by employer, location, years of experience, and qualifications. The median salary for web developers, according to the Bureau of Labor Statistics (2014), is just under $65,000 annually. A quick search of web-based job postings will provide additional information about the level of salary one might expect from working in this important career in education.

EMPLOYMENT OUTLOOK
The importance of a company, school, or business web presence has increased dramatically over the past 10 years. This trend is expected to continue, and job growth is expected to remain strong in both the near and long term. This demand will be fueled by continued improvements in mobile technology, e-commerce, gaming, cloud storage, versatility of multimedia, and Internet connectedness.

FURTHER INFORMATION FOR EXPLORATION
For additional information about a career in web design, see www .webprofessionals.org, the International Webmasters Association (www .iwanet.org), the National Association of Government Web Professionals (www.nagw.org), and the HTML Writers Guild (www.hwg.org).

97. INSTRUCTIONAL DESIGNER

BASIC DESCRIPTION
Instructional designers (instructional systems designers, instructional coordinators) work with content experts to identify learning goals, objectives, and expected competencies. They then use that knowledge to develop instructional practices, strategies, training tools, and other resources that work to optimize learning through use of multimedia, technology, and other supporting documents. These training strategies and resources are then tested and refined for use. In addition, instructional designers develop assessments to determine whether learning goals have been met. Discovering the most effective methods by which others learn is the key focus of this career in education.

CORE COMPETENCIES AND SKILLS NEEDED

Core competencies related to using technology (e.g., software, basic HTML, graphic design, web-page editors) effectively within teaching practices are needed. This includes effectively planning and implementing instructional practices. Excellent writing skills are needed. The ability to juggle multiple responsibilities and projects under tight deadlines is essential for this position. Effective interpersonal and communication skills are needed. Working as a part of a team and seeing projects through from start to finish are especially important for an instructional designer.

EDUCATIONAL REQUIREMENTS

A bachelor's degree in instructional design, education, curriculum, or a related field is expected. Additional graduate work that enhances specialty knowledge can be helpful when entering this career or as a part of continuing education. A comprehensive understanding of learning theory and optimized learning is required. Graduate programs in instructional design or instructional design for e-learning are available at many universities.

EXPERIENCE NECESSARY

A prior history of working within the field of instructional coordination or professional development is expected. The ability to work as a member of a team to develop and implement projects should be evident.

CERTIFICATION, LICENSURE, AND CONTINUING EDUCATION REQUIREMENTS

No particular certification or licensure is required to be an instructional designer, although certifications are available and connected to related professional associations (e.g., certified professional in learning and performance).

SALARY/COMPENSATION

Typically salaries for an instructional designer range from $40,000 to $50,000 but will vary widely based on years of experience, degree, and geographic location. Business or industry employment settings may provide higher salaries. School- or government-based settings may provide more modest salaries. Reviewing job openings in this career on Internet websites will help to estimate salaries more accurately for the area/ setting in which you are interested in working.

EMPLOYMENT OUTLOOK
The employment outlook for instructional designers appears to be steady for the years to come. An increase in online education, a greater focus on accountability with respect to student competency development, and the anticipated rapid expansion of new technology pertaining to optimized learning will further enhance the need for individuals to enter this career in education.

FURTHER INFORMATION FOR EXPLORATION
For additional information and resources about the field of instructional design, see www.instructionaldesigncentral.com and the website of the Society for Applied Learning Technology (www.salt.org).

98.   ONLINE DEGREE COORDINATOR (UNIVERSITY)

BASIC DESCRIPTION
Online degree (distance education) coordinators are responsible for overseeing recruitment, admissions, retention, and graduation of students who are completing an online degree. They may also be responsible for ensuring that course content meets national training standards. Development, maintenance, and continuous improvements in program offerings, recruitment materials, and the program website are especially important for those working in this coordinator position. This position requires a close working relationship with individuals in other programs and departments within the university. Partnering with those involved in other distance learning activities and online programs across campus is especially important.

CORE COMPETENCIES AND SKILLS NEEDED
Considerable knowledge about online learning, learning management systems, and degree program coordination is very important for those working as online degree program coordinators. Strong communication skills and the ability to work as a member of a team are particularly important in this leadership position.

EDUCATIONAL REQUIREMENTS

An advanced degree in educational technology, curriculum and instruction, distance education, educational leadership, or a related field is required. Prior coursework in learning theory, program development, instructional technology, or marketing all would link well to the skills necessary in this position.

EXPERIENCE NECESSARY

Previous employment related to online education at the university level is highly desired. Prior program coordination experience is necessary. If a candidate has no prior experience with online education delivery systems, then experience in the field of education or community education will likely be required. Experience working as a member of a team and strong interpersonal skills are needed given the need to interface frequently with potential students interested in or accepted into the program. Proficiency in use of social media, technology, and other marketing tools may link well to the requirements necessary for success in this position.

CERTIFICATION, LICENSURE, AND CONTINUING EDUCATION REQUIREMENTS

No specific certification or licensure is required for this position, although online degree coordinators in the field of education may have a background and training in teacher education and possibly be certified teachers. Staying informed about issues of training and changes in degree requirements within the field of study is especially important within this position. Staying up to date on the trends in online education and best practices in using technology to enhance instruction is also required.

SALARY/COMPENSATION

Salaries vary considerable according to years of experience, location, and type of online degree. Typical salaries may fall between $35,000 and $45,000.

EMPLOYMENT OUTLOOK

The proliferation of online education has resulted in a substantial increase in the need for degree program coordinators. Given the growth in information technology and use of technology in education, and the necessity of meeting the needs of a workforce wanting to pursue advanced degrees, it is likely that this career will grow substantially in the years ahead.

FURTHER INFORMATION FOR EXPLORATION
A close look at online degree program offerings at a university that may be familiar (e.g., education.msu.edu/academics/online) can help to better understand the nature of this career in education. The United States Distance Learning Association (www.usdla.org) or the Distance Education Accrediting Commission (www.deac.org) might also be consulted.

99.   MULTIMEDIA COORDINATOR

BASIC DESCRIPTION
Multimedia coordinators (digital media coordinators) are specialists in managing digital information (e.g., websites, blogs), desktop publishing, marketing and branding, and educating others. They are responsible for the development and implementation of media-based strategies to meet identified goals and objectives. Use of multimedia in instruction and training is a common focus within this career in education, although this position may be found in industry (e.g., gaming, websites), nonprofit agencies, or government (e.g., databases, professional training) settings. Individuals in this position will work closely with the director of communications, or they may assume a dual role that includes the responsibilities of the director of communications position within an organization.

CORE COMPETENCIES AND SKILLS NEEDED
Knowledge and skills pertaining to desktop publishing, web development, video production, graphic design, and programming (e.g., HTML) are necessary. In addition, exceptional communications skills (e.g., visual, written), creativity, and the ability to work closely with others are needed. Exceptional time-management skills and the ability to see projects to completion are essential. When working under the pressure of tight deadlines, the ability to maintain a high degree of professionalism, to juggle multiple projects at one time, and to provide strong leadership is important in this career in education. Coordination of people, technology, and resources is especially important in this role.

EDUCATIONAL REQUIREMENTS

A bachelor's degree in graphic design, video production, communications, marketing, media, journalism, or a related field is required. Coursework in educational technology, visual communications, content delivery, and social media is important for the work to be accomplished in this position.

EXPERIENCE NECESSARY

Prior experience in developing, writing, or editing content for web-based platforms is necessary. A history of and prior success in building, maintaining, and engaging active online audiences through social media may be needed.

CERTIFICATION, LICENSURE, AND CONTINUING EDUCATION REQUIREMENTS

Staying up to date on trends in technology is required. This includes familiarity with search engine trends, new media, content delivery, and best practices in growing and engaging audiences.

SALARY/COMPENSATION

Salaries for multimedia coordinators will depend on location, years of experience, type of degree earned, and the breadth of the position's responsibilities. A typical salary would be expected to fall in the $45,000 to $55,000 range.

EMPLOYMENT OUTLOOK

Use of educational technology has grown tremendously in the past decade. This trend is expected to increase in the years ahead given the emergence of new technologies, the role of multimedia in content delivery, and the ability to reach vast audiences through the Internet.

FURTHER INFORMATION FOR EXPLORATION

For additional information about the multimedia field, see the website of the International Federation of Multimedia Associations (www.fiam.org) or the website of the Association for the Advancement of Computing in Education (www.aace.org).

100. E-LEARNING DEVELOPER

BASIC DESCRIPTION

E-learning developers (instructional designers) create courses or trainings that can be taken online. This includes the use of technology in the development of course materials, training modules, learning activities, methods of assessment, and interactive discussion forums. Content development can take many forms and may include the creation of tutorials, simulations, quizzes, and troubleshooting guides. Digital learning curriculum must meet the needs of the target population. Testing and refining the content prior to implementation is essential. E-learning developers may work independently, but more typically will work as a part of a team of specialists that may include curriculum designers, graphic artists, video producers, subject specialists, and learners. This career in education may be in either the public or private sector.

CORE COMPETENCIES AND SKILLS NEEDED

Creativity, technical skills, and specialization in content knowledge are needed within this position. Skills in effectively completing a needs assessment within the population of interest, working as a part of multidisciplinary team, and working under pressure to meet deadlines are essential competencies needed by e-learning developers. Excellent written, verbal, and visual communication skills are necessary within this career in education. A commitment to quality and attention to detail are especially important in this position given the complexity of the system being developed to carry forward the goals of the curriculum.

EDUCATIONAL REQUIREMENTS

A bachelor's or master's degree in instructional design, communication, educational technology, multimedia/graphic design, curriculum and instruction, or a related field is necessary. An associate's degree may be acceptable with demonstrated competencies in the effective development and delivery of e-learning modules. Coursework and training in a wide variety of software applications, hardware, and multimedia approaches used to enhance learning are required. In addition to having the technological know-how to build a meaningful and creative e-learning course/module, a service-minded, team player who can relate well to others will be especially well suited for this career.

EXPERIENCE NECESSARY

A background in teaching, curriculum, web design, audio visual technology, e-learning development, or instructional design is necessary. A history of effectively working collaboratively as a member of a project development team is important for this career. Prior experience in designing online learning materials, websites, or computer-based activities is needed.

CERTIFICATION, LICENSURE, AND CONTINUING EDUCATION REQUIREMENTS

Many universities offer an e-learning design- and- development certificate. This certificate provides evidence of training in e-learning development, instructional design, scripting, and production and delivery of online training curriculum. A commitment to continuing education and keeping up to date with technological advances is required.

SALARY/COMPENSATION

The average salary for an e-learning developer, according to a recent salary and compensation report by the eLearning Guild, is just under $80,000. Salary range will vary based on location, degree held, experience, and technological expertise.

EMPLOYMENT OUTLOOK

The growth of online learning has created a very positive employment outlook for this profession. Advances in technology, improvements in online instruction, and use of multimedia will continue to create new innovations. The potential for growth in this career is substantial.

FURTHER INFORMATION FOR EXPLORATION

A number of helpful resources can be further explored at the website of the E-Learning Guild (www.elearningguild.com), a community for e-learning professionals.

101. EDUCATIONAL DESIGN STUDIO DIRECTOR

BASIC DESCRIPTION

The director of an educational design studio oversees all aspects of a studio that is set up to provide a high degree of technological innovation to online learning activities. The studio serves as a workplace for conceiving, designing, developing, implementing, and evaluating new e-learning products. Within a university setting, the studio supports various technologies (e.g., green screen technology, multimedia, synchronous audio/visual technologies, software applications, video capture/streaming/publishing, mobile computing, course management systems) for teaching and learning. Staff members (i.e., project teams) working within the educational design studio typically work with faculty to collaboratively create teaching tools that enhance the learning process. The studio director is responsible for hiring staff, overseeing resources and finances, purchasing new equipment, and working with vendors to explore the latest in educational technology trends. Bringing technological innovation into the online classroom and facilitating innovative practices within courses are the primary goals of an educational design studio director.

CORE COMPETENCIES AND SKILLS NEEDED

A firm understanding of the value of and need for bringing technological advances and innovation to enhance the teaching and learning process is necessary. Strong communication skills are especially important for this leadership position. The ability to think creatively about solutions and efficiently/effectively problem solve are key characteristics of a strong leader in this position. The ability to work across multiple colleges and departments within a university is essential. Skills in project development and evidence of efficiently bringing projects to the point of completion are especially necessary within this position.

EDUCATIONAL REQUIREMENTS

An advanced degree in educational technology, instructional design, e-learning, or a closely related field is required. Leadership and management coursework is typically evident. A strong background in educational theory and research-based practices is especially essential given the active learning that is taking place within the studio itself. Continuous improvement through a high level of investigation of instructional practices and dissemination of studio activities to a diverse audience (e.g., students, administrators, community members, online audiences) is expected.

EXPERIENCE NECESSARY

Prior experience in educational technology, e-learning, or instructional design is necessary. A background in educational administration or leadership within the field of educational technology is typical for those who assume the director position. A history of working with a diverse array of students, faculty, and administrators is required.

CERTIFICATION, LICENSURE, AND CONTINUING EDUCATION REQUIREMENTS
Continuing education and keeping a close eye on the field of educational technology are necessary. No specific certification or licensure is associated with this director position.

SALARY/COMPENSATION
The concept of an educational design studio is both innovative and unique within college campuses. Salaries for those in this position will likely depend on an employee's background, training, and degree. The rarity of studios focus on enhancing student learning via technology is quite substantial. Thus, salaries are best conceptualized within the context of the setting, as well as the background and training of the applicant. Director positions may range from $80,000 to $90,000.

EMPLOYMENT OUTLOOK
Currently, educational design studios are relatively rare. For those studios that are set up within university settings, the need for strong leadership and a vast background in instructional design results in a need for more leaders to assume positions within this emerging discipline.

FURTHER INFORMATION FOR EXPLORATION
To further explore the types of activities and projects taking place in one university-based educational design studio, see the website of the CEPSE/COE Design Studio at Michigan State University (designstudio .educ.msu.edu).

Career-in-Education Profile
EDUCATIONAL DESIGN STUDIO DIRECTOR

Interview with John Bell (BS, Computer Science; MS, Computer Science; PhD, Computer Science)

Describe your educational background.

My work with both computers and teaching began informally when I grew up in a home of educators who were passionate about how technology could positively impact teaching and learning. So throughout my K–12 education, I did a lot of learning on my own. I pursued this interest in technology in college while also continuing my work outside of school. My interest in teaching was entirely in an informal setting until I completed a year as a postdoctoral research in education. That position was very significant for me because it brought together these two interests of technology and teaching and learning. I also pursued a seminary degree with an emphasis on the support of learning.

Describe your prior experiences and the path you took to get to this career.

My career began with a focus on using technology to support those working in K–12 education, with a primary focus on leadership issues. My task was to create technology tools to support educational leaders as well as teachers in their own responsibilities in the school setting. I then spent many years teaching teachers how to think about and use technology in ways that supported teaching and learning. My current position is a natural next step toward helping people use technology in ways that further their goals. Both then and now, I am looking for ways to help teachers maximize the effectiveness of their teaching to enhance meaningful understanding by students.

Describe the work that you do.

The mission of the design studio is to support faculty in the use of online technologies in their teaching, whether that teaching is face to

(*continued*)

(continued)

face or online. As such, my task has several elements, a few of which I have outlined as follows:

- Understanding faculty, their teaching strategies, and their educational goals
- Understanding students, their learning strategies, and their situations
- Bringing these pieces together: My task is to find an approach to technology-integrated teaching and learning that effectively serves faculty and the students.

What is a typical day like for you in this career?

A typical day (although almost no day is just like this) might involve:

- Completing tasks quickly and effectively
- Talking with faculty who are at various stages (i.e., advanced planning, meeting with partners to get their go-ahead) of course development
- Working with the technology director in order to achieve an educational goal. Sometimes that work is developing web-based applications; other times, it is learning how to use new technology

What is the most challenging part of your career?

Probably the most challenging part of this work is trying to piece together multiple strands that often seem to be pulling apart. For example:

- Each instructor has a vision for his or her teaching, and we want to support that vision. Yet we do not have the resources to do everything that each person wants. So we spend a lot of time looking for ways to relate the work of different people. Faculty members want the technology they use to take on a high degree of transparency. That is, they don't want their own thinking or their students' thinking to be taken up by focusing on the technology. My job is to be looking for, preparing for, and developing

(continued)

(*continued*)

new technologies and new strategies. In sum, we need to have an eye on the present and the future, walking carefully in a mixture of the two.

What is the most rewarding part of your career?

The most rewarding part of this work is seeing faculty, students in classes, and students in the studio benefit. Hearing faculty describe with satisfaction how technology enabled them to do what they were trying to do in class is very gratifying. Hearing and seeing students in classes who experience considerable learning gains through the use of educational technology is quite significant.

What advice do you have for someone in high school or currently at the undergraduate level who might be interested in this career?

I would encourage anyone interested in this career to look for any opportunity available to learn how to work better with a range of people in helping them achieve their goals. In this work, one must be able to find ways in which to help people work together, and to use technology to help people achieve their goals. In some sense, the "customer is always right." It takes skill, experience, confidence, and humility to do that well. I would also encourage people to look for ways to use technology to meet educational needs in their placements. Thinking critically about the uses of technology is so important for this work!

What advice do you have for someone currently in a different career/field who might be interested in your career?

I would suggest that someone considering a change in direction take every opportunity to explore critically the intersection of technology and learning. Ask questions like:

- Is technology helping learning? If so, in what ways?
- What are the side effects of using the technology? Are those side effects desirable or not?

(*continued*)

(continued)

- What is the relationship between the teaching strategy and the technology? In what ways do they work well together?
- What new technologies and/or strategies could make this learning situation more conducive to learning?

If you decided to advance your career, what steps would you take and what career(s) might you seek out?

Within my context, "disciplined inquiry" is of very high value. It is easy to have my work dominated by the desire to get the work done. My career will be helped to the degree that, while completing the work, I also am able to do research on what we do. Our goals include:

- Gaining a better understanding what we do, what we could do, and why some strategies and technologies are more, or less, effective
- Improving what we do by finding what works and enhancing it, and by finding what is not working and changing it
- Sharing what we are learning with others

REFERENCE

Bureau of Labor Statistics, U.S. Department of Labor. (2014). *Occupational outlook handbook, 2014-2015 edition, Web Developers.* Retrieved July 13, 2015, from http://www.bls.gov/ooh/computer-and-information-technology/web-developers.htm

VI ■ THE FUTURE OF EDUCATION

12 ■ PROFESSIONAL DEVELOPMENT AND CAREER GROWTH

Self-assessment (i.e., understanding your own strengths and weaknesses) is critical for those entering a career in education. Educators who are committed to personal excellence through continuous improvement (e.g., addressing personal areas of weakness) are especially valued. Continuing education to address weaknesses and build on strengths can position one successfully for professional advancement and leadership opportunities.

In each of the 101 career descriptions a brief overview of continuing education requirements was provided. As a general rule of thumb, when a certificate or a license is secured for employment there is a need to demonstrate involvement in regular and ongoing formal professional development activities. The reason for this is simple: Knowledge and best practices evolve.

The evolving body of knowledge with respect to a discipline that is largely funded by public tax dollars makes professional development not only important, but absolutely necessary. Ultimately, requiring continuing education for certification/licensure renewal is a means to protect the public and enhance the value of educational services. Individuals in industry or government agencies also must be up to date with their knowledge in order to maintain relevance and importance to their organizations.

Individuals who are working in the field of education with a bachelor's degree may choose to complete graduate coursework to earn a master's or doctoral degree. This additional training typically is meant to enhance one's ability to perform within his or her current roles and responsibilities. These graduate educational pursuits can provide familiarity with contemporary teaching practices and enhance discipline-specific knowledge.

There are also a number of salary benefits to furthering one's education, especially for those who are working in schools. Large financial incentives or significant merit increases to retain exceptional educators have not traditionally been a part of public schools (e.g., Head Start, K–12 systems, universities). Earning an advanced degree is one way to step up on a district's salary scale, or it can provide a competitive edge in securing a higher paying position in a different educational system (e.g., industry, government). Large jumps in salary within public education careers are often only afforded to those who can demonstrate their value to other educational systems.

Career growth opportunities are plentiful in the field of education, as is evident in many of the 23 career interviews featured in this book. Those interviewees provide specific examples of the mobility afforded to individuals with the talents and skills of an educator. They show how career changes are possible within an educational system or across systems (e.g., school districts, businesses, government agencies).

The volume of pending retirements of a large segment of current leaders within all educational systems won't be filled by only hiring personnel new to the system. This need for future leaders in schools will require training and education of those who are already a part of the system. This need for internal career development especially highlights the importance and focus that will be placed on continuing education in the decade to come.

Knowing that professional advancement and continuing education are important and necessary parts of the field of education, the big question becomes how to effectively and efficiently update the workforce's knowledge and skills. Educational technology and distance education (i.e., online courses) have revolutionized this process. The possibilities for continuous improvement in professional development approaches through the use and investigation of technological effectiveness appear endless.

A new discipline has emerged in the area of instructional effectiveness, learner outcomes, and educational technology. The recent substantial growth in this emerging area within education led to our focus on a handful of educational technology careers within this book. The increased science and study of effectiveness of online instructional approaches is just beginning. The data are emerging daily on these teaching practices and will further improve this promising method of continuing education in the years ahead.

Online education and educational technology have the potential to fill educators' need for continuing education expectations within the time demands of the profession. Many opportunities are available for continuing education during the summer months. In addition, the advent of online education and the availability of evening courses allow individuals to seek these learning opportunities during the school year. Many local community colleges and regional/national universities now offer these courses. In addition, many professional associations sponsor continuing education credit opportunities through podcasts, seminars, conferences, webinars, and other web-based techniques.

The ease of knowledge dissemination and availability of resources on the Internet also appear to be making a big difference in improving the knowledge and training of current educators. Numerous foundations and government-supported agencies are in place to promote effective educational practices. Although there are many sources available, we have selected four to briefly feature in our book. These include the following:

What Works Clearinghouse (ies.ed.gov/ncee/wwc). The What Works Clearinghouse (WWC) is funded by the Institute of Educational Sciences (IES), a division of the Department of Education. The purpose of the WWC is to provide educators with the information necessary to make data-based decisions about their practices. The website of the WWC provides a repository of information on the research associated with educational practices, programs, products, and policies. Using the metric of "high-quality research," the WWC provides guidance as to which instructional practices actually make a difference in the field of education. The WWC is organized by topic and is quite diverse in its coverage. Examples of specific topics reviewed include math, literacy, science, dropout prevention, educational technology, early childhood education, teacher effectiveness, and school choice.

Center for Public Education (www.centerforpubliceducation .org). The Center for Public Education (CPE) is associated with the National School Boards Association and the National School Boards Foundation. The center is a national resource for information about public education and its importance within our country. The CPE provides up-to-date research, data, and analysis of current education-related issues. The primary focus of this analysis is to explore ways to improve student achievement. By providing this important information to the public, the mission of the CPE is to increase support for public schools. Numerous helpful resources on school improvement are available to school personnel to assist with continuing education. Resources provided include original studies and reviews of education research. Examples of school districts' application of research-based practices are also highlighted. Helping the public to understand education terminology, statistics, and unique school-related topics is also a major focus of the work of the CPE.

Edutopia (www.edutopia.org). Edutopia is funded by the George Lucas Educational Foundation, which was created by George Lucas, the famous movie director. As found on the Edutopia website, the mission and purpose of the foundation is to think creatively about how to best help students learn. The foundation's focus on professional development is especially geared primarily at educators and school leaders (see www .edutopia.org/teacher-development). The website includes a set of diverse blogs, videos related to professional development, and features on important topics commonly associated with continuing education within the teaching profession (e.g., game-based learning, differentiated instruction, culturally relevant teaching, formative assessment). The foundation also supports a research division, called George Lucas Research, with a mission to build evidence for innovative teaching practices.

***Education Week Teacher PD Sourcebook* (www.edweek .org/tsb).** This professional development website is associated with the publication *Education Week*, which is funded by the nonprofit group Editorial Projects in Education (EPE). The EPE produces a number of publications and online products associated with K–12 education. The mission of the EPE is to raise awareness and understanding of critical issues facing teachers and schools in the United States. The *Teacher PD Sourcebook* provides valuable information and resources to educators pertaining to more than 35 topics. Examples include blended learning, character education, social–emotional learning, at-risk students, special education, English language learning, Response to Intervention (RtI), classroom management, and all major aspects of education (reading, writing, math). Access to publications, webinars, and professional conference opportunities are among the many methods provided to teachers to promote their continuing education.

13 ■ THE JOB-SEARCH PROCESS: RESOURCES AND APPROACHES

At this point in the book you have been exposed to 101 possible careers in education and the types of background and training that are necessary to compete successfully for these positions. You now know that these careers in education can be found in a diverse array of settings, including schools, industry, religious organizations, and government agencies. With your newfound appreciation for the breadth and depth of the field and the background/training required, we hope that you are ready to pursue one or more careers in education that may be of particular interest to your commitment to serve and educate others. With an updated résumé polished, professional references confirmed, necessary credentials/licensure obtained, and possibly a portfolio of your related work ready to go, it is time to embark on the job-search process.

The job-search process for a career in education should be viewed as an exciting one. This is a chance to turn your thoughts and ideas about a career in education into reality. Planning, persistence, and perseverance are necessary for any job-search process, but especially within the field of education, where the supply of well-qualified personnel can substantially overshadow the demand, depending on the community in which one lives.

Job-search approaches usually follow one of three types. These include a search that is national in scope, which affords the opportunity to go where the jobs are available. Conducting and securing a position in a location that is divergent from where an individual grew up or studied is an effective way to create national mobility and expand one's potential employment opportunities for the future. In many cases one's professional credentials or one's family situation may restrict his or her ability to conduct a national search. A regional or state-focused search allows one to work on balancing professional and personal geographic restrictions. The third type of job search is one that is restricted to a local community or city. These more narrow searches are the most restrictive and potentially most challenging, especially in places where highly qualified applicants may be plentiful. Distinguishing oneself from other applicants via training, experience, or credentials is essential to increase the chance to compete successfully for these local openings.

NATIONAL JOB-SEARCH APPROACH

If your personal circumstances allow and your professional qualifications afford the opportunity for mobility, we highly recommend that you be willing to search nationally for a position in education. To assist you in a national job search for one of the many careers available within schools, you are strongly encouraged to first review the annual report produced by the U.S. Department of Education, Office of Postsecondary Education (2015), titled *Teacher Shortage Areas Nationwide Listing: 1990–1991 through 2014–2015*. Not only does this annual report present information about the geographic areas of the country that are in greatest need of teachers, it also provides very helpful information about the financial incentives (e.g., student loan forgiveness, scholarships) that are available to those who get jobs in these government-identified teacher-shortage careers.

Although it is essential to remember that this annual report is not a job-listing report, as the shortages might not be able to be filled due to funding issues, the report can be a helpful starting point when conducting a national search or even for those first contemplating a career in education. This is especially true for those who may be in high school or those who might be considering a career change. Specifically, the report identifies six careers in education that have clearly demonstrated persistent national shortages for well-qualified personnel. Embarking on an education to someday enter into one of these careers has the potential to lead to much success within the job-search process. These shortages include the following areas of education:

Bilingual education and English language acquisition
Foreign language
Mathematics
Reading specialists
Science
Special education

It is also important to recognize that these severe teacher shortages are consistent with a number of national priorities and initiatives (e.g., training grants, scholarship programs, retraining programs) aimed at bettering the educational system's readiness to (a) prepare individuals for science, technology, engineering, and math (STEM) careers and (b) educate those who struggle with access to education due to disabilities or other disadvantage (e.g., low income, immigrant status).

The following Internet search engines are particularly helpful when looking for education career openings across the country. It is important to note that most of these also allow results to be limited to one or more states or regions of the country, making them useful for anyone who is engaged in an education job search—nationally, regionally, or locally. The setting (school, industry, government) in which these search engines are predominantly focused helps to organize these resources.

> School: www.topschooljobs.com (*Education Week*)
> School: www.K12jobs.com
> School: www.educationamerica.net
> School: www.teach.org/jobsearch
> Industry: www.monster.com
> Industry: www.indeed.com
> Industry: www.simplyhired.com
> Federal government: www.usajobs.gov
> State government (example): www.jobcenterofwisconsin.com

There are also numerous discipline-specific job-search resources that can be located through a search of the Internet or via professional publications distributed by those organizations. Some examples include the following:

> Educational technology jobs: The International Society for Technology in Education (iste-jobs.jobtarget.com/jobseeker/search/results)
> Museum educator jobs: American Alliance of Museums (www.aam-us.org/resources/careers)
> School administrator jobs: The School Superintendents Association (www.aasa.org/jobs.aspx)
> School psychology positions: National Association of School Psychologists (nasponline-jobs.jobtarget.com) or listings by state associations (www.maspweb.com)
> Summer camp jobs: American Camp Association (www.acacamps.org/jobs)
> University/college jobs: *The Chronicle of Higher Education* (www.chronicle.com) or www.higheredjobs.com

REGIONAL/STATE JOB-SEARCH APPROACH

Those who need to conduct a search within a specific region of the country or a specific state will benefit from the adaptability of the search tools suggested in the previous section. However, regional or state-level professional association groups might be especially important to seek out, as many provide listings or serve as a clearinghouse for job openings. If you already have a career in education, opportunity for career changes can be especially enhanced if you are actively engaged in a professional association, given the chance to network with colleagues throughout the state. In addition, it is important to use the professional contacts made through your degree or training programs when conducting a regional/state-based job search.

In addition to understanding the landscape of national shortages, it is worth the time necessary to uncover regional and state-level shortages prior to embarking on a job search or when first considering a training program to become an educator. For example, in the state of Michigan there has been widespread media attention on the need for many more teachers who can (a) help prepare personnel for manufacturing/trade/technical jobs, and (b) meet the needs of students within failing and high-need (e.g., low-income communities) schools, and (c) address the need for well-qualified personnel to educate students with disabilities, especially those students who are diagnosed with autism spectrum disorder). These education personnel needs also can be seen in Michigan's 2014–2015 reporting within the *Teacher Shortage Areas Nationwide Listing* document prepared by the U.S. Department of Education, Office of Postsecondary Education (2015). The following careers were highlighted in this annual report as experiencing current and expected future shortages in the state of Michigan:

Early childhood special education
Language teachers
   American sign language
   Bilingual education
   English as a second language
   Native American languages
Occupational/technical training
   Automobile technician
   Collision repair technician
   Construction trades
   Cosmetology
   Graphics and printing technology

Communications
Personal and culinary services
Public safety/protective services
Radio and TV broadcasting technician
Therapeutic services
Welding, brazing, and soldering
Special education teachers—all categories

LOCAL/CITY JOB-SEARCH APPROACH

Networking with professional associates is an exceptional way to do a local/city job search. If your professional circle is limited or you are new to the education profession, then it is recommended to begin in an entry-level position within an organization that hires educational personnel (e.g., school, business, government agency). Being a part of such an organization, even if that means volunteering, can afford opportunities for advancement, an important foundation of experience, and specific knowledge about the administrative structure or professional networks available in that employment setting. Those experiences and the knowledge you will gain of that system can be instrumental in creating opportunities for parallel career moves or advancement/promotion to other positions.

REFERENCE

U.S. Department of Education, Office of Postsecondary Education. (2015). *Teacher shortage areas nationwide listing: 1990–1991 through 2014–2015*. Retrieved from http://www2.ed.gov/about/offices/list/ope/pol/tsa.html

■ INDEX